"*Infants and Children in the Church: Five Views on Theology and Ministry* makes a significant contribution to the growing field of child theology. The Orthodox, Roman Catholic, Lutheran, Reformed, and Baptist authors in this edited volume offer thoughtful explanations of their traditions' theological understandings of baptism and sin with regard to infants and children. I have been looking for a book such as this for two decades—a book that drills deep into the interlinking theological issues of sin and guilt, the status of children before God, and infant baptism (and believers' baptism)—and how beliefs on such complex issues impact how we receive and welcome children in our faith communities. The book held two surprises for me: 1) these five streams of Christianity reflected more commonalities than I had anticipated; they overlapped significantly, exhibiting more congruence than I had expected (though differences were explicit and profound as well), and 2) the authors penned fairly nuanced explanations of infant death and salvation that contrasted somewhat with past more straightforward teachings that unbaptized infants who die could not be saved.

What one believes about children, their status before God, sin, culpability, and baptism matters deeply in how churches teach their young. Indeed, church leaders—in particular, children's ministers—should possess a robust understanding of their own tradition's theology regarding children; however, one of the best ways to deepen, broaden, and enrich one's ministry with children is to examine what other Christian traditions believe and how they have received, welcomed, and taught children in the past. We have much to learn from each other's stories; this text provides an excellent means for beginning that journey."

—**Holly Allen**, professor of family studies and Christian ministries, Lipscomb University

"This book represents an example of what can be done in new ecumenical exchanges that reflect a true dialogue. What better place to focus than children and their place in the life of the church?"

—**Archpriest Chad Hatfield**, president, St. Vladimir's Orthodox Theological Seminary

"One of the advantages of living in an ecumenical age is the opportunity for Christians to take another look at old controversies without feeling compelled to hurl anathemas at each other. Each of the five contributors to *Infants and Children* represents a different faith tradition and provides a rationale for the treatment of children in his own church, including but not limited to baptism. While differences are acknowledged, caricatures are avoided. The result is an enlightening and engaging volume. In an age that trumpets abortion as a fundamental right, this book reminds us that whatever their differences otherwise, the faithful recognize children as God's creation and the object of his love in Jesus Christ; and in the church, they should be treated as such."

—**Cameron A. MacKenzie**, Forest E. and Frances H. Ellis Professor of Historical Theology, Concordia Theological Seminary

"I can think of no issue more important in the practical life of the church than that of the place of children. After all, a church that does not cultivate the next generation is a church that dies. At the same time, the issue is theologically fraught, with many of our denominational divisions coming right at this point. This book brilliantly puts together a respectful and convictional conversation on these crucial issues. This book will leave you better able to articulate your view, and better able to see why others might disagree. I highly recommend this book, and hope it is the beginning of long reflection of what it means for the church to be child-like in our dependence and child-friendly in our mission."

—**Russell Moore**, president, The Ethics and Religious Liberty Commission of the Southern Baptist Convention

INFANTS and CHILDREN in the CHURCH

ADAM HARWOOD *and* KEVIN E. LAWSON

EDITORS

INFANTS
and
CHILDREN
in the
CHURCH

FIVE VIEWS ON

THEOLOGY AND MINISTRY

NASHVILLE, TENNESSEE

Infants and Children in the Church: Five Views on Theology and Ministry

Copyright © 2017 Adam Harwood and Kevin E. Lawson

Published by B&H Academic
Nashville, Tennessee

All rights reserved.

ISBN: 978-1-4627-5110-5 (print)
ISBN: 978-1-4336-4652-2 (eBook)

Dewey Decimal Classification: 248.82
Subject Heading: INFANTS \ CHILDREN AND SPIRITUAL LIFE \ CHURCH WORK WITH CHILDREN

Scripture quotations marked (ESV) are taken from the ESV® Bible (The Holy Bible, English Standard Version®). ESV® Permanent Text Edition® (2016). Copyright © 2001 by Crossway, a publishing ministry of Good News Publishers. The ESV® text has been reproduced in cooperation with and by permission of Good News Publishers. Unauthorized reproduction of this publication is prohibited. All rights reserved.

Scripture quotations marked (RSV) are from the Revised Standard Version of the Bible, copyright © 1946, 1952, and 1971 the Division of Christian Education of the National Council of the Churches of Christ in the United States of America. Used by permission. All rights reserved.

Scripture quotations marked (NASB) are taken from the New American Standard Bible®, Copyright © 1960, 1962, 1963, 1968, 1971, 1972, 1973, 1975, 1977, 1995 by The Lockman Foundation. Used by permission.

Scripture quotations marked (NKJV) are taken from the New King James Version®. Copyright © 1982 by Thomas Nelson. Used by permission. All rights reserved.

The Orthodox Study Bible: Copyright 2008 by St. Athanasius Academy of Orthodox Theology. Old Testament Text: St. Athanasius Academy Septuagint. Copyright 2008 by St. Athanasius Academy of Orthodox Theology. New Testament Text: New King James Version. Copyright 1982 by Thomas Nelson, Inc.

Printed in the United States of America

First printing in 2017

To all who invested in the spiritual birth and growth of the writers herein
when all of us were but infants and children.
And to those who continue to serve in ministry to little ones.
Your labor of love is deeply important.

CONTENTS

Acknowledgments	xi
Contributors	xiii
Introduction—Kevin E. Lawson	**1**
An Orthodox View—Jason Foster	**11**
Responses	37
A Roman Catholic View—David Liberto	**47**
Responses	70
A Lutheran View—David P. Scaer	**81**
Responses	104
A Reformed View—Gregg Strawbridge	**113**
Responses	143
A Baptist View—Adam Harwood	**155**
Responses	183
Welcoming Children—Kevin E. Lawson	**193**
Name Index	207
Subject Index	211
Scripture Index	215

ACKNOWLEDGMENTS

We are deeply indebted to the many people who have supported this writing effort. Grateful appreciation extends to the theologians of differing denominational and theological traditions who agreed to join us in this writing venture. They first developed and shared their papers at a 2015 conference hosted and funded by the New Orleans Baptist Theological Seminary (NOBTS) Baptist Center for Theology and Ministry as well as the Christian Education Division. Following that event, the contributors revised their presentations for this publication; they also offered their responses to the chapters submitted by their colleagues. Their compiled work stands as a wonderful gift to the church, and we deeply appreciate the investments they made to the body of Christ.

We are also appreciative of the hospitality and financial support for this project offered by the NOBTS Baptist Center for Theology and Ministry and that of the school's Christian Education Division. The school and its leaders were gracious hosts for the conference, and their support of this resource has been invaluable.

We also want to thank B&H Academic for accepting this book and working with us to bring it to publication. We are grateful for their confidence in this project and for their support of us throughout the compilation and editing process.

And finally, on behalf of all the writers associated with this resource, we offer gratitude to the supportive family members, friends, and colleagues who have borne with all of us in this season of writing, travel, and even more writing. This project would not exist without your support, and we thank God for you.

—Adam Harwood and Kevin E. Lawson

CONTRIBUTORS

A list of the theologians contributing to this volume, as well as information on their respective traditions, appears below in order of the chapters each penned.

Kevin E. Lawson (EdD, University of Maine, Orono) serves as co-editor of this book and contributes the introduction and the conclusion. He is professor of Christian education and former director of the PhD and EdD programs in educational studies at Talbot School of Theology, Biola University in La Mirada, California. He is editor of the *Christian Education Journal*. He also served as a board member of The Society for Children's Spirituality: Christian Perspectives from 2001 to 2012. Among other books, he edited *Understanding Children's Spirituality: Theology, Research, and Practice* (2012).

Jason Foster (PhD, Durham University) advocates for an Orthodox view. He is priest of Holy Nativity of our Lord Orthodox Church in Bossier City, Louisiana. He holds master's degrees from Dallas Theological Seminary, Cranmer Theological House, and Oxford University. His PhD dissertation is entitled "*Sursum Corda*: Ritual and Meaning of the Liturgical Command in the First Five Centuries of the Church."

David Liberto (PhD, Marquette University) advocates for a Roman Catholic view. He is professor of historical and dogmatic theology at Notre Dame Seminary and Graduate School of Theology in New Orleans, Louisiana. He has published several articles in academic, peer-reviewed publications and is currently working on a book-length treatment of the psychological analogy of the Trinity.

David P. Scaer (ThD, Concordia Seminary) advocates for a Lutheran view. He is professor of systematic theology and New Testament as well as editor of *Concordia Theological Quarterly* at Concordia Theological Seminary in Fort Wayne, Indiana. Among other works, he is the author of *Infant Baptism in Nineteenth Century Lutheran Theology* (2011) and contributor to *Understanding Four Views on the Lord's Supper* (2007).

Gregg Strawbridge (PhD, University of Southern Mississippi) advocates for a Reformed view. He is pastor of All Saints Presbyterian Church in Lancaster, Pennsylvania, and is the founder and creative director of *www.WordMp3.com*, an online audio library of Christian worldview resources. He edited and contributed to *The Case for Covenantal Infant Baptism* (2003) and *The Case for Covenant Communion* (2006).

Adam Harwood (PhD, Southwestern Baptist Theological Seminary) serves as co-editor of this volume and advocates for a Baptist view. He is associate professor of theology, McFarland Chair of Theology, director of the Baptist Center for Theology and Ministry, and editor of the *Journal for Baptist Theology and Ministry* at New Orleans Baptist Theological Seminary in New Orleans, Louisiana. He is the author of *The Spiritual Condition of Infants* (2011) and *Born Guilty?* (2013).

INTRODUCTION: INFANTS AND CHILDREN IN THE CHURCH

Kevin E. Lawson

> Behold, children are a heritage from the Lord,
> the fruit of the womb a reward.
> (Psalm 127:3, ESV)[1]

Have you ever received a gift that left you feeling uncertain about what you should do with it? I have many times, and while I welcome such gifts and appreciate the loving intentions of the givers, such presents leave me puzzled. Scripture declares, and followers of Jesus affirm whole-heartedly, that children

---

[1] All Scripture references in this introduction are taken from the English Standard Version (ESV).

are a heritage from God, a gift to us; thus, we Christians rejoice whenever a child is born into our families and into our churches. And yet, as the church we sometimes find ourselves a bit perplexed about what to do with these so-called gifts once the celebration is over. The dilemma comes down to this: just how are we to faithfully steward these precious little ones? How are we to minister to them, to encourage their spiritual growth, and to support their developing relationships with God—their Creator and Father?

Over the last hundred years, churches of all denominations have posed theological questions related to children and childhood, seeking guidance in the development of the church's ministry to the children God has given them. They ask,

- What is the spiritual condition of children, and how can and should they relate to God during this early phase of life?
- In what ways should Christians include them within the fellowship and community of the church?
- In what sacraments or ordinances should children participate at particular ages or stages, and what does their participation mean to them and to the church?
- How might believers effectively raise children toward love and faith in God, toward trusting reception of God's grace through faith in Christ, and toward spiritual maturity?
- What responsibilities should the church in general and parents or caregivers in particular take in the spiritual instruction and nurture of children?
- How can Christians work together for our children's good?

Churches today have diverse understandings of how to answer these questions—a reality leading various denominations to follow different practices with children. For instance, in some traditions, infants are baptized; in others, baptism is delayed until such time as a child expresses personal faith in Christ. Moreover, some traditions include children in celebrations of the Lord's Supper, or Eucharist; others delay participation until a certain age is reached or until a personal experience of faith is vocalized. And although some churches include children in the full experience of corporate worship, others create separate worship and instruction experiences for them. In many cases, these diverse practices are deeply rooted in a theological understanding of the needs of children and of their place within the church body. In others, there has been little serious reflection on how or even whether theology should impact the way Christians train their young.

Though most believers would express a desire to be faithful to God in the care and spiritual training of his gift of children, answering questions like those above proves difficult for many. Marcia Bunge, reflecting on the current state of theological thought on issues regarding children observes that this has led to some negative impacts: "The absence of well-developed and historically and biblically informed teachings about children in contemporary theology helps explain why many churches often struggle to create and to sustain strong programs in religious education and in child-advocacy ministry."[2]

This book is designed to foster the kind of theological reflection for ministry practice that will help the church better respond to the gift of children in our midst. Christians need to give more attention and thought to the theological principles underlying this topic and to their implications for ministry practice. By carefully examining our own beliefs and practices, as well as those of other major branches of the Christian church, we hope to stimulate more thoughtful reflection and greater discernment concerning how God would have us minister to, for, and with children—both those within our congregations and those within our communities.

A Few Biblical Foundations

In anticipating the church's questions on this topic, God provided foundational instruction in Scripture that relates to his people's responsibility to

---

[2] Marcia J. Bunge, "Introduction," in *The Child in Christian Thought*, ed. Marcia J. Bunge (Grand Rapids, MI: Eerdmans, 2001), 4.

instruct children regarding God's law and mighty works. In the Shema, the nation of Israel is commanded to teach their children the commands of God:

> Hear, O Israel: The Lord our God, the Lord is one. You shall love the Lord your God with all your heart and with all your soul and with all your might. And these words that I command you today shall be on your heart. *You shall teach them diligently to your children, and shall talk of them when you sit in your house, and when you walk by the way, and when you lie down, and when you rise.* You shall bind them as a sign on your hand, and they shall be as frontlets between your eyes. You shall write them on the doorposts of your house and on your gates. (Deuteronomy 6:4–9, emphasis added)

Later, in the Psalms, we see how this command to Israel had become a commitment affirmed by the psalmist, Asaph:

> Give ear, O my people, to my teaching;
>   incline your ears to the words of my mouth!
> I will open my mouth in a parable;
>   I will utter dark sayings from of old,
> things that we have heard and known,
>   that our fathers have told us.
> *We will not hide them from their children,
>   but tell to the coming generation
> the glorious deeds of the Lord, and his might,
>   and the wonders that he has done.*
>
> *He established a testimony in Jacob
>   and appointed a law in Israel,
> which he commanded our fathers
>   to teach to their children,
> that the next generation might know them,
>   the children yet unborn,
> and arise and tell them to their children,*

> *so that they should set their hope in God*
> *and not forget the works of God,*
> > *but keep his commandments;*
> *and that they should not be like their fathers,*
> > *a stubborn and rebellious generation,*
> *a generation whose heart was not steadfast,*
> > whose spirit was not faithful to God. (Psalm 78:1–8, emphasis added)

In the New Testament, Jesus welcomes and blesses children, affirming that the kingdom of heaven belongs to such as them: "Then children were brought to him that he might lay his hands on them and pray. The disciples rebuked the people, but Jesus said, *'Let the little children come to me and do not hinder them, for to such belongs the kingdom of heaven.'* And he laid his hands on them and went away" (Matt 19:13–15, emphasis added).

Later, Paul writes to help first-generation church leaders and members understand how to follow Christ together. He reaffirms the important role that parents have in the instruction of children in matters of the Christian faith: "Fathers, do not provoke your children to anger, but bring them up in the discipline and instruction of the Lord" (Eph 6:4).

These passages affirm both that children are important to God and that his people bear the responsibility for raising them toward saving faith in Jesus Christ.

A Brief Historical Overview

While the Christian understanding of the value and importance of children and of their instruction in the faith is firmly rooted in Scripture, historically believers have struggled with how best to apply these truths. And church leaders over the centuries have not always addressed such matters well—in part because of their own failure to properly understand the impact of sin on human nature, how that applies to infants and children, how baptism functions in the lives of those who are baptized, the role and impact of the

Eucharist/Lord's Supper in the lives of believers, and the nature of the church and how children relate to it.

For example, even in the early church leaders struggled with whether or not infants should be baptized. Some said baptism should be delayed, possibly until after adolescence.[3] In most cases children were included in the corporate worship of the church, but instruction in the faith was primarily seen as the responsibility of parents.[4] As time progressed, infant baptism became the norm in both the Eastern and Western branches of the church, but confirmation (an anointing of the newly baptized by the bishop as a symbol of the indwelling of the Holy Spirit) became a separate event, eventually moving into early adolescence and becoming a time for focused instruction in the faith for those ready to take responsibility for following Christ.[5] In the West, in the eleventh century, the doctrine of transubstantiation resulted in young children no longer being able to participate in the Eucharist out of a concern that they might accidentally spit out the body and blood of Christ.[6] Following the Fourth Lateran Council in 1215, with a renewed emphasis on the Eucharist, confession, and instruction in the faith, catechisms (brief curriculum that addressed basic doctrines and faith practices) received increased attention leading to the development and publication of written catechisms and their sporadic use by church leaders and parents.[7]

---

[3] For example, see Tertullian, *Baptism* 18:3–6, for an early argument against infant baptism, and Origen, *Homilies on Luke* 14:5, for an early argument for infant baptism. See also Paul Turner's book, *Ages of initiation: The First Two Christian Millennia* (Collegeville, MN: Liturgical, 2000).

[4] O. M. Bakke, *When Children Became People: The Birth of Childhood in Early Christianity* (Minneapolis, MN: Fortress, 2005), 153–58.

[5] J. D. C. Fisher, *Christian Initiation: Baptism in the Medieval West* (London, England: Alcuin Club, 1965), 114–20.

[6] Ibid, 115.

[7] Kevin E. Lawson, "Learning the Faith in England in the Later Middle Ages: Contributions of the Franciscan Friars," *Religious Education* 107, no. 2 (2012): 147–48.

With the Reformation in the early-sixteenth century came renewed emphasis on teaching the basics of the faith through catechisms and the importance of confirmation as a time of instruction for children on the verge of assuming adult responsibilities. Both within the Catholic Church and in Protestant churches, receiving instruction in the catechism became a normal part of growing up within the faith community.[8] In fact, this remained the dominant model for instructing children in the faith for a few hundred years, particularly for those groups—Catholic and Protestant—who practiced infant baptism. The Protestant Sunday school, begun in the late eighteenth century, became an alternate model for training children in spiritual matters; it placed more emphasis on teaching the stories of the Bible than on following a systematic theological formula.[9] The Pietist movements of the seventeenth and eighteenth centuries emphasized the importance of a person's religious experience, and the Great Awakenings of the eighteenth and early nineteenth centuries focused attention on the experience of conversion. In response, Horace Bushnell, writing from a covenantal theological perspective, emphasized the spiritual instruction and nurture of children and his confidence in the formative power of Christian parents' faith on that of their children.[10] His views greatly influenced the religious education movement of the late nineteenth and early twentieth centuries.[11]

The Purpose and Structure of This Book

As this summary of church history on the matter shows, Christian traditions have proposed various answers to the theological and pragmatic ministry

---

[8] Maxwell Johnson, *The Rites of Christian Initiation: Their Evolution and Interpretation* (Collegeville, MN: Liturgical, 1999), 270.

[9] Anne M. Boylan, *Sunday School: The Formation of an American Institution, 1790–1880* (New Haven, CT: Yale University Press, 1988), 133–49.

[10] Horace Bushnell, *Views on Christian Nurture, and of Subjects Adjacent Thereto* (Delmar, NY: Scholars' Facsimiles and Reprints, 1847/1975), 183–209.

[11] See Boylan, *Sunday School*, 91–92, 147–52.

questions concerning infants and children—and each provides a unique perspective worthy of reflection.

This resource was born out of a conversation held at an academic conference following the presentation of a paper by Adam Harwood, my co-editor and a contributing writer to this book. He and I were keenly aware that the church as a whole wrestles, both in its theology and in its practice, with how best to minister to, for, and with the children God brings to his people. Out of our shared passion for the subject, we created a proposal to bring together theologians with diverse pastoral experience to address four major questions that contribute to the way churches approach ministry to children:

1. How are infants and children impacted by sin? The way a congregation views the possible inheritance of a sin nature, personal responsibility for sin, and the impact of other's sins on a child all play into how it instructs its little ones. Responses to this question prove foundational for how the remaining questions will be answered within a particular tradition.

2. How does God treat people who die in infancy or childhood? Historically, high infant mortality rates brought a sense of urgency to discussions about this issue. Today, the high rates of abortion, the prevalence of miscarriages, and the continuing challenges of high infant mortality rates in the majority world continue to make this a major pastoral concern and one that bears on the way infants and children are treated within the church and without.

3. When and how are children considered members of the church? Traditions wrestle with whether children are "insiders" or "outsiders" in terms of the body of Christ. How a denomination answers the first two questions often contributes to what aspects of the life of the church children are allowed to participate in and defines which aspects should be reserved for the time when individuals reach adolescence or adulthood.

4. When and how are children instructed in Christian doctrine? Most Christians understand intuitively that children should be instructed in the faith as they grow, but who bears this responsibility? And how should such teaching be carried out? Different traditions shed varying lights on these matters.

To aid understanding of the complex issues and implications raised by each view included in the chapters ahead, Adam and I chose to follow each author's presentation with the responses of the authors holding other theological positions. After the presentation of each of the five theological traditions as well as the feedback each received, we close the book with a chapter focused on helping the church as a whole to be more faithful in its ministry to little ones. It is our sincere hope that this work will help believers draw informed conclusions regarding this topic and will serve as a catalyst that encourages Christians of all traditions to make the most of every opportunity God gives us to instruct boys and girls in the faith.

Infants and Children in the Church:
An Orthodox View

Jason Foster

Introduction

The question of the relationship between God and infants is fundamentally an inquiry into the nature, condition, and purpose of human existence in its purest and most primal form. Life's celebratory and critical situations relating to young ones engender the deepest feelings of joy and sorrow. All Christian pastors are called to participate in these life events and to provide a response to the matter of how God relates to humanity's youngest. This work will seek to demonstrate how the Orthodox Christian Church answers the following questions pertaining to infants and children:

1. How are infants and children impacted by sin?
2. When and how are children considered members of the church?[1]
3. How does God treat people who die in infancy or childhood?
4. When and how are children instructed in Christian doctrine?

The Orthodox response to these queries is realized first and foremost within the liturgical praxis of the church—*lex orandi, lex credendi* (the rule

---

[1] Herein the terms *infant* and *child* will be used interchangeably.

of prayer is the rule of faith). Therefore, the method employed in presenting answers will be a systematic summary of the rites that compose the mystery of baptism.[2] The sacramental journey of an infant from the first day of his life to his union with Christ in baptism provides not only a theoretical but also a pastoral context by which to engage the theological topics presented. This chapter will also look to the early church fathers and leading contemporary scholars to shed light on the traditional understandings of the theological themes encountered and considered. The inclusion of the Orthodox treatment of these questions provides an ancient Eastern Christian response that is unique for the following reasons: the Reformation and the theological debate that birthed varying confessions took place in the West, not the East; the advent of a formulated doctrine of penal substitutionary atonement set forth by Anselm of Canterbury took place after the Great Schism; and many of St. Augustine of Hippo's writings were inaccessible in the East until the fourteenth century.[3] Therefore, the Orthodox position is another tradition that offers an ancient, Christian point of view.

Question 1: How Are Infants Impacted by Sin?

On the day an Orthodox Christian woman gives birth to a child, the priest makes a pastoral visit to offer up prayers for her and the newborn. After the completion of the *Trisagion*,[4] the pastor says the following set of petitions:

---

[2] Due to the numerous hypothetical situations and syllogisms this study can present, the topics discussed will be presented in the normal context and order of church life. Reference to infants, therefore, will be common since it is uncommon for Orthodox children not to be baptized before they are two to three months of age.

[3] There is some debate whether Theodore of Mopsuestia interacts with an Augustinian text in the fifth century and the Fifth Ecumenical Council held in Constantinople in AD 533 listed Augustine among the Fathers of the Church. However, Demetrios Cydones did not translate most of his works into Greek until 1360.

[4] A set of prayers to the Holy Trinity ending with the "Our Father."

O Sovereign Master and Lord Almighty, Who heals every sickness and every weakness: do You Yourself heal this Your servant/handmaiden (Name) who this day has borne a child, and raise her up from the bed on which she lies. For according to the words of Your Prophet David, in sin were we conceived and all are defiled before you; protect her, and this child which she has borne; shelter her under the covering of your wings from this day to her last; through the intercession of the all pure *Theotokos* and of all the Saints, for blessed are You to ages of Ages. Amen.

Sovereign Master and Lord our God, Who was born of our all pure Lady *Theotokos* and Ever Virgin Mary, Who as a Babe was laid in a manger, and as a Child was held up to be seen, do You Yourself have mercy on this Your servant (Name) who this day has borne this child, and be gracious unto her voluntary and involuntary offenses, protecting her from every diabolical cruelty; preserve the child she has borne from every bane, from every harm, from every hostile rage, from evil spirits of the day and night ... and of the infant which has been born of her do You account worthy to worship in the earthly Temple which You have prepared for the glorification of Your Holy Name ...

O Lord our God, Who was well pleased to come down from the Heavens, and to be born of the holy *Theotokos* and Ever Virgin Mary for the salvation of us sinners, Who knows the frailty of human nature: according to the multitude of Your compassions forgive the sins of Your servant (Name), who this day has borne a child ... and be gracious to Your Servant (Name) and to all the house in which the child has been born ... Amen.

The priest concludes the first-day prayers with the *Apolysis*: "Glory to You, O Christ our God and our Hope, glory to You. May Christ our true God, Who was born in a cave and laid in a manger for our salvation ..."

The Orthodox Church's teaching on how infants are impacted by sin is witnessed in these first-day prayers for the mother and child.[5] The reference to Psalm 51:5 (50:7 in the Septuagint) speaks to the condition of the mother: "For behold, I was conceived in transgressions, And in sins my mother bore me," resulting in defilement.[6] However, this language is not used in this liturgical context to describe the theological and anthropological condition of the infant. Instead, the prayers call on God to protect the baby from his first breath to his last, to count the child worthy to enter and worship in the earthly temple, and to grant grace to the household to which the child was born. Lastly, the faithful gathered for this occasion are reminded throughout the petitions that Christ assumed humanity and "lay in a manger for our salvation." Thus, he ontologically and soteriologically identifies with the frailty of the human state of the mother and child by becoming flesh, and there is a way of salvation. However, the silence pertaining to the sins of the little one that has just come from the womb speaks to the personal culpability of the infant.

---

[5] In the West, the teachings of St. Augustine of Hippo (c. 354–430) were instrumental in the formation of the Latin theological anthropology. The North African bishop found himself in a theological debate with Pelagius, who opposed the idea that the divine gift of grace was prerequisite to performing the will of God. Augustine argued there was a radical change in the human condition after the fall that left man in a totally corrupt/depraved state and therefore man's will was enslaved and not truly free. Papanikolaou summarizes Augustine's teaching on original sin in what he refers to as five principal tenets: (1) the actual sin of Adam, as well as its punishment, was inherited; (2) the post-lapsarian condition left every dimension of the human person subject to sin; (3) original sin was transmitted to offspring through the concupiscence associated with procreation; (4) the infant soul was guilty; and (5) salvation required baptism for infants. See *Orthodox Readings of Augustine*, ed. George E. Demacopoulos and Aristotle Papanikolaou (Crestwood, NY: St. Vladimir Seminary Press, 1976), 30.

[6] All Scripture references in this chapter are from the *Orthodox Study Bible* (Nashville, TN: Thomas Nelson, 2008). The OT texts are from the St. Athanasius Academy Septuagint; the NT texts are from the New King James Version.

The spiritual condition of a child, in its archetypical form, is witnessed in the narrative of Adam and Eve in Genesis 1–3. There is a symphony of theological interpretations among the church fathers pertaining to the creation account recorded in the first book of the Bible. In light of the proposed subject matter, St. Irenaeus's (c. 130–202) account in *Against Heresies* 3.22.4–5 and 4.38.1–2, whether literal or metaphorical, seems of particular relevance.[7] According to the second-century bishop of Lugdunum in Gaul, when the Creator fashioned man and woman and placed them in the garden, he did so in order that the sole creation endowed with the divine image would grow from *infancy* to perfection, i.e. deification.[8] Thus, for the Bishop, *perfected* adulthood is not the starting point of humanity in the Genesis account. This potential was not realized in Adam.

When the serpent tempted Eve in the garden (Gen 2:16–17), the evil one contradicted God's Word. He promised her that if she broke the divinely commanded fast and ate of the forbidden tree she would not die, as God had foretold. Instead, she and Adam "would become like gods, knowing good and evil." As spiritual infants, endowed with free will, Eve and Adam believed the lie and sought deification through disobedience. Their actions resulted in broken communion with the Creator, the source of all life. Consequently, according to St. Ephrem the Syrian in his *Commentary of Genesis* 2.35.1, they were removed from the garden so as not to eat of the tree of life and remain in

---

[7] Irenaeus, *Against Heresies* 3.22.4–5, 4.38.1–2, in *The Apostolic Fathers with Justin Martyr and Irenaeus*, trans. Alexander Roberts and W. H. Rambut, ed. Alexander Roberts and James Donaldson. In *The Ante-Nicene Fathers*, vol. 1 (Buffalo, NY: Christian Literature, 1885; reprint, New York, NY: Charles Scribner's Sons, 1903), 455, 521.

[8] Peter Bouteneff explains that *deification* can be understood as "'Christification,' or becoming ever-more Christ-like." Peter Bouteneff, "Christ and Salvation," in *The Oxford Companion to Orthodox Christian Theology*, ed. Mary B. Cunningham and Elizabeth Theokritoff (Cambridge, UK: Cambridge University Press, 2008), 104. See also Panayiotis Nellas, *Deification in Christ: Orthodox Perspectives on the Nature of the Human Person* (Crestwood, NY: St. Vladimir Seminary Press, 1987), 115–59.

this state forever, became subject to mortality, and, in turn, developed a propensity toward sin.[9] They, along with all creation, suffered. The divine image is now scarred but remains, as well as humanity's potential for union and communion with God—the potential to move from infancy to adulthood in Christ, the Second Adam.[10]

The world, received by every person, is a world inherited from Adam and his descendants. This includes the consequences of the collective sin of all humanity throughout the ages. Andrew Louth describes the Eastern conviction on this anthropological reality:

> The Greek Fathers speak in this connexion of 'ancestral sin,' *propaterikon amartema*, sin of our forefathers, inherited sin. We are born into a ruined cosmos, ruined at a moral, rather than a physical level (though there are areas—disease for instance—where it is difficult to draw a line); we add our bit to the devastation, but most of it was already laid waste long before we came along. The story of Adam speaks of the very beginning of this process, but just as we are implicated in a sin that is bigger than we are, so, too, Adam has unleashed consequences of sin that are more than he could be regarded as personally responsible for.[11]

Louth's reflection sees Adam as the "genesis" of the human spiritual condition; however, each individual, through the exercise of personal free will, also hears the Word of God walking in the garden, asking, "Why are you hiding?" Every

---

[9] *Selected Prose Works: Commentary on Genesis, Commentary on Exodus, Homily on Our Lord, Letter to Publius*, trans. Edward G. Mathews Jr. and Joseph P. Amar, ed. Kathleen McVey, *The Fathers of the Church* 91 (Washington, DC: Catholic University of America Press, 1994), 122–23. St. Paul comments on this theological transformation in Romans 6.

[10] For a comparison of the terms *image* and *likeness* and an overview of the Orthodox teaching on deification, see Georgios I. Mantzaridis, *The Deification of Man: St Gregory Palamas and the Orthodox Tradition*, trans. Liadain Sherrard (Crestwood, NY: St. Vladimir Seminary Press, 1984), 15–40.

[11] Andrew Louth, *Introducing Eastern Orthodox Theology* (Downers Grove, IL: InterVarsity, 2013), 73.

child is born into a fallen creation that all his or her ancestors, not just Adam and Eve, by their own volition helped to create. In the womb, each baby thus realizes the cumulative effect of gluttony, lust, covetousness, anger, sadness, despondency, vainglory, and pride. This notion of anthropology is less historical and individualistic; it is not centered on Adam.[12] Rather, it is a timeless narrative that brings all of humanity into the story, into the garden. Thus, as humans, infants inherit the fallen condition as victims and not as perpetrators. They are not active causes as they are incapable of participating in the further dissemination of the ancestral sin. Their human stories have yet to be written; but, as infants of the church, their stories begin in the rites associated with and in the mystery of baptism.

Question 2: When and How Are Children Considered Members of the Church?

In the Orthodox Church, membership is realized when one is united to Christ in baptism, regardless of age.[13] In the normal practice of the church, infants are baptized on or soon after the fortieth day following their births.[14]

---

[12] Ibid.

[13] The earliest liturgical text of the baptismal rite of Constantinople is found in the Barberini 336 *Euchologion* of the eighth century. As noted by scholars, this rite shows considerable continuity to the other fourth century practices in Antioch, as witnessed in the writings of St. John Chrysostom, Theodore of Mopsuestia, and the *Apostolic Constitutions*. For an overview, see Bryan Spinks, *Early and Medieval Rituals and Theologies of Baptism: From the New Testament to the Council of Trent* (Burlington, VT: Ashgate, 2006). The early occurrence of the rite is witnessed in the first or second-century document known as the *Didache*. For a comprehensive work on the history of baptism in the first five centuries, see Everett Ferguson, *Baptism in the Early Church: History, Theology, and Liturgy in the First Five Centuries* (Grand Rapids, MI: Eerdmans, 2009).

[14] Tertullian (c. 160–255), in *On Baptism* 18.4, "Of the Persons to Whom, and the Time When, Baptism is to be Administered," argued that infant baptism should be delayed to an older age when they can rationally comprehend the Christian faith and its demands. He writes, "And so, according to the circumstances and disposition, and even age, of each individual, the delay of baptism is

However, prior to this event, two other rites are performed that are ritually connected to baptism.

---

preferable; principally, however, in the case of little children. For why is it necessary—if (baptism itself) is not so necessary—that the sponsors likewise should be thrust into danger? Who both themselves, by reason of mortality, may fail to fulfil[1] their promises, and may be disappointed by the development of an evil disposition, in those for whom they stood? The Lord does indeed say, 'Forbid them not to come unto me.' Let them 'come,' then, while they are growing up; let them 'come' while they are learning, while they are learning whither to come; let them become Christians when they have become able to know Christ." His commentary demonstrates that the practice of infant baptism was the accepted norm and/or tradition of the church. Moreover, his concern for the souls of the children speaks to the efficacy of the rite of baptism to bring out the remission of sins and procure the seminal position of salvation. He writes, "Why does the innocent period of life hasten to the 'remission of sins?' More caution will be exercised in worldly matters: so that one who is not trusted with earthly substance is trusted with divine! Let them know how to 'ask' for salvation, that you may seem (at least) to have given 'to him that asks.'" Also, Tertullian extends his pastoral warning to the unmarried: "For no less cause must the unwedded also be deferred—in whom the ground of temptation is prepared, alike in such as never were wedded by means of their maturity, and in the widowed by means of their freedom—until they either marry, or else be more fully strengthened for continence. If any understand the weighty import of baptism, they will fear its reception more than its delay: sound faith is secure of salvation." Certain fathers of the fourth century were baptized later in life. Examples include, but are not limited to, St. John Chrysostom, St. Basil of Caesarea, and St. Gregory of Nazianzus. However, once again, the delay in their baptisms was due to a misunderstanding of the theological nature of the rite—what to do with sins committed after they were remitted. Each of these fathers employed infant or young-child baptism and spoke of the spiritual benefits of the rite. The only formal, ecclesiastical dispute recorded on the matter took place in third-century North Africa. St. Cyprian, in *Letters* 64.2, is not debating with Fidus over the practice of infant baptism, but on what day it should be administered, when he writes: "As to what pertains to the case of infants: You [Fidus] said that they ought not to be baptized within the second or third day after their birth, that the old law of circumcision must be taken into consideration, and that you did not think that one should be baptized and sanctified within the eighth day after his birth. In our council it seemed to us far otherwise." Other fathers who address the Orthodox tradition of paedobaptism include St. Irenaeus, *Against Heresies* 2.22.4; St. Hippolytus, *The*

Naming the Child—A New Identity

On the eighth day after birth, the priest once again visits the mother and child and offers the "naming prayers" following the example set forth in the Gospel of Luke when Christ was taken to the temple to be circumcised and named on the eighth day.[15] After making the sign of the cross on the forehead, lips, and chest of the infant, the pastor prays:

> O Lord our God, we entreat You, and we supplicate You, that the light of Your countenance be signed on this, Your servant (handmaiden), [Name], and that the Cross of Your Only-begotten Son be signed in his (her) heart and understanding, so that he (she) may flee from the vanity of the world and from every evil snare of the enemy, and may follow after Your commandments. And grant, O Lord, that Your holy name may remain unrejected by him (her), and that, in due time, he (she) may be joined to Your Holy Church, and that he (she) may be perfected by the dread Mysteries of Your Christ, so that, having lived according to Your commandments, and having preserved the seal unbroken, he (she) may receive the blessedness of the elect in Your kingdom: By the grace and love for mankind of Your Only-begotten Son, with Whom You are blessed, together with Your Most-holy, Good and Life-creating Spirit, now and ever, and unto ages of ages. Amen.

The new infant receives his Christian name as a sign of his new identity in the faith community. Although the child is not considered a member of the church, the prayers offered by the priest communicate the expectation of responsibility and anticipate soteriological advancement. Moreover, the notion of being signed with the cross identifies the infant with Christ and

---

Apostolic Tradition 21.16; and Origen, *Homilies on Leviticus* 8:3, and *Commentary on Romans* 5:9.

[15] In the new covenant, baptism—that is, the circumcision of Christ—is an act of God joining a person to Christ (Col 2:11–14).

his sufferings. It is through the path of spiritual struggle, discipline, and daily dying that he is to appropriate the redemptive works of the Crucified One, to partake of his life-giving body and blood, and to progress toward his true human potential, Christlikeness.[16]

Churching of the Child—Entering the Temple

On the fortieth day, the infant child participates in the rite of churching; at that point he is considered a peripheral member. This practice follows the ancient Jewish tradition established in Leviticus 12. It is believed Jesus sanctified the event by his own identification with it as recorded by St. Luke in his Gospel (2:22–40). On this day, Joseph and Mary took the Christ child back to the temple to be "presented to the Lord." The Orthodox rite takes place in the vestibule (a location corresponding to the outer court or Court of the Gentiles in the temple); there the priest meets the mother, sponsor(s), and the child.[17] After the pastor makes the sign of the cross over the mother and infant, he recites the following after his prayer for the mother:

> And bless this child which hath been born of her; increase him; sanctify him; enlighten him; give virtue unto him; and endow him with a good understanding. For thou hast brought him into being, and hast shown him the physical light and has appointed him to be vouchsafed the spiritual light in due time, and that he may be numbered among Thy chosen flock, through the Only-begotten Son, with

---

[16] To be a true human is to be alive in Christ. In the words of the St. Irenaeus, "The glory of God is a living human being" (*Against Heresies* 4.20.6).

[17] Sponsor(s) or godparent(s) serve as additional parents for the child and seek to offer spiritual advice and counsel throughout the baby's life, assisting in good and difficult times. Typically, in the case of the death of a child's parents, a sponsor will raise the child as his or her own.

whom Thou are blessed, together with Thine all-holy, and good, and life-giving Spirit; now and ever unto ages of ages. Amen.

When the petition ends, the priest carries the child into the nave, while reciting Psalm 5:7 (5:8 in the Septuagint): "In the fullness of Your mercy I will come into Your house; In fear of You I will worship toward Your Holy temple." If the infant is male, the priest carries him through the holy doors and around the altar. If the child is female, the priest stands with her before the holy doors only. In either case, the pastor holds the child and recites the words of St. Simeon as recorded in Luke 2:29–32: "Lord, now You are letting Your servant depart in peace, according to Your word; for my eyes have seen Your salvation which You have prepared before the face of all peoples, a light to bring revelation to the Gentiles, and the glory of Your people Israel." At the conclusion of the churching, the child is returned to the mother.

Thus far, in the infant's spiritual journey toward baptism from the first to the fortieth day of his life, the church—the body of Christ—has prayed for his protection and for the blessing to enter and worship in God's temple; and the infant has been sealed with the sign of the cross. The church has also prayed for the child's obedience and faithfulness to Christ throughout his life, for his illumination and entrance into Christ's holy church, and for his reception of life-giving Holy Communion. Therefore, while the infant is neither sacramentally united to Christ nor considered a formal member of the church, he is under the watchful care of God and his people. The conclusion of this membership process is the mystery of baptism.

The Mystery of Baptism—Church Membership: Reception into the Catechumenate

As the infant is carried to the narthex of the church for baptism, he is first received in the catechumenate (the period during which one begins to become a disciple of Christ and enter his holy Church). The priest comes out of the sanctuary and lays his hand on the baby. This ritual action signifies that from that time forth the child belongs to God (Matt 13:30).[18] During his entrance, the child, along with the sponsor(s), participates in the rite of exorcism.[19] In this portion of the service, the priest commands all evil influences, realized or potential, to flee from the child. Then the sponsor—speaking for the infant—confesses he has renounced the Devil, united himself to Christ, and believes in him as King and God. Next, the godparents recite the symbol of faith, the Nicene-Constantinopolitan Creed. These actions represent that the initial declaration of the death of the old man and the reception of the new in the resurrected Christ has begun. After it the sponsor(s) bow low with the child in worship before the Holy Trinity. Thus, the godparents, throughout the exorcisms, are articulating the faith of the little one.[20]

---

[18] This act recalls Jesus's parable about the wheat being gathered into the Lord's barn (Luke 13:30).

[19] The rite of exorcism is described in the early third-century document known as the *Apostolic Tradition*. In 21:1–15 of this writing, generally attributed to St. Hippolytus of Rome, the children are instructed to speak for themselves if they are able to do so. If they are unable, then a parent or sponsor speaks for them. The document states, "At the time appointed for baptism, the bishop shall give thanks over some oil, which he puts in a vessel. It is called the Oil of Thanksgiving. He shall take a portion of the oil and exorcise it. It is called the Oil of Exorcism.... When the elder takes hold of each of them who are to receive baptism, he asks each of them to renounce Satan, saying, 'I renounce you Satan, all your service, and all your works.' After he has said this, he shall anoint each with the Oil of Exorcism, saying, 'Let every evil spirit depart from you.'" Following a Trinitarian confession of faith, the deacon anoints the newly baptized with the Oil of Thanksgiving in the name of Jesus Christ.

[20] Matthew 15:28 provides an example of the faith of one person impacting another when a woman approaches Christ about her sick daughter. "Then Jesus answered and said to her, 'O Woman, great is your faith! Let it be to you as you desire.' And her daughter was healed from that very hour." Another example is found in Mark 2:4–5, where the faith of others results in the forgiveness of sins. The text states, "And when they could not come near Him because of the crowd, they uncovered the roof where He was. So when they had broken through, they let down the bed on which the paralytic was lying. When Jesus saw their faith, He said to the paralytic, 'Son, your sins are forgiven you.'"

In *Of the Water and the Spirit: A Liturgical Study of Baptism*, Father Alexander Schmemann discusses whether there is a need for stated personal faith in the rite of baptism. He argues, "The sacrament then is precisely this: the decisive encounter of faith and the Divine response to it, the fulfillment of the one by the other."[21] Anticipating the question of why infants would be baptized who have neither a personal faith nor a desire to be baptized, Schmemann explains that this question could be asked at every baptism: "If what we have said about faith and desire were understood as implying that the reality and the efficacy of Baptism depends on personal faith, is contingent upon the conscious desire of the individual, then the 'validity' of each Baptism, be it infant or adult, should be questioned. For to whom is it given to measure faith, to pass judgment on the degree of 'comprehension' and 'desire' in it?"[22]

He continues his argument by distinguishing between "personal faith" and "Christ's faith." For Schmemann, Christ's faith, that which is necessary, is "given to us, becoming our faith and our desire, the faith by which, in the words of St. Paul, 'Christ may dwell in your hearts . . . that being rooted and grounded in love (we) may be able to comprehend with all the saints what is the breadth and length and depth and height (Eph. 3:17–18)."[23] Clarifying his point, he continues by explaining that there is a difference between the faith of an adolescent or adult convert to Christianity and that type of faith

> which constitutes the very life of the Church and of her members and which St. Paul defines as having in us Christ's mind, i.e. His faith, His love, His desire. Both are gifts of God. But the former is a *response* to God's call while the latter is the very reality of that to which the call summons. . . . It is personal faith in Christ that brings

---

[21] Alexander Schmemann, *Of Water and the Spirit: A Liturgical Study of Baptism* (Crestwood, NY: St. Vladimir Seminary Press, 1974), 66.
[22] Ibid., 67.
[23] Ibid.

the catechumen to the Church; it is the Church that will instruct him in and bestow upon him Christ's faith by which she lives.[24]

For Schmemann, the faith of the church is the presence of Christ's faith within her. Applying this logic to the case of infants as well as to adults, he writes, "For now we know why Baptism does not and indeed cannot 'depend' for its reality (i.e. for truly being our death, our resurrection with Christ) on personal faith however 'adult' or 'mature' it may be." Also, "Baptism depends—totally and exclusively—on Christ's faith; it is the very gift of his Faith, its true grace."[25] He concludes, "Thus it is on the faith of the Church which *knows* and *desires* it to be—and, therefore makes Baptism that which it is—both 'tomb' and 'mother.'"[26]

Infants, as mentioned previously, are brought to the ecclesia on the fortieth day and "churched." This ritual act identifies a little one as belonging to a Christian family (a holy offspring, according to 1 Cor 7:14) and, therefore, to the church where the faith of Christ is present. The confession by the sponsor(s) on behalf of the infant confirms this position. Moreover, their consent is necessary due to the fact that "they have the power to offer their child to God and to be responsible for his growth in the 'newness of life.'"[27] At the conclusion of the exorcism in the narthex, the child is carried to the baptismal font to further symbolize death and resurrection, or new life movement from the fallen world to the kingdom of God (Romans 6). His sponsors are given a lighted candle, which represents that the infant will soon be united to Christ, the light of the world, in baptism. The newly illumined child is to share in that light.

The Order of Holy Baptism—The Blessing of the Baptismal Water

The celebrant, after offering up petitions for the forgiveness of his own sins before he conducts the mystery, prays for God's blessing upon the baptismal

---

[24] Ibid., 66–67.
[25] Ibid., 68.
[26] Ibid., 69.
[27] Ibid., 70.

waters and breathes on them the shape of the cross three times. He then chants, "Wherefore, O King Who lovest mankind, come Thou now and sanctify this water, by the indwelling of Your Holy Spirit." (As recorded in Genesis 1 and noted by Tertullian in the third century, the Spirit of God throughout salvation history operated with or within the element of water to bring about life and death.)[28] After that, he prays: "And grant to it the grace of redemption, the blessing of the Jordan. Make it a fountain of incorruption, the gift of sanctification, the remission of sins, the remedy of infirmities." (This language recalls the baptism of Christ in the Jordan by St. John the Baptist in John 3:13–17; Christ's entrance into the water sanctified it.) And then, making the sign of the cross in the water with his hand, signifying the destruction of all evil, the priest prays:

> [Lord,] manifest Thyself in this water, and grant that he may put away from himself the old man, which is corrupt through the lust of the flesh, and that he may be clothed upon with the new man, and renewed after the image of Him Who created him: that being buried, after the pattern of Thy death, in baptism, he may, in like manner, be a partaker of Thy Resurrection; and having preserved the gift of Thy Holy Spirit, and increased the measure of grace committed unto him he may receive the prize of his high calling and be numbered with the firstborn whose names are written in heaven, in Thee our God and Lord, Jesus Christ.

Throughout the preparatory process, Orthodox Christians, through faith, see the ritual words, signs, and symbols as communicating the spiritual reality of the operation and effect of the Holy Spirit upon the infant within the mystery.

The Blessing of the Oil of the Catechumens

In the final ritual act before the infant is baptized, the priest anoints him with the oil of gladness. This portion of the service is thematically connected

---

[28] See Tertullian, *On Baptism*, where he sets forth God's use of water in the salvation history of his people as recorded in the biblical texts.

to the event recorded in Gen 8:11. A dove sent out by Noah after the flood returned with an olive branch. This represents, as revealed by the words of the priest, the sacramental place of the oil in conjunction with the Holy Spirit as the water is prepared to receive the infant. The priest refers to "the token of reconciliation and of salvation from the flood, the foreshadowing of the mystery of grace (baptism), and didst provide the fruit of the olive for the fulfilling of Thy Holy Mysteries, Who thereby dost fill them that were under the law with Thy Holy Spirit, and dost perfect them that are under grace." The oil, after the celebrant's request that it be blessed by the operation and indwelling of the Holy Spirit, is employed as a means of protection and renewal for the one who will be baptized. The celebrant pours it into the font three times, making the sign of the cross. To conclude this rite, the infant is anointed with oil on the forehead, ears, hands, and feet. This signifies the healing nature of the action and the enabling of obedience in thought, word, and deed. The child is now prepared to die and be born again of the water and the Spirit (John 3:5; Titus 3:5–6), to enter into the waters of salvation (1 Pet 3:21).

The Mystery of Baptism—Membership in the Church

At this point in the proceedings, the priest takes the child from his sponsor(s), stands on the western end of the baptismal font, and faces east. (According to tradition, west represents the fallen world while east represents the heavenly Jerusalem from whence the Lord will return at the Parousia.[29] It is therefore in this spiritual direction that the dead in Christ shall rise in the rite of baptism and at the Parousia.) Then, following the doctrinal pattern commanded by Christ in Matt 28:19, the priest immerses the child in the baptismal water three times, saying, "The servant of God (Name) is baptized, in the name of the Father, Amen (Immerse). And of the Son, Amen (Immerse). And of

---

[29] St. John Chrysostom discusses the significance of facing east in baptism in his *Baptismal Instructions* 10.14–15.

the Holy Spirit, Amen (Immerse)." This rite, as described in Acts 2:38 and in the Creed, is for "the remission of sins." This is reflected liturgically as the priest and people recite Psalm 32 (31 in the Septuagint) as the newly baptized receives a new white garment of clothing, spiritually signifying the robe of righteousness and the light of Christ. Furthermore, as read during the following rite of chrismation, St. Paul in his letter to the Romans (6:3–11) informs the faithful that this mystery brings about the infant's death, burial, and resurrection-union with Jesus Christ: "As many of us as were baptized into Christ were baptized into His death . . . we were buried with Him through baptism into death, that just as Christ was raised from the dead by the glory of the Father, even so we should also walk in newness of life." Thus, the infant, as a member of the church, the living body of Christ, enters the kingdom of God (John 3:5) and eternal life. He is chrismated (anointed) with holy chrism, oil consecrated by a bishop, and thereby sealed with the gift of the Holy Spirit as the priest makes the sign of the cross on his forehead, eyes, nostrils, lips, ears, chest, hands, and feet (cf. Acts 2:38).

The theological effects of the baptismal rite are summarized in the concluding rite of ablution. Therein the priest, dipping a sponge in clean water, proclaims to the newly illumined, "You are justified. You are illumined. You are sanctified. You are washed: in the name of the Father and the Son and the Holy Spirit." Then, with the sponge, he washes the oil from the child, saying, "You are baptized. You are illumined. You have been chrismated. You are sanctified. You are washed: in the Name of the Father, and of the Son, and of the Holy Spirit." Then, to conclude the ceremony, the infant gives a first offering of the hair of his head and receives a cross. At that point, the newly enlisted soldier of Christ is admonished, within the congregation of the faithful, to daily die to himself by taking up his cross and following Christ. The priest, holding the cross and Gospel Book in his hands, then leads the newly illumined, his sponsor(s), family, and all the little baptized children gathered in a procession around the font, singing, "As many have been baptized into Christ have put on Christ: Alleluia, Alleluia, Alleluia." The final act of his new membership is the reception of Christ in Holy Communion, where he receives the "medicine of immortality."[30]

Question 3: How Does God Treat People Who Die in Their Infancy or Childhood?

When an Orthodox child dies, it is extremely uncommon for him not to have been baptized first.[31] Therefore, when an infant reposes, the funeral liturgy celebrated is the same as that given an adult—with a few exceptions. The reason for this is that the little one has been born again of the water and Spirit in the mystery of baptism. He, by "putting on Christ," has participated sacramentally in the death and resurrection of our Lord; he is thus a member of the body of Christ and sacramentally privy to all that entails. The liturgical language of the service sets forth the mind of the church on this issue of how God treats baptized infants.

The Orthodox Funeral Service for Children

In the Orthodox funeral rite for departed little ones who were two years old or younger, the customary petitions for the forgiveness of sins are omitted. They are replaced with this prayer:

> O Lord Who watches over children in the present life and in the world to come because of their simplicity and innocence of mind, abundantly satisfying them with a place in Abraham's bosom, bringing them to live in radiantly shining places where the spirits of the righteous dwell; receive in peace the soul of Your little servant (Name), for You Yourself have said: "Let the little children come to Me, for of such is the Kingdom of Heaven."

---

[30] St. Ignatius of Antioch, *Letters to the Ephesians* 20.
[31] Infants that fall asleep in the Lord are buried in their white baptismal garments.

The theme of protection and reception as first encountered in the first-day prayers for the infant are echoed in the petitions for newly departed babies. The Gospel reading referenced here and later read by the priest in the service sets forth the Orthodox answer to the question being considered:

> At that time, they were bringing even infants to him, that he might touch them; and when the disciples saw it, they rebuked them. But Jesus called them to him, saying, "Let the children come to me, and do not hinder them; for to such belongs the kingdom of God. Truly I say to you, whoever does not receive the kingdom of God like a child shall not enter it." ... Those who heard it said, "Then who can be saved?" But he said, "What is impossible with men is possible with God." (Luke 18:15–17, 26–27)

The reoccurring theme of the Gospel chosen by the Orthodox Church in the funeral rite reveals her theology relating to the deaths of baptized infants. They are understood to be received by Christ and granted rest in the place where the just repose: the kingdom of heaven.

In the Case of Unbaptized Infants

Following the Eastern tradition of apophatic theology, a theology that recognizes the inadequacy of human language to describe the essence of God and therefore attempts to describe God by negation or to speak of him only in absolute terms and to avoid what may not be said, the early Greek Fathers remained silent regarding this question of unbaptized infants with the exception of the fourth-century Father, Gregory of Nyssa.[32] A Vatican-approved

---

[32] For further study, see *On Infants' Early Deaths*, trans. William Moore, in *Selected Writings and Letters of Gregory, Bishop of Nyssa*, Nicene and Post-Nicene Fathers of the Christian Church, Second Series, ed. Philip Schaff and Henry Wace, vol. 5 (New York, NY: Christian Literature Company, 1893), 372–81. It is currently the practice of the Orthodox Church to administer emergency baptisms as the need arises. In turn, it is the normal course of action that if an infant

document set forth by the International Theological Commission provides a concise summary of the Eastern tradition: "Few Greek Fathers dealt with the destiny of infants who die without Baptism because there was no controversy about this issue in the East. Furthermore, they had a different view of the present condition of humanity."[33] This comment is a reference to the Orthodox doctrine of ancestral sin discussed previously in this work. The document continues by contrasting ancestral sin with the Western view of original sin first formally set forth by St. Augustine of Hippo (c. 354–430).[34] The Commission explains:

> For the Greek Fathers, as the consequence of Adam's sin, human beings inherited corruption, volatility, and mortality, from which they could be restored by a process of deification made possible through the redemptive work of Christ. The idea of an inheritance of

---

is critically ill or otherwise in danger of death, the priest will baptize, chrismate, and serve him or her Holy Communion if possible.

[33] International Theological Commission, "The Hope of Salvation for Infants Who Die Without Being Baptized," 1.2.11, available at http://www.vatican.va/roman_curia/congregations/cfaith/cti_documents/rc_con_cfaith_doc_20070419_un-baptised-infants_en.html.

[34] Some Western fathers seemed to consider infants as innocent in the eyes of God: *Shepherd of Hermas* (c. 150): "They are as infant children in whose hearts no evil originates; nor did they know what wickedness is, but always remain as children. Such accordingly without doubt, dwell in the kingdom of God, because they defiled in nothing the commandments of God.... (A)ll infants are honorable before God, and are first in persons with Him."; Justin Martyr, *First Apology* XVIII, (ca. 155), "For you let even necromancy, and the divinations, whom you practice on immaculate children, and the invoking of departed human souls."; and Tertullian in his work *A Treatise of the Soul* 56, "If you mean the bad, even now the souls of the wicked deserve to be consigned to those abodes; if you mean the good why should you judge to be unworthy of such a resting-place the souls of infants and of virgins, and those which, by reason of their condition in life were pure and innocent?"

sin or guilt—common in the Western tradition—was foreign to this perspective, since in their view sin could only be a free, personal act.[35]

The work continues: "Alone among the Greek Fathers, Gregory of Nyssa wrote a work specifically on the destiny of infants who die, *De infantibus praemature abreptis libellum*. The anguish of the Church appears in the questions he puts to himself: the destiny of these infants is a mystery, "something much greater than the human mind can grasp."[36]

Although Gregory concedes to deep mystery, he concludes by contrasting the death of an infant with that of an adult: "Since the innocent infant does not need purification from personal sins, he shares in this life corresponding to his nature a sort of regular progress, according to his capacity.... The premature death of newborn infants does not provide a basis for the presupposition that they will suffer torments or that they will be in the state as those who have been purified in this life by all the virtues."[37] Thus, in the death of an unbaptized infant, Gregory concedes: "Apostolic contemplation fortifies our inquiry, for the One who has done everything well, with wisdom (Psalm 104:24), is able to bring good out of evil."[38] In regards to the place where

---

[35] International Theological Commission, "The Hope of Salvation for Infants Who Die Without Being Baptized," 1.2.11. While the Orthodox Church does not subscribe to notion of original guilt, Patriarch Jeremiah II—in his discussion with certain Lutheran representatives from Tübingen from 1572–79—does seem to find some common ground with the Protestants on the issue of original sin. See George Mastrantonis, *Augsburg and Constantinople: The Correspondence between the Tübingen Theologians and Patriarch Jeremiah II of Constantinople on the Augsburg Confession* (Brookline, MA: Holy Cross Orthodox Press, 1982), 36.

[36] International Theological Commission, "The Hope of Salvation for Infants Who Die Without Being Baptized," 1.2.12. For an English translation of *De infantibus praemature abreptis libellum*, see Gregory of Nyssa, *On Infants' Early Deaths*.

[37] Gregory of Nyssa, *De infantibus praemature abreptis labellum*, in International Theological Commission, "The Hope of Salvation for Infants Who Die Without Being Baptized," 1.2.12.

[38] Ibid.

unbaptized infants find themselves in death, the Eastern Fathers stress that they do not suffer the eternal reality of hell. Beyond this, they remain silent.

Although these Fathers do not offer in-depth insight into the question at hand, an Orthodox funeral service drafted and performed for a stillborn child includes the following petitions: "O Savior and Master of life: comfort the faithful parents of this departed child with the knowledge that to innocent children, who have done no deeds worthy of tears, are granted the righteousness, peace and joy of Thy kingdom."[39] Thus, in the case of how God treats baptized and unbaptized deceased infants, the Orthodox Church approaches God in its liturgy with assurance of his grace and mercy and of the infants' participation in the joy of his kingdom.

Question 4: When and How Are Children Instructed in Christian Doctrine?

As noted throughout this chapter, Orthodox soteriology is understood as a process, not a point in time, which begins for infants in baptism. Unlike in many Western churches today, confirmation or chrismation (the seal of the gift of the Holy Spirit) in the Eastern Orthodox Church is still performed during the greater rite of baptism. Throughout their entire lives, then, those who have been baptized into Christ are to grow in the grace and knowledge of what took place via their rite of entrance into the church. And, with gentleness and respect, they are to be able to give a good account for the hope within them (1 Pet 3:15). Historically, however, the Orthodox Church has not developed a formal systematic set of texts didactically employed according to the age and mental development of the participant—a formal recognized catechism.[40] Rather, instruction has always been understood as organic

---

[39] Reference taken from a service performed at St. Vladimir's Orthodox Theological Seminary in Crestwood, New York.

[40] This is not to say there have not been Orthodox catechism books drafted in the form of Reformation-type documents. These works are helpful tools, but their use is not mandated by the church. Arguably, another reason for the lack of

or quite often "caught" rather than "taught." As a result, infants and children receive their proper theological education through participation in the liturgical life of the church.[41] According to the Orthodox tradition, "If you are a theologian, you will truly pray, and if you truly pray, you will be a theologian."[42] Although formal catechetical instruction takes place as one participates in the daily liturgical services and the Sunday Divine Liturgy, a personal catechism leading to a more in-depth understanding of the biblical and theological dogmas found within the Nicene-Constantinopolitan Creed is arguably brought to fruition in the Orthodox home.

Instruction through Participation in the Liturgical Life of the Church

Orthodox worship engages all five senses and demands work (*leitourgia*) and learning through repetition. The acronym EPIC, coined by Leonard Sweet and used to describe postmodern worship, seems to describe the 1,650 year-old liturgical experience of the Orthodox Christian: worship is to be Experiential, Participatory, Image Driven, and Connected.[43] In the liturgy, children encounter and participate in the story of salvation told through the iconography surrounding them; they hear the litanies of the people as incense

---

formal catechetical material is the practice of infant communion; there is not a time of instruction between baptism and first communion.

[41] It is not uncommon, however, for Orthodox parishes to host Vacation Bible Schools and other special events during the year. For an insightful commentary on children's education in the church, see the study by Andrew Estocin, "Is it time to do away with Sunday School?," at http://myocn.net/is-it-time-to-do-away-with-sunday-school/?fb_action_ids=10153270804879083&fb_action_types=og.likes.

[42] Evagrius Ponticus, *On Prayer* 61, in *Evagrius Ponticus*, ed. A. M. Casiday, The Early Church Fathers, ed. Carol Harrison (New York, NY: Routledge, 2006), 192. English translation of *On Prayer* by Simon Tugwell.

[43] Leonard Sweet, *Post-Modern Pilgrims: First Century Passion for the 21st Century* World (Nashville, TN: B&H, 2000).

fills the air, and they cross themselves at the mention of the name of the Holy Trinity. The singing of the Psalter tells of the coming of the Lord. The reader shares aloud the epistle lesson from the apostles. The vested priest proclaims the words of Christ in the Gospels and delivers his homily exhorting the believers to imitate those things they have heard. The Symbol of Faith (a biblical summary of the essential Christian dogmas) is recited by all. Tithes and offerings are offered to the Lord. Collectively hands and voices are raised in the saying of the "Our Father." And as the gifts of bread and wine are offered to God "on behalf of all and for all," they bow low with the community as the Spirit of God transforms the gifts into the body and blood of Christ. Then, with all those who have been baptized into Christ, they approach Christ and receive him in Holy Communion, physically partaking of the gospel.

In such services the doctrines of the church are made alive in worship. To participate in the services is to participate in the doctrines of the faith.[44] They are not simply memorized, but are rather progressively actualized throughout the life of the Christian. In summary, the formal liturgical life of the church provides a living tradition by which children are taught to pray, use the Bible, hear the stories of the saints, make offering to God, and are transformed by his presence and power in the reading of the sacred texts and the divine mysteries. This being said, daily instruction and guidance are offered by families in their homes as they seek to incorporate the rule of prayer daily.

Catechism in the Home—A Way of Life

For the Orthodox, the primary teaching mechanism of the church is the home. And the primary task of the parents is to raise saints, those who will be

---

[44] According to ancient practice, infants and children attend every liturgical service offered by the local parish. In a normal church week, this may consist of Wednesday night vespers, Saturday Great Vespers, Sunday Matins, and Divine Liturgy. This is not to say there are no other services offered during the week. In some Orthodox parishes, matins and vespers are served on a daily basis along with the third, sixth, and ninth hour prayers.

able to give a good account before the awesome judgment seat of Christ. Saint John Chrysostom describes the accountability of Christian parents: "We are so concerned with our children's schooling [and worldly success]; if only we were equally zealous in bringing them up in the discipline and instruction of the Lord." Also, "This, then, is our task: to educate both ourselves and our children in godliness; otherwise what answer will we have before Christ's judgment seat?"[45]

Every Orthodox home has a place set apart as holy. There the Bible, icons, candles, censers, prayer books, and other sacramental items are placed for daily collective and personal prayer. The father and mother are to teach first and foremost by demonstration so the children will follow in imitation. This means the family will gather for daily prayers, the reading of the Scriptures, and discussion about where the church is during the liturgical year and why it is important. Saint John Chrysostom further speaks to the necessity of the parents setting an example for their children: "Generally the children acquire the character of their parents, are formed in the mold of their parents' temperament, love the same things their parents love, talk in the same fashion, and work for the same ends."[46] Moreover, when the household attends formal church services, the adults are to keep their children engaged by explaining the ritual signs and symbols they see and experience. If a monastery is nearby, the family can visit with the monks or nuns for practical advice, spiritual insight, rest, and prayer. Also, the priest can bless the family home and have a meal with the family during the season of theophany. And throughout the year, he can listen to each family member's confession and offer spiritual guidance. In summary, instructing children in the tradition of the church is a collective effort. It involves the liturgical life of the local ecclesia, the priest, the monastic community, and the daily instruction of the parents—for in the Orthodox Church no person is ever saved alone.

---

[45] St. John Chrysostom, *On Marriage and Family Life* (Crestwood, NY: St. Vladimir Seminary Press, 1986), 64.
[46] Ibid. 64.

Conclusion

This chapter set forth a liturgical context by which certain questions regarding infants and children could be addressed from an Orthodox perspective. It was demonstrated that infants are born into a world contaminated by ancestral sin. They are not guilty for the actions of their primal parents that led to the fall, or for the sinful actions of any other ancestor proceeding from it. The cumulative effects of historical disobedience, however, impact them from the moment of conception until physical death: the ultimate consequence of sin suffered by all. Therefore, as children of Christian parents, these "holy ones" are immediately given over to the watchful care of God and the church where they are signed, named, and received by him in the rites pertaining to baptism.

According to the Orthodox Church, formal membership and the soteriological process of salvation begins when infants are sacramentally united to the conquering death and resurrection of Christ and are sealed with the Holy Spirit in the mystery of baptism; they are born again via water and the Spirit. By participation in the liturgical life of the church, they thus become "partakers of the divine nature" (2 Pet 1:4) and overcome, by God's grace and their cooperation with it, the effects of the fall and dwell once again in communion with God in paradise.

If one of these little baptized ones should die, the church does not pray for the forgiveness of his or her sins—for the infant is not considered personally sinful. Rather, the body of Christ prays for the child's reception by Christ, who said, "Suffer little children, and forbid them not, to come unto me: for such is the kingdom of Heaven." In the case of non-baptized infants, the church expectantly, as set forth in the liturgical rites, looks to God for grace and mercy, citing the same Gospel passage.

Throughout the child's life as a Christian, he will participate in the living tradition of mother church, both among the ecclesia and in his home. He will be catechized weekly by the formal liturgical theology of the church and by the domestic example he experiences daily. Thus, the little one will be instructed to become a rationally-endowed sheep that hears and understands the voice of the Good Shepherd. This true knowledge, contrary to that proclaimed by the world and developed in various shades of darkness, is gained only through the continual acquisition of the Holy Spirit. It is fostered by the child's parents, and preserved, protected, and passed on from one generation to the next. To conclude, this study was timely and relevant "in the beginning" and it still is today as people continue to ask, "What about the children?" and look to the church, the living body of Christ, for answers pertaining to life and death.

Responses to an Orthodox View of Infants and Children in the Church

A Roman Catholic Response by David Liberto

Fr. Jason Foster has presented the Orthodox position on the topic of infants and children in the church. My response will employ the *modus operandi* of citation and response. I will cite a brief passage from the paper, and then I will respond by way of questions, analysis, and critique. For ease of presentation, I will cite the various passages in the order in which they are given in Foster's essay.

> Citation 1: "This notion of anthropology is less historical and individualistic; it is not centered on Adam. Rather, it is a timeless narrative that brings all of humanity into the story, into the garden. Thus, as humans, infants inherit the fallen condition as victims not as perpetrators."

This point leads me to ask, But what about the curses of Genesis 3? These are given as direct consequences of the fall. And what other sources can one marshal for this position? Irenaeus, one of the main patristic sources for this, offered a very defined soteriology very early. His is hardly the most developed anthropology in the patristic period.

Moreover, if humans inherit this guilt, how is that not traceable to Adam? Does this tracing back to him accord better with Paul's understanding that in Adam all have sinned (Rom 5:12)? How is this different from the Catholic understanding of original sin, which is contracted by propagation? If the terminology of ancestral sin is to emphasize the universality of the problem of sin, in this we (Catholics and Orthodox) agree. However, this understanding is not opposed to the Catholic understanding of original sin, but it is not a full explanation of the cause and effects as found in latter teaching either.

> Citation 2: "This comment [referring to a quotation from the International Theological Commission document on the fate of unbaptized infants, a commission of the Roman Catholic Church] is a reference to the Orthodox doctrine of ancestral sin discussed previously in this work. The document continues by contrasting ancestral sin with the Western view of original sin first formally set forth by St. Augustine of Hippo (c. 354–430)."

It should be noted, however, that a Catholic does not hold to a doctrine of original sin merely because it was propounded by the Bishop of Hippo. Councils and popes upheld Augustine's teaching on the matter as opposed to the Pelagian denial of original sin and its consequences.

> Citation 3: "Thus, in the case of how God treats baptized and unbaptized deceased infants, the Orthodox Church approaches God in its liturgy with assurance of his grace and mercy and of the infants' participation in the joy of his kingdom."

The baptismal rite cited by the author includes an exorcism for the baptism of an infant. Why would this be if not because, until the infant is baptized, the child is not a child of light, but is instead in need of God's grace as found in baptism? Therefore, to assert that all infants enjoy participation in the life of God seems to empty the need and efficacy of Baptism—something that the Orthodox liturgy does not support.

A LUTHERAN RESPONSE BY DAVID P. SCAER

Orthodoxy correctly holds that how a church worships reflects its faith. Doctrine and practice exist in a reciprocal relationship. A consistent liturgy inculcates the church's faith in adults and infants; the Orthodox ritual of baptism rehearses biblical realities so that Christ in his infancy is identified with the frailty of our human nature. Naming the child signifies the child's new life in baptism by immersion, symbolizing Christ's death and resurrection. Lutheran liturgies do not have the anointing and processing with the child from the narthex to the sanctuary, but they retain exorcism, renunciation of Satan, recitation of the creed, and baptism in the name of the Triune God. The Orthodox formula, "you are baptized in the name of the Father" rather than "I baptize you in the name of the Father" follows the biblical usage where the passive voice of the verb indicates that God baptizes, which is a very Lutheran thought indeed. Sponsors speak for the faith of the child who by baptism becomes a member of the body of Christ. Quotations by Alexander Schmemann that baptism does not depend on faith could easily be attributed to Martin Luther. Lutherans do not have a rite of blessing of the font, but they do hold that baptism is the water through which God led Israel out of captivity and in which Jesus was baptized.

Similarities between Lutheran and Orthodox rites for infant baptism are striking, but each understands man's creation and fall into sin differently. They agree that the condition in which man was created in Eden was probationary. If Adam had been allowed to remain in paradise and had eaten from the tree of life after he sinned, then his and his descendants' misery would have been compounded by permanent separation from God. He was given the choice of deification by following God's word, but he listened to Satan, who could not rightly offer it. While Lutherans speak of the promise of permanent holiness, the Orthodox speaking of deification provides a perspective on Adam's transgression not as ordinary sin, but being lured by Satan to become like God. Lutherans challenge the Orthodox view that Adam's descendants—including infants—share in his guilt and suffer the consequences of death, while remaining morally intact with only an inclination to sin. So each person, including children, sins by his own volition. Lutherans hold that since all were present in Adam, all participated in his sin (Rom 5:12). Sin's universality was remedied by the universality of salvation in Christ, the second and greater Adam (Rom 5:15; 1 Cor 15:22). Lutherans do not know the state of moral neutrality in which the will is free to choose between good and evil. Not even Adam had a free will in this sense. Rather, he crossed the boundary from holiness to sinfulness—an option not given to his descendants.

Christ was conceived in a supernatural way without sin and chose to suffer sin's consequences. Here we bring up a peripheral question of why God provided a remedy for Adam's descendants, but not for angels. Each angel sinned of his own accord. We participated in Adam's treachery, but the decision was his, not ours. Out of this dilemma God provided a solution in baptism as the new creation in Christ.

The Orthodox correctly interpret Ps 51:5, "Behold . . . and in sin did my mother conceive me" (RSV), as the mother's sinfulness in conceiving, though they add that it does not "describe the theological and anthropological condition of the infant." But it does. The first part of the passage, "I was brought forth in iniquity" (Ps 51:5, RSV) indicates that from birth humans are permeated with sin. Setting aside differences of interpretation on this passage, other passages describe humankind's innate opposition to the things of God; "the imagination of man's heart is evil from his youth" (Gen 8:21, RSV); "out of the heart come evil thoughts, murder, adultery, fornication, theft, false witness, slander. These are what defile a man" (Matt 15:19–20, RSV).

Orthodox—along with Lutherans—wrestle with the fate of infants born to non-Christians and dying without baptism; they agree no definitive answer exists for this conundrum. Rather than speaking of children's innocence, it might be preferable to say their evil inclinations have not fully developed.

Anyone proposing that children are not morally responsible should consider 2 Kings 2:23–24 where the taunters of Elisha are small boys who pay the consequences of their actions.

A Reformed Response by Gregg Strawbridge

Father Foster has provided a fascinating glimpse into some rites of the Eastern Church that illuminates the Orthodox view of children and infants.[47] We agree on several points, three of which are particularly noteworthy: (1) Participation in the liturgical life of the church, from infancy, is a potent means of shaping children. (2) The home is a primary teaching mechanism, not an alternative to the church. (3) Baptized children should be nourished in Christ in Holy Communion, without delay.[48]

I do, however, have some criticisms of the Eastern view as presented. The primary concern is the relative complexity of this set of rites. Is this forty-day program what Jesus had in mind when he commanded the baptism of the nations (Matt 28:19–20)? I suggest it was not.

First, the Orthodox view of original sin does not comport with biblical teaching (Psalm 51; Romans 3). We confess together that "there is one baptism for the remission of sins" as the Nicene Creed indicates. But what can this mean for an allegedly sinless infant? Prior to union with Christ, Adam is our covenantal head. Therefore, humans stand condemned in him and through him receive innately our own depravity. Infants and young children

---

[47] I want to thank my research assistant, Scott Cline, for helping me interact with all of these positions. Any faults in my responses or position are mine alone.

[48] Paedocommunion (allowing infants to participate in Communion) is a disputed issue among Reformed churches. For a Reformed theologian who argues that Communion should be reserved for only those who have made a profession of faith, see Cornelis P. Venema, *Children at the Lord's Table?: Assessing the Case for Paedocommunion* (Grand Rapids, MI: Reformation Heritage, 2009).

are thus sinful. This Augustinian position provides the clearest and most biblical explanation.

Second, delaying baptism until the fortieth day is unwarranted and unbiblical. Leviticus 12 was referenced as a basis for the practice, but this passage is concerned with the purification of the mother during the antecedent age when such purifications were necessary under Torah. The world has since been cleansed by the blood of Christ; no such ceremonial cleansing is now required for her or the baby. The circumcision of the child (far more parallel to baptism) was to be on the symbolic eighth day (as the passage states, Lev 12:3). Jesus was presented in the temple on the fortieth day, but he had already been officially incorporated into the covenant community by circumcision.[49]

Third, if a child is named on the eighth day "as a sign of his new identity in the faith community," but baptism is the basis for this identity, there is a strange confusion on a child's identity over his first forty days. I doubt that parents are confused about the child's identity. Surely faithful parents would consider the infant to be part of the church and people of God, or functionally a covenant child. A covenantal view of incorporation is a more robustly biblical understanding of the identities of such children.

Fourth, I can see no scriptural basis for the "oil of gladness" as a preparatory sacrament prior to baptism. Oil is unnecessary if Christian water baptism is identified with the baptism of the Holy Spirit, which was symbolized in the priestly ordination by oil. As Peter recalled, "John baptized with water, but you will be baptized with the Holy Spirit" (Acts 11:16, NASB). In Eastern Orthodoxy, the simplicity of the Great Commission baptism has

---

[49] In AD 254, sixty-six bishops convened in Carthage and declared that baptism need not be delayed until the eighth day; they never considered whether it may be delayed longer than that (George Pretyman, *Elements of Christian Theology* [London: Luke Hansard & Sons, 1815], 472). The "eighth" day circumcision is symbolic of the resurrection (e.g., the "first day" of the week is the eighth day). Thus, a better type-fulfillment timing for baptism is simply on the nearest possible Sunday.

been drowned by layers of unnecessary tradition that distract from baptism's singular glory: the washing of sinners in the Triune name.

Finally, the destiny of the unbaptized child dying in infancy turns out to be a mystery in Eastern Orthodoxy. But if salvation simply comes through baptism, then the question is easy to answer: either baptism saves or it does not. The Reformed view is nuanced regarding the efficacy and necessity of baptism.[50] I am also dissatisfied that Fr. Jason did not provide an answer to the fate of non-Christian children dying in infancy. The example from the funeral service clearly presupposes a child born into a family from the church. What of a child with no such link to the church?

A Baptist Response by Adam Harwood

Orthodox and Baptist views on infants and children in the church are similar in some respects. Baptists, like the Orthodox, affirm that sin results in the defilement of precious newborns (Ps 51:5), as stated in their first-day prayers for a mother and child. Baptists also affirm that the disobedience in the garden resulted from Adam and Eve's misuse of their free will. As Article 3 of the Baptist Faith and Message (BFM) states, "In the beginning man was innocent of sin and was endowed by his Creator with freedom of choice. By his free choice man sinned against God and brought sin into the human race."

Louth's description of ancestral sin is consistent with the effects of sin mentioned in the BFM.[51] Specifically, Louth notes that people are born into a "ruined cosmos" and that "Adam has unleashed consequences of sin" which

---

[50] "Although it is a great sin to contemn or neglect this ordinance, yet grace and salvation are not so inseparably annexed unto it, as that no person can be regenerated, or saved, without it: or, that all that are baptized are undoubtedly regenerated" (Westminster Confession 28.5).

[51] Since many Baptists regard the BFM to summarize the major teachings of the Bible, those Baptists regard concordance with the BFM to be concordance with the teachings of Scripture.

devastate God's creation. The BFM describes the results of Adam's sin on creation in similar ways, noting that Adam's "posterity inherit a nature and an environment inclined toward sin" (Article 3). Foster clarifies the Orthodox view of the impact of ancestral sin: "Thus, as human beings, infants inherit the fallen condition as victims not as perpetrators." Also, they are not "active causes" or participants in ancestral sin. Foster's comments are consistent with this remark in the BFM about Adam's posterity: "Therefore, as soon as they are capable of moral action, they become transgressors and are under condemnation." Like the Orthodox view, some Baptists consider humans to be responsible for sin only after they are capable of moral action. Other Baptists, however, consider all people to be born guilty due to the sin of Adam. In both Baptist views, all people—even as infants—are negatively impacted in their nature and environment by sin.

Orthodox ceremonies for naming and "churching" the child function in ways that bear some similarity to the Baptist parent-baby dedication. Here too the infant is not yet a full member of the church. Rather, the family and church pray for the future spiritual growth of the child. The Orthodox view should be commended for its seriousness in nurturing the spiritual growth of families and because these and other ceremonies attempt to identify with biblical precedent. For example, the naming ceremony correlates loosely to the instance when the infant Jesus was presented at the temple (Luke 2:22–38). Another similarity between the Orthodox and Baptist views is that both are certain no infants will occupy hell, although Baptists differ with one another concerning the theological details of infant salvation.

Baptists diverge from the Orthodox, however, at three crucial points: (1) union with Christ, (2) water baptism, and (3) entrance into the church. Baptists regard union with Christ to be a relationship one enters by repenting of sin and trusting in Jesus. Based on their views of union with Christ and the New Testament example of confession prior to baptism, Baptists would receive as church members only those people who have voluntarily united with Christ then confessed that faith through water baptism by immersion.[52] Neither a sponsor's faith nor following ritual can substitute for the necessity of having a personal faith relationship with Jesus.

Foster is correct, however, in citing Matt 15:28 as an example of the faith of one person impacting another person. But this example of God physically healing a demon-possessed daughter due to the Canaanite mother's faith is disanalogous to a sponsor attempting to confess faith in Christ on behalf of an infant at his baptism. Many Scriptures exhort believers to pray for one another, and this text indicates that God responded to the mother's prayers by delivering her daughter from demonization. In this episode, Jesus clarified for the Jews that even a Gentile could call on God in genuine faith, which resulted in God healing her daughter. It is not clear from this text, however, that a person can repent of another person's sin or trust Christ on behalf of another. Foster offers stronger support for his case when he cites the four men carrying the paralytic to Jesus. Mark 2:4–5 indicates Jesus saw "their faith" and declared the man's sins forgiven. Even so, the paralytic man's faith could have been included in the pronoun "their." In this case, the man was capable of consciously trusting Jesus—something that infants likely cannot do.

The Orthodox and Baptist views are united at several points concerning original sin and infant salvation, but the primary distinction centers on the Baptist theology and practice of baptizing and affirming as united with Christ only those individuals who repent of sin and believe in Jesus. This excludes infants from church membership.

---

[52] For the sequence of confession before water baptism, see Acts 2:36–41; 8:4–12, 26–38; 10:44–48; 16:13–15, 25–34; and other texts.

Infants and Children in the Church:
A Roman Catholic View

David Liberto

Introduction

Anyone who holds a baby is struck by how delicate, how dependent, and how defenseless an infant is. Surely little ones are precious—precious to the parents and siblings, to the grandparents, to caregivers, and they are no doubt precious to God. Because they are so innocent, infants are often described as little angels, and it is rare to find a reaction to them like that of the great St. Augustine who thought he discerned anger and jealousy in an infant who watched another infant nursing.[1] Thus, if one only developed his theological thinking by what he experienced—notwithstanding the assessment of St. Augustine—one would probably assume that all infants and young children are in good spiritual health.

Augustine may have been wrong in assessing what he witnessed with the "jealous" infant, but he would go on to defend an understanding of sin, grace, and salvation that would, in the main, represent the Catholic soteriological position as the church would define it in subsequent teaching. For

---

[1] St. Augustine, *Confessions*, 2nd ed., trans. F. J. Sheed, ed. Michael Foley (Indianapolis, IN: Hackett, 2006), 9.

that reason, Augustine will be visited again below. But before expounding the Catholic position on the spiritual state of infants, it is important to first give a brief exposition of the sources utilized by the Catholic Church to discern the truth of the faith.

One's theological knowledge, which includes one's understanding of the state of the souls of infants, is a matter of dealing with the mysteries of the faith—many of which are never directly empirically verifiable. Knowledge of these mysteries comes through revelation, and they are apprehended by faith. This is not to say that one's experiences have no bearing on theological thinking;[2] nevertheless, Christian doctrines are not formulated merely by a reflection on one's experiences *per se*; they are informed first and foremost by God's revelation about his plan of salvation for the human family.

For a Catholic, this revelation is found in the Holy Scriptures and in the Apostolic Tradition. These two distinct sources of revelation coalesce to provide "one sacred deposit of the Word of God."[3] The magisterium, or teaching authority of the church—namely all the popes throughout history and all those bishops who are/were in communion with them—are charged with "the task of authentically interpreting the word of God, whether written or handed on."[4] The Catholic position on any given datum of revelation, therefore, can be found in those magisterial teachings of popes, councils, and synods where the authentic understanding of the Scriptures and the Tradition

---

[2] If we define "theology" as *fides quarens intellectum*, then we should distinguish the contents of the faith from the efforts of the theologian. An example of the faith is the Symbol of Nicaea. It posits what the Catholic faithful are to believe. It is recited at Sunday Mass. On the other hand, St. Augustine's psychological analogies for the Trinity, as found in his *De trinitate*, constitute a work of theological reflection. His purpose there is to illuminate and explicate the mystery of the Trinity as found in the Scriptures and in the teaching of the church as found in the Creed of Nicaea.

[3] *Dei verbum* 10 (Dogmatic Constitution on Revelation), in *The Documents of Vatican II*, ed. Walter M. Abbott, S.J. (New York, NY: Guild, 1966), 117. The Latin reads, "*unum verbi Dei sacrum depositum.*"

[4] Ibid.

are expounded for the faithful.[5] Discerning what the teaching of the Catholic Church is on the spiritual condition of infants requires an examination of the Sacred Scriptures, to be sure, but must also include the magisterial teaching of the Catholic Church. According to *Dei verbum*, the Second Vatican Council's document on revelation, it is the magisterium that provides the only sure guide for interpreting the Sacred Scriptures correctly.[6] Therefore, although quoting from Rom 5:12 might be part of a Catholic understanding on the universality of sin, the Catholic position is never merely a matter of exegesis; it must include the church's explication and understanding of that verse of the Bible, as well as her understanding of other verses of the Sacred Scriptures that are related to the question at hand. Finding the mind of the church on any given theological question, then, is a matter of knowing the magisterial teaching on that question. This is the reason why an exposition of the Catholic position on a topic must include citations from such sources as councils, synods, and papal documents. Discovering what the teaching of the Catholic Church is requires the use of these sources.

---

[5] A compendium of magisterial teaching is found in *Denzinger: Enchiridion symbolorum definitionum et declarationum de rebus fidei et morum*, 43rd ed., ed. by Peter Hünermann et al. (San Francisco, CA: Ignatius, 2012). Although this volume only bears the name of the first editor/compiler, another editor of the *Enchiridion* was Adolph Schönmetzer, who reworked the marginal numbering system of his predecessor. For this reason, marginal numbers of the present edition will bear the prefix DS, for Denzinger/Schönmetzer, followed by the index number as assigned in this edition.

[6] *Dei verbum* 10 (DS 4214): "But the task of authentically interpreting the word of God, whether written or handed on, has been entrusted exclusively to the living teaching office of the church, whose authority is exercised in the name of Jesus Christ. This teaching office is not above the word of God, but serves it, teaching only what has been handed on, listening to it devoutly, guarding it scrupulously and explaining it faithfully in accord with a divine commission and with the help of the Holy Spirit; it draws from this one deposit of faith everything which it presents for belief as divinely revealed."

Question 1: How Are Infants and Children Impacted by Sin?

In giving a Catholic response to this question, I feel a brief recounting of the Catholic Church's understanding of the original state of man, the fall, and its consequences for all humans is important.

The church understands that the first man "was not only created good, but was also established in friendship with his Creator."[7] Man was created with natural endowments, including the gift of reason whereby he would image his Creator and preside over all of the visible creation. Added to his natural endowments was the supernatural gift of grace, which elevated man above what was his by nature. That man had friendship or fellowship with God and was in a state of holiness and justice due to the grace bestowed on him from the beginning. This state is called "original justice" in Catholic teaching.

Being a rational creature, Adam also was endowed with free will. Although he enjoyed friendship with God, he was first a creature of Almighty God with the responsibilities and obligations that were the due of a rational, embodied, creaturely being. God gave instructions to Adam, including a prohibition against eating from the tree of the knowledge of good and evil. When Adam disobeyed God on this matter, he fell from grace, lost original justice, forfeited the friendship he had with God, and incurred penalties—including death. In the state of original justice, Adam enjoyed a harmony of soul and body; he was rightly ordered. His spiritual faculties of soul, intellect, and will, would have had control over his passions.[8] With the fall, this right ordering

---

[7] *Catechism of the Catholic Church* (hereafter cited as CCC), 2nd ed. (Washington DC: United States Catholic Conference, 1997), no. 374. Citations of CCC refer to catechism numbers rather than page numbers.

[8] "Passions" are understood to be natural faculties of the human soul. Man, a rational creature, possesses senses and appetites that are attracted to the good and shun evil. CCC, 1767 states, "In themselves passions are neither good nor evil. They are morally qualified only to the extent that they effectively engage

was destroyed. Importantly, the Catholic position is not that human nature was destroyed by the fall, but that it was wounded.[9] Adam fell from grace and lost the original integrity with which he was created.

The Catholic Church, since the time of the Pelagian controversy in the early fifth century, developed a teaching on original sin. The teaching is that all humans are implicated in the sin of Adam.[10] Original sin, so understood, is not referring only to the disobedience of Adam, but especially to the consequences of the first sin on all humans, infants included. In the year 418 the Council of Carthage met to oppose the teaching of the Pelagians. Its second canon addresses the spiritual state of infants:

> Likewise, it has been decided: Whoever says that little children right from their mothers' wombs ought not to be baptized or says that they are indeed baptized for the forgiveness of sins but that they derive from Adam no trace of original sin that would have to be removed by the bath of rebirth, whence it follows that in their case the baptismal formula "for the remission of sins" is to be understood as not true but false, let him be anathema.[11]

Again in the sixteenth century, the Catholic Church would promulgate teaching on original sin at the Council of Trent's fifth session. Like the Council of Carthage and the Second Council of Orange held in AD 529, it would address the spiritual condition of infants. In fact, Canon 4 of the

---

reason and will. . . . It belongs to the perfection of the moral or human good that the passions be governed by reason."

[9] *CCC*, 405.

[10] Second Council of Orange, canon 2 (*DS* 372): "If anyone maintains that the fall harmed Adam alone and not his descendants or declares that only bodily death which is the punishment of sin, but not sin itself, which is the death of the soul, was passed on to the whole human race by one man, he ascribes injustice to God and contradicts the words of the apostle: 'Sin came into the world through one man, and death through sin, and so [death] spread to all men as all sinned in him.'" The Councils of Carthage and Trent contain similar teaching.

[11] *DS* 223.

fifth session of Trent, recognizing the magisterial authority of the Council of Carthage, quotes from the latter's canon 2, cited above.

This chapter began by describing our experience of infants. The innocence of these little ones is our common experience. Certainly it is common sense to make the point that these babies are innocent. Catholic teaching agrees with this—in part. Original sin "does not have the character of personal fault."[12] In other words, although infants contract original sin, they are innocent of any personal sin. Sin, as the *Catechism of the Catholic Church* defines it, is "an offense against reason, truth, and right conscience."[13] Until children reach the age of reason or discretion, they are unable to sin "an utterance, a deed, or a desire contrary to the eternal law."[14] Nevertheless, because all contract original sin, infants are deprived of the original holiness and justice that was Adam's in the beginning. They will, in due time, experience the full effects of original sin whereby "human nature is weakened in its powers; subject to ignorance, suffering, and the domination of death; and inclined to sin."[15] Some of these natural powers affected by original sin are latent in the infant or young child. For instance, there is not yet the power to deliberate or choose based on the truth of the natural moral law accessible to all who are able to utilize reason. Effects of original sin include a darkening of the intellect and a weakening of the will. In an infant in whom the age of reason and deliberation have not been reached, however, one cannot detect any effect with regard to these powers. What is sure is that without the grace of God that heals and elevates the soul, the infant, "born with a fallen nature,"[16] would continue to be in bondage to the power of sin and darkness; this would eventually manifest itself in due course. That does not mean that every unbaptized person is going to be as bad as possible. Nor does the Catholic Church teach that everything that is

---

[12] CCC, 405.
[13] Ibid., 1849.
[14] St. Augustine, *Contra Faustum*, 22, as quoted in the CCC, 1849.
[15] CCC, 418.
[16] Ibid., 1250.

done by someone who is not in a state of grace is sinful.[17] In fact, the church teaching, as found at the Council of Trent, is that someone not in a state of grace—like the unbaptized—can do morally good things, performing actions that fall under the moral or cardinal virtues.

According to the Catholic Church, there is only one remedy for the sickness of original sin—baptism. Our Lord himself taught, "Unless one is born of water and the Spirit, he cannot enter the kingdom of God" (John 3:5).[18] The Catholic Church understands that Christ is here speaking about baptism. Baptism, in Catholic thought, is one of the seven sacraments of the New Testament. It is the one that is necessary if one is to be born a child of God. The Catholic Church "does not know of any means other than baptism that assures entry into eternal beatitude."[19] Because the Catholic Church understands that original sin is the state of all humans who enter the world, it is

---

[17] Council of Trent, sixth session, can. 7 (DS 1557): "If anyone says that all works performed before justification, no matter how they are performed, are truly sins or deserve God's hatred; or that the more earnestly one tries to dispose himself for grace, the more grievously he sins, let him be anathema."

[18] All Scripture references in this chapter are from the English Standard Version (ESV).

[19] CCC, 1257. Although the church is clear as to the necessity of baptism for one to be saved, she does not rule out the possibility that some who, due to no fault of their own, have not heard and responded to the gospel, and thereby have not had the possibility of asking for baptism. This "invincible" ignorance does not save, however; somehow the grace of Christ must be offered to them by God, and doing what they know to be right by the light of the natural law and ready to obey God, they can, in some mysterious way, come to saving faith. The *locus classicus* for this magisterial teaching is found in Pope Pius IX's *Quanto conficiamur moerore* (DS 2866): "We know as well as you that those who suffer from invincible ignorance with regard to our most holy religion, by carefully keeping the natural law and its precepts, which have been written by God in the hearts of all, by being disposed to obey God and to live a virtuous and correct life, can by the power of divine light and grace, attain to eternal life. For God who sees, examines, and knows completely the minds and souls, the thoughts and qualities of all, will not permit, in his infinite goodness and mercy, anyone who is not guilty of voluntary fault to suffer eternal punishment."

incumbent upon all Catholic parents to bring the newly born to the laver of regeneration. The Catholic Church would not be so insistent on this if it were not based on her understanding that original sin is universal in scope.

What does the Catholic Church teach about the state of those infants who are baptized? Does the power of sin still hold some grip on them? First, baptism's spiritual significance for the recipient can be discerned in the rite of baptism itself. Whether by immersion or by pouring, the matter and mode of baptism signify the cleansing from sin and the newness of life in the Holy Spirit. Immersion, more specifically, signifies the person being buried with Christ and rising to new life (Rom 6:3–4). Pouring signifies the cleansing from sin and the springs of living water that now flow into the soul of the recipient. The infant who receives baptism is a "new creation in Christ" (2 Cor 5:17); thus, those baptized infants become "partakers of the divine nature" (2 Pet 1:4).

However, although the recipient of grace through baptism is no longer in a state of original sin, and, in the case of an adult who is baptized, has all past personal sins forgiven, baptism does not remove all of the temporal consequences associated with original sin. Baptized persons will still suffer, get sick, and experience physical death. There remains what the Catholic tradition calls the *fomes peccati* (the kindling of sin), or an inclination to sin called concupiscence.[20] The Catholic Church does not consider this inclination to sin to be a sin itself, but merely a weakness and disorder that remains after original sin is remitted. Despite the presence of concupiscence, the baptized person receives grace to overcome the inclination to sin. He can and should strive to obey the commandments of God.[21] With grace, the believer has the theological virtues of faith, hope, and love infused within his soul. Although

---

[20] The Council of Trent, fifth session, can. 5 (*DS* 1515). See also CCC, 1264.

[21] *DS* 1570: "If anyone says that a justified man, however perfect he may be, is not bound to observe the commandments of God and of the Church but is bound only to believe, as if the Gospel were merely an absolute promise of eternal life without the condition that the commandments be observed, let him be anathema."

present in the soul in a habitual (ever-present) manner, these virtues are given precisely so that the child of God may act in a supernatural manner, a manner befitting a son or daughter of God. With these virtues, along with the gifts of the Holy Spirit, the believer is equipped to collaborate in the divine plan and to cooperate in the work of God—both for the salvation of his own soul and for the souls of others.[22]

Baptized infants, although receiving justifying grace, the theological virtues, and the gifts of the Holy Spirit, are unable to utilize the gifts or have them come to fruition in holy actions until they are able to know the truth of the gospel for themselves and to act in accord with that truth. It was for the same reason that infants and very young children were not to be charged with any personal sin. Someone who has not reached the age of reason,[23] therefore, cannot be charged with a morally good or meritorious action any more than he can be charged with an immoral or punishable action.

Question 2: How Does God Treat People Who Die in Infancy or Childhood?

If a baptized little one dies, the Catholic Church is clear about that child's eternal destiny. Since such a person would have no way of sinning subsequent to baptism, he would be in a state of grace. There would be nothing that would prevent him from the ultimate supernatural end of the human person, the beatific vision.

The case of infants and children[24] who die without being baptized is a much more difficult matter to discern from Catholic teaching. That is not to say that there is no teaching to inform a Catholic theological response to

---

[22] CCC, 2003.

[23] The "age of reason" is a stage of human development reached by an individual; the stage is probably reached at a chronological age unique to each child.

[24] The words "infants" and "children" will be used interchangeably in this section, with the understanding that children are those who have not reached the age of reason.

such a question; there is magisterial and even dogmatic teaching that either directly or indirectly informs one's theological response. Nevertheless, it must be stated that there is no dogmatic statement of the church that definitively addresses the final destination of the souls of deceased unbaptized children.

Three clear teachings of the Catholic Church bear upon the question of the destiny of the souls of unbaptized infants, however. First, as stated above, the Catholic Church has dogmatic teaching concerning the universal extent of original sin. Infants are not exempt from the guilt oft original sin. No one in such a state can inherit the kingdom of God. Second, the Catholic Church only knows one sure way for someone to have original sin remitted; that is the laver of regeneration as found in the sacrament of baptism. Third, unbaptized infants cannot be charged with personal sin.

Starting with St. Augustine, there is a steady stream of theological opinion on the state of unbaptized infants utilizing the dogmatic teaching of the Catholic Church to form such opinions.[25] Augustine clearly assented to all three of the teachings above. His theological opinion was that unbaptized infants are damned to hell, although with the mildest of punishments (*mitissima poena*).[26] For him, there is no salvation without grace, and there is no grace outside baptism. There simply is no way, in Augustine's theological reasoning, that the unbaptized infant could be saved. Although there is no penalty incurred for any personal sin, even infants sinned in Adam.[27] Augustine's view, although harsh to modern sensibilities, was adopted by other Fathers

---

[25] In this section, the theological positions on limbo will be discussed. The Catholic Church has never pronounced a dogmatic teaching directly on the subject. The theological positions discussed here are all in keeping with the dogmatic teaching on original sin and the necessity of baptism for salvation. Even Augustine's position, which will seem harsh to the modern ear, is still a valid theological position—even if there might be few, if any, adherents presently.

[26] St. Augustine, *De pecc. mer.*, 1.16.21.

[27] Augustine utilized a Latin translation of Romans that translated the *eph hō* ("because") of Rom 5:12 as *in quo* ("in whom").

of the church. In the Middle Ages, Anselm of Canterbury expounded the Augustinian position.[28]

In the Scholastic period, new and varied positions on limbo were developed. Limbo of the infants is the place for the souls of unbaptized infants who are excluded from the beatific vision due to original sin.[29] Peter Lombard defended a view in his *Sentences* (Bk. II, dist. 33) that understood Augustine's "mildest penalty" to refer to the fact that unbaptized infants do not have the beatific vision.[30] In this version of limbo, the souls of unbaptized infants would experience the *poena damni* (pain of loss), but not the *poena sensus* (pain of sense) experienced by those who suffer due to personal sins. This is a softening of the Augustinian position whereby these souls are not enjoying the beatific vision, but neither are they to be lumped with the *massa damnata*, as was done by Augustine.

The final Scholastic theory of limbo to be examined is the one put forth by St. Thomas Aquinas. His mature position on the souls in limbo is found in his *Quaestiones disputatae de malo*. It is here, in this later work written around 1270, that St. Thomas would build his theory of limbo on the teaching of the church and on his own theological anthropology as found in *De malo*. Thomas understands that original sin (unlike personal sin) leaves man's nature basically intact. Based on this understanding, he asserts that the souls in limbo come to possess perfect natural knowledge. Yet, because these souls never received grace, a gift that would elevate them to the supernatural order, they are not able to possess knowledge of the beatific vision. Theirs is a knowledge of natural beatitude. The souls in limbo, according to this position, do not suffer any pain of loss because they do not know that they have

---

[28] Anselm of Canterbury, *De conceptu virginali et de originali peccato*, in Opera omnia, 6 vols., ed. F. S. Schmitt (Edinburgh, Scotland: T. Nelson, 1946–1961) 2:170–71.

[29] The beatific vision is the immediate knowledge of God that human souls and angels will enjoy in heaven.

[30] Peter Lombard, *The Sentences Book II: On Creation*, trans. Giulio Silano (Toronto, Canada: Pontifical Institute of Medieval Studies, 2008), 164–70.

been deprived: they have no knowledge of a supernatural end, which is only known through faith. St. Thomas sums up his position: "The souls of children dying in Original Sin indeed know of beatitude in general and according to its broad definition, but they do no know the specifics. And therefore they do not grieve over its loss."[31]

In asserting this reason why the souls do not experience anguish, St. Thomas contributes a new version of limbo that while observing all the relevant Catholic dogmas, incorporates his own theological anthropology of the natural and supernatural orders into the mix. These two orders have their own ends and their own proper operations whereby one can distinguish between natural and supernatural knowledge, natural and supernatural beatitude.[32] Serge-Thomas Bonino summarizes the theological import of St. Thomas's position:

> There are degrees in the ordering of man to the vision of God, and the doctrine of limbo pleads in favor of the relative consistency of a natural order defined by its own finalities, by the *immediate* ordering the natural end, the one that it can obtain by its own proper activity, the one that the soul in limbo enjoys.
>
> Man, in fact, is not immediately ordered to the supernatural end, and his distant ordering does not create an exigency. In the *De*

---

[31] St. Thomas Aquinas, *De malo* (Leonine Edition, vol. 23, 1982), q. 5, a. 3, ad 1: "*Animae puerorum in peccato originali decedentium cognoscunt quidem beatitudinem in generali secundum communem rationem, non autem in speciali; et ideo de eius amissione non dolent.*"

[32] Ibid., co.: "*Quia ergo pueri post mortem sciunt se nunquam potuisse illam gloriam caelestem adipisci, ex eius carentia non dolebunt. Possumus tamen utrumque coniungentes mediam viam tenere, ut dicamus quod animae puerorum naturali quidem cognitione non carent, qualis debetur animae separatae secundum suam naturam, sed carent supernaturali cognitione, quae hic in nobis per fidem plantatur, eo quod nec hic fidem habuerunt in actu, nec sacramentum fidei susceperunt. Pertinet autem ad naturalem cognitionem quod anima sciat se propter beatitudinem creatam, et quod beatitudo consistit in adeptione perfecti boni; sed quod illud bonum perfectum, ad quod homo factus est, sit illa gloria quam sancti possident, est supra cognitionem naturalem.*"

malo (q. 5, a. 3, ad 3), St. Thomas explains that the degree of gravity of a punishment may be taken either from the nature of the good of which someone is deprived—and in that case the punishment of loss is the greatest there is since it deprives of an infinite Good—or from the relationship that the subject has with the good of which it is deprived. In this case the punishment of damnation, for infants, is the slightest there is because they are deprived of what is the least connatural to them. The ordering to the vision of the divine essence, although inscribed in their nature, is for them extremely remote, since they have never had the means to actualize this orientation.[33]

Lastly, of all the positions on limbo, that of Thomas Aquinas seems to work better with the teaching that infants do not commit any personal sin. Although the lack of grace is due to the lack of baptism, the lack of any personal sin would seem to require a position that did not have any suffering—not even of the mildest form—for those who die innocent of any personal sin.

Until recently, the theological position of limbo enjoyed a certain acceptance in Catholic thought and culture. Although no one theory was ever raised to the status of dogma by the Catholic Church, limbo was accepted as a doctrine of the Church—at least inasmuch as it was found in the writings of various Catholic theologians of prominence. In 2007, the International Theological Commission (ITC) expressed it this way:

> [T]he affirmation that infants who die without Baptism suffer the privation of the beatific vision has long been the common doctrine of the Church, which must be distinguished from the faith of the Church. As for the theory that the privation of the beatific vision is their sole punishment, to the exclusion of any other pain, this is a

---

[33] Serge-Thomas Bonino, "The Theory of Limbo and the Mystery of the Supernatural in St. Thomas Aquinas," in *Surnaturel: A Controversy at the Heart of Twentieth-Century Thomistic Thought*, ed. Serge-Thomas Bonino (Ave Maria, FL: Sapientia, 2009), 145.

theological opinion, despite its long acceptance in the West. The particular theological thesis concerning a "natural happiness" sometimes ascribed to these infants likewise constitutes a theological opinion.[34]

A new theological opinion surfaced in the *Catechism of the Catholic Church*. Here the church holds out the hope that unbaptized infants who die will receive the grace of God and be saved:

> As regards children who have died without Baptism, the Church can only entrust them to the mercy of God, as she does in her funeral rites for them. Indeed, the great mercy of God who desires that all men should be saved, and Jesus' tenderness toward children which caused him to say: "Let the children come to me, do not hinder them," allow us to hope that there is a way of salvation for children who have died without Baptism. All the more urgent is the Church's call not to prevent little children coming to Christ through the gift of holy Baptism.[35]

It is this position that the International Theological Commission is forwarding in the document cited. After a thorough recounting of how theologians dealt with this problem in the past, including the various renditions of a limbo of the infants, it is clear that the ITC offers the view that there is reason to hope that unbaptized infants will be saved outside the sacrament of baptism. The difference between all the theories of limbo recounted by the document and the position that is forwarded by the ITC document is that the former theories of limbo are theological positions informed and framed by the church's dogmatic teaching on original sin and the need for baptism for salvation. The latter and more recent position is a theological opinion that emphasizes the

---

[34] International Theological Commission, "The Hope of Salvation for Infants Who Die Without Being Baptized," 1.7.40, available at http://www.vatican.va/roman_curia/congregations/cfaith/cti_documents/rc_con_cfaith_doc_20070419_un-baptised-infants_en.html.

[35] CCC, 1261.

mercy of God and the exigencies of current pastoral situations. No matter what theological position one might hold on the fate of unbaptized infants who die, we can all "hope" that God saves them. However, there simply is no revelation on this matter in order to pronounce in any definitive way the fate of these innocent ones.[36] On this point, the ITC document is clear and sober:

> It must be clearly acknowledged that the Church does not have sure knowledge about the salvation of unbaptized infants who die. She knows and celebrates the glory of the Holy Innocents, but the destiny of the generality of infants who die without Baptism has not been revealed to us, and the Church teaches and judges only with regard to what has been revealed.[37]

Question 3: When and How Are Children Considered Members of the Church?

A child is incorporated into the church in and through baptism.[38] All the rights and privileges that belong to a church member belong to the baptized child. These rights include the right to a Catholic home where the faith is lived and taught. When the child arrives at the age of reason, in a progressive and developmental manner, he will take on the responsibilities and duties that

---

[36] It is the opinion of the present writer that the Thomistic position contains much to merit its consideration. It takes the relevant dogmas into consideration while doing justice to the fact that an infant cannot do anything to deserve condemnation. It also renders a position that supplies a natural end of human creatures.

[37] ITC, *Infants*, n. 79.

[38] *Code of Canon Law* (henceforth CIC), c. 849, in *Code of Canon Law: Latin-English Edition* (Washington, DC: Canon Law Society of America, 1999), 321: "Baptism, the gateway to the sacraments and necessary for salvation by actual reception or at least by desire, is validly conferred only by a washing of true water with the proper form of words. Through baptism men and women are freed from sin, are reborn as children of God, and, configured to Christ by an indelible character, are incorporated into the Church."

come with church membership.[39] Being born into a Christian home is not enough. It is not natural birth but the regeneration of baptism—supernatural birth—that places one into the church. That is why the Church insists that Catholic parents are to have their children baptized only a few weeks after birth, and sooner if there is danger of death.[40]

The Catholic Church understands that the sacraments of confirmation and the Eucharist follow baptism. These three sacraments together make up

---

[39] It is important to clarify what is meant by "the Church." Catholics tend to capitalize the word church when speaking of "the" Church. That is because it serves as the proper name of the People of God. The Church, in Catholic teaching, is to be identified with the visible Roman Catholic Church. This is the traditional teaching, explicitly taught by the magisterium. Despite opinions to the contrary, the Second Vatican Council maintained this dogmatic teaching. *Lumen gentium* no. 8 (DS 4118–19):

> Christ, the one Mediator, established and continually sustains here on earth His holy Church, the community of faith, hope and charity, as an entity with visible delineation through which He communicated truth and grace to all. But, the society structured with hierarchical organs and the Mystical Body of Christ, are not to be considered as two realities, nor are the visible assembly and the spiritual community, nor the earthly Church and the Church enriched with heavenly things; rather they form one complex reality which coalesces from a divine and a human element. For this reason, by no weak analogy, it is compared to the mystery of the incarnate Word. As the assumed nature inseparably united to Him, serves the divine Word as a living organ of salvation, so, in a similar way, does the visible social structure of the Church serve the Spirit of Christ, who vivifies it, in the building up of the body.
>
> This is the one Church of Christ which in the Creed is professed as one, holy, catholic and apostolic, which our Savior, after His Resurrection, commissioned Peter to shepherd, and him and the other apostles to extend and direct with authority, which He erected for all ages as "the pillar and mainstay of the truth." This Church constituted and organized in the world as a society, subsists in the Catholic Church, which is governed by the successor of Peter and by the Bishops in communion with him, although many elements of sanctification and of truth are found outside of its visible structure.

[40] *CIC*, c. 867.

the sacraments of initiation. Confirmation is important since it completes the baptismal grace received in baptism.[41] The bond to the Church, begun in baptism, is perfected in confirmation where recipients are strengthened or "confirmed" by the Holy Spirit so as to be able to bear witness to and defend the faith given in baptism. Although all sacraments, worthily received, give the recipient sanctifying grace, each sacrament also dispenses a grace peculiar to it.

Until the early twentieth century, the order of reception of the sacraments of initiation was baptism, confirmation, and Eucharist. Under Pope Pius X, receiving the Eucharist was allowed before confirmation. This was done for pastoral reasons. The Eucharist was not offered to some until the age of twelve or thirteen. This delay was due to the fact that confirmation, whose ordinary minister is a bishop, was, for logistical reasons, not being administered until later. Thus, first Communion was being delayed as a matter of course since the traditional order of reception of the sacraments was being followed. The pope thought it not good to delay reception of the Eucharist and to thereby deprive youth so great a grace. Unfortunately, following Pope Pius X's permission for First Communion to come before confirmation, the latter was practically detached from Holy Communion, with the age of confirmation varying from place to place, and from one generation to the next.[42]

Some bishops have decided to restore the sequence of the sacraments of initiation to the traditional order. In those dioceses, seven or eight-year-old children are confirmed and receive their First Communion at the same mass. This seems to be the more theologically and pastorally sound age and

---

[41] CCC, 1285.

[42] The 1983 Code of Canon Law gives minimum age for confirmation as the age of discretion (*CIC*, c. 889). *CIC*, c. 891 suggests that confirmation take place around the age of discretion, but leaves it up to the conference of bishops in a given territory to determine another age. In 2002, the United States Conference of Catholic Bishops designated the span between seven and sixteen years of age as being the age of confirmation. It became prevalent in most dioceses to confirm at age sixteen.

order for confirmation. The Eucharist is the summit of the sacramental life of the church. Having confirmation after one's First Communion does not accord with the progressive nature of the sacraments of initiation where the Eucharist is the height of one's full communion with the Church.

Perhaps some bishops favored a late age because they felt the recipients needed to be more mature. After all, confirmation is considered by many to be the sacrament of Christian maturity. However, this is not really the case. Below are the effects of confirmation, as given by the *Catechism of the Catholic Church*:

> It brings an increase and deepening of baptismal grace;
> it roots us more deeply in the divine filiation which makes us cry, "Abba! Father!";
> it unites us more firmly to Christ;
> it increases the gifts of the Holy Spirit in us;
> it renders our bond with the Church more perfect; and
> it gives us a special strength of the Holy Spirit to spread and defend the faith by word and action as true witnesses of Christ, to confess the name of Christ boldly, and never to be ashamed of the Cross.[43]

Nowhere is the word maturity used in the listing of the effects. But more importantly, one should realize that the sacrament of confirmation does not presuppose the effects that it causes in the recipient. Confirmation is a perfecting of baptismal grace. It provides people the strength to live a more perfect spiritual life. Having those graces sooner rather than later in the traditional sequence seems the better pastoral response to an era dominated by a strange brew of secularism, skepticism, and materialism. Add to that the emergence of the New Atheism, and one can make a strong case for confirming at a younger age. Graces will be needed to combat such a tide of forces that would see to the ruin of the young and vulnerable.

---

[43] CCC, 1303.

Question 4: When and How Are Children Instructed in Christian Doctrine?

It is never too early to teach children about the faith. Young children learn by imitation. Thus, although their little ones might not understand deep theological truths, parents should not underestimate the powerful and long-lasting impressions made on children who learn first and foremost by imitating their parents, siblings, and other family members. Even before there is any formal instruction about the faith at home, the child is already learning valuable lessons regarding what is right and wrong, about how to treat others with respect, and about love and forgiveness. It is clear and consistent Catholic teaching that the primary place for instruction in the faith is within the family. The Church understands the important and irreplaceable influence that parents and the home environment have on a child. Parents are to provide models of virtuous living to their children. They are to give instruction in the faith in both word and deed. Even two- and three-years-olds can develop a sense of the sacred. It is especially at this age, in fact, that children have very active religious imaginations. Parents should foster their openness to the sacred.

Thomas Aquinas was fond of the axiom, "that which is received is received in the mode of the receptor." With this axiom in view, it is important that children be instructed in a manner befitting their stages of life. Much of this comes down to common sense. When adults speak to an infant, their tone is different than when speaking to other adults; the vocabulary they use is different. This serves as a reminder that parents should be careful to provide their offspring age-appropriate instruction in the faith.

A Catholic can go many places to get magisterial teaching on the importance of the family for instructing little ones in the faith. One important source for teaching on marriage and the family is Pope Pius XI's magisterial letter *Casti conubii* of 1930. In the encyclical he writes,

> The blessing of offspring, however, is not completed by the mere begetting of them, but something else must be added, namely the

proper education of the offspring. For the most wise God would have failed to make sufficient provision for children that had been born, and so for the whole human race, if He had not given to those to whom He had entrusted the power and right to beget them, the power also and the right to educate them. For no one can fail to see that children are incapable of providing wholly for themselves, even in matters pertaining to their natural life, and much less in those pertaining to the supernatural, but require for many years to be helped, instructed, and educated by others. Now it is certain that both by the law of nature and of God this right and duty of educating their offspring belongs in the first place to those who began the work of nature by giving them birth, and they are indeed forbidden to leave unfinished this work and so expose it to certain ruin. But in matrimony provision has been made in the best possible way for this education of children that is so necessary, for, since the parents are bound together by an indissoluble bond, the care and mutual help of each is always at hand.

If the duty of educating children is primarily the responsibility of the parents,[44] the Church herself is also aware of the role she must play in assisting the parents in this holy endeavor.[45] The Catholic Church has built and maintained schools for children for centuries. These schools afford children

---

[44] *CIC*, c. 793, §1: "Parents as well as those who take their place are obliged and enjoy the right to educate their offspring; Catholic parents also have the duty and the right to select those means and institutions through which they can provide more suitably for the Catholic education of the children according to local circumstances."

[45] Ibid., c. 794, §1: "The duty and right of educating belongs in a unique way to the Church which has been divinely entrusted with the mission to assist men and women so that they can arrive at the fullness of the Christian life."

from Catholic families the opportunity to be educated in the faith.[46] Here the education is typically more formal in nature. Using various educational methods that are age-appropriate, Catholic school teachers are an important resource for families who want to reinforce and supplement the formation in the faith they have begun in their children. Catholic schools are charged with the responsibility to nurture, protect, and develop what has begun in the home. Again, Pius XI provides guidance in this area in his encyclical of 1929, *Divini Illius Magistri*:

> Education belongs preeminently to the Church, by reason of a double title in the supernatural order, conferred exclusively upon her by God Himself; absolutely superior therefore to any other title in the natural order.
>
> The first title is founded upon the express mission and supreme authority to teach, given her by her divine Founder: "All power is given to me in heaven and in earth. Going therefore teach ye all nations, baptizing them in the name of the Father, and of the Son, and of the Holy Ghost, teaching them to observe all things whatsoever I have commanded you, and behold I am with you all days, even to the consummation of the world." Upon this magisterial office Christ conferred infallibility, together with the command to teach His doctrine. Hence the Church "was set by her divine Author as the pillar and ground of truth, in order to teach the divine Faith to men, and keep whole and inviolate the deposit confided to her; to direct and fashion men, in all their actions individually and socially, to purity of morals and integrity of life, in accordance with revealed doctrine."

---

[46] Ibid., c. 796, §1: "Among educational means the Christian faithful should greatly value schools, which are of principal assistance to parents in fulfilling their educational task."

> The second title is the supernatural motherhood, in virtue of which the Church, spotless spouse of Christ, generates, nurtures and educates souls in the divine life of grace, with her Sacraments and her doctrine. With good reason then does St. Augustine maintain: "He has not God for father who refuses to have the Church as mother."[47]

Pope Pius thus ties together the magisterial and the maternal natures of the Church. In the life of the believer, the Church is first a mother in the supernatural order. That order has its own supernatural operations and end. The Church is teacher in that she instructs her children so they can do the will of God, thereby fulfilling the responsibilities incumbent on the child of God.

Many magisterial documents address the importance of Christian education in the faith. But why, if grace is conferred by baptism and the other sacraments, is education so important? One document that supplies the rationale for proper instruction of children in the faith is the Second Vatican Council's *Declaration on Christian Education* (*Gravissimum educationis*), promulgated on October 28, 1965. The document states,

> Since every Christian has become a new creature by rebirth from water and the Holy Spirit, so that he may be called what he truly is, a child of God, he is entitled to a Christian education. Such an education does not merely strive to foster in the human person the maturity already described. Rather, its principle aims are these: that as the baptized person is gradually introduced into a knowledge of the mystery of salvation, he may daily grow more conscious of the gift of faith which he has received; that he may learn to adore God the Father in spirit and in truth, especially through liturgical worship; that he may be trained to conduct his personal life in righteousness and in the sanctity of truth, according to his new standard of manhood (Eph 4:22–34).

---

[47] DS 3686.

Thus, indeed, he may grow into manhood according to the mature measure of Christ (cf. Eph 4:13), and devote himself to the upbuilding of the Mystical Body. Moreover, aware of his calling, he should grow accustomed to giving witness to the hope that is in him (1 Pet 3:15), and to promoting that Christian transformation of the world by which natural values, viewed in the full perspective of humanity as redeemed by Christ, may contribute to the good of society as a whole. Therefore this holy Synod reminds pastors of souls of their acutely serious duty to make every effort to see that all the faithful enjoy a Christian education of this sort, especially young people, who are the hope of the Church.[48]

Just as every child needs food and water in order to grow and flourish, the child of God, born in and through the waters of baptism, needs to grow and mature spiritually. This is why Catholic parents, always with the support of the Church, are to nurture their children in the faith. In this way, the child of God can grow into a mature and responsible Christian adult who can live worthy of the high calling of the Christian vocation and contribute to the good of society as this life provides a witness of hope, faith, and love for all to see.

Conclusion

This chapter began with the idea that experience and common sense would tell us that infants and small children are innocent. Catholic theology would agree that they are wholly innocent of any actual sins, yet it admits that they remain diseased by an invisible contagion that all humans contract—original sin. The Catholic Church knows of no other remedy for this universal malady other than baptism. And once baptized, the infant is a new creature in Christ

---

[48] *Gravissimum educationis* 2 (Declaration on Christian Education) in *The Documents of Vatican II*, ed. Walter M. Abbott, S.J. (New York, NY: Guild, 1966), 640–41.

and a member of God's family, the Church. Grace is infused into the baptized baby's soul. Catholic parents then have the grave responsibility to provide an ongoing education for their children so that these supernatural gifts, once given at baptism and completed in confirmation, are allowed to develop and mature so that along with the natural development of the child, there might be a concurrent supernatural development of those gifts God bestowed in and through the sacraments.

If parents bear a grave responsibility to see to the natural needs of their children, how much more is it the church's duty to provide for their spiritual needs, education, and development? The Catholic Church, both *Mater et Magistra*, understands that Catholic parents require the assistance of the Church in many and varied ways. It is in and through the Church that children receive the sacraments of initiation. The Catholic Church has established schools to assist parents in providing a sound education in things secular and sacred. Parents and the Church can work cooperatively to provide boys and girls all they need to mature as healthy and holy children of God.

Responses to a Roman Catholic View of Infants and Children in the Church

An Orthodox Response by Jason Foster

The Eastern Orthodox Church and the Roman Catholic Church share the first millennium of church history. This is evidenced in part by our appeal to common sacred texts *and* church tradition in answering theological questions; for us, the two cannot be separated logically. But while the ancient East and West both claim to be the "One, Holy, Catholic and Apostolic Church," they have historically diverged on the anthropological and soteriological ramifications of the sin of Adam and Eve and how their choices infected their progeny.

It is not difficult to see in the views presented how the teachings of the sixteenth century Roman Catholic Church, originally systematized by St. Augustine of Hippo (AD 354–430), influenced the historical Protestant understandings of original sin (guilt); and, consequently, how it relates to infants. Therefore the Baptist, Lutheran, Presbyterian, and Roman Catholic positions share a common source and derivations of it that are unfamiliar to the Eastern Orthodox Church. However, contrary to the Baptist and Reformed (Presbyterian) views but similar to the Lutheran perspective, the sacramental remedy of baptism—as offered by David Liberto in a coherent and faithful presentation to the teaching of the magisterium (*obsequium religiosum*)—is analogous, to some extent, to the theology and praxis of the Orthodox Church regarding infants and children: the necessity of mystical incorporation (baptism) into the church for the remission of sins and union with Christ in his death and resurrection, the efficacy of the liturgical rites of confirmation and Holy Communion, and the need for family, parish, and parochial education.

While there are numerous similarities between the East and the West, another major difference between the Orthodox Church and the Roman Catholic Church is the understanding of church dogma. Orthodoxy sees the final deposit of faith given by Christ to the church. Roman Catholics subscribe to what Cardinal Henry Newman referred to as the "Development of Doctrine," whereby the church grows in her understanding of dogma. In relation to Adam and infants, Roman Catholics, as set forth in Liberto's work, have arguably transitioned in their theological anthropology. The 1885 Baltimore Catechism confirmed the position taken at the Council of Trent in 1546 (Session V) by proclaiming original sin as that which "comes down to us from our first parents, and we are brought into the world with its guilt on our soul" (Q. 266). Liberto, in his chapter, references the 1997 version of the *Catechism of the Catholic Church* in which "new theological opinions surfaced." There the doctrine of original sin is still present; however, it is rearticulated in words that seem to avoid the notion of original guilt (a position not ascribed to by the Orthodox Church and briefly referenced in Liberto's chapter in his section on the eternal state of unbaptized infants). In this new catechism, human nature is "wounded by (Adam's) first sin," "weakened" by ignorance, suffering, and death, and "inclined to sin" (416). These conclusions are in close theological proximity with the Orthodox teaching on ancestral sin. Thus, this new or emerging Roman Catholic theological anthropology explaining how sin impacts little ones may serve to further realign the West with the East on the issue of how sin impacts them. However, there are also certain theological ideas that developed in the Roman Catholic Church after the Great Schism in AD 1054 that are foreign to Orthodoxy, such as the development of the doctrine of limbo for infants and the separation in time between the sacraments of confirmation and Holy Communion from baptism. (The Fourth Lateran Council of 1215 ended the ancient Western practice of paedocommunion.)

While many questions may be asked regarding these innovations and decisions, they find their place in a greater system that can, arguably, only be understood within it. Ultimately, Roman Catholics and Eastern Orthodox Christians, like the other traditions presented, desire to understand God's heart regarding the place of infants and children in the economy of salvation offered to them and us by a "good God who loves mankind, and unto [Him] we ascribe glory, to the Father, and the Son, and the Holy Spirit, now and ever and unto the ages of ages. Amen."[49]

A LUTHERAN RESPONSE BY DAVID P. SCAER

Lutheran and Catholic doctrine were shaped during the sixteenth-century Reformation; thus, their respective doctrines and practices are best understood in tandem. To show their agreement with the Catholics against the Anabaptists, who were refusing to baptize infants and were rebaptizing those baptized in infancy, Lutherans set forth their views on baptism before Emperor

---

[49] This is part of a common conclusion to various litanies in Orthodox services, e.g., matins, vespers, or Divine Liturgy.

Charles V in the Augsburg Confession of 1530. In the Confutation of the Augsburg Confession, the Catholics responded favorably to the Lutheran positions on baptism, but grave differences soon surfaced requiring Lutherans to respond in the Apology of the Augsburg Confession the next year. The Peace of Augsburg (1555) recognized both Lutheranism and Catholicism as legal religions of the Holy Roman Empire of the German nation and baptism in either church bestowed citizenship.

In those days infant baptism was as much a cultural phenomenon as it was a religious one. But no longer does infant baptism enjoy this privileged status, and the years have long passed when families with long Christian roots in North America were expected to have their children baptized. Still, however, Lutherans and Catholics administer infant baptism with virtually identical liturgies. Close relatives or family favorites serve as sponsors to speak for the child in renouncing Satan and confessing the Creed.

Both Lutherans and Catholics believe all humanity is corrupted by sin for which God provided a remedy in baptism through which the Holy Spirit gives rebirth into the kingdom of God. Baptized children who die in infancy are received by Christ into eternal bliss. Parents have the prime responsibility of nurturing the faith given in baptism, but the church shares in this responsibility by maintaining parochial and Sunday schools. Before being confirmed, baptized children are instructed in the catechism with attention given first to the Ten Commandments, the Apostles' Creed, and the Lord's Prayer. This is followed by instruction on baptism, confession and absolution, and the Lord's Supper. Thus, the general outlines of the faiths are similar.

Lutheran and Catholic differences center on Luther's doctrine of justification that God, on account of Christ, justifies believers through faith that necessarily produces good works; faith—not works—determine one's relation to God. However, differences first emerged regarding the view of original sin. Both agreed that original sin embraces all humanity for which God provides a remedy in baptism.

While Catholics hold that baptism eradicates original sin, they say it does not forgive actual sins. Lutherans disagree. For Catholics, the remaining inclination to sin can be overcome by cooperating with grace given in the other sacraments. For Lutherans, original sin is such an absolute corruption of the human nature that man opposes all the things of God. The baptized Christian is born again, but struggles with sin until death. This radical understanding of sin is matched by an equally radical understanding of baptism, in which, for the sake of Christ, God forgives both original and actual sin. Any thought that anyone can contribute to his salvation not only lacks biblical support, but compromises Christ's all sufficient sacrifice. Actual sins are seen as original sin taking form in thoughts, words, and deeds. So the difference between original and actual sin is a distinction without a difference.

At the heart of Catholic teaching is the belief that after Adam was created, he was given grace. In the fall, man lost grace—but not his natural endowments including reason. Death and other miseries followed the fall, but man's reason remains essentially intact. This allows the Catholic doctrine of salvation to advance in two opposite directions. On one hand, baptism is absolutely necessary for salvation even for infants; on the other hand, those who have no direct knowledge of the gospel are able to use reason to attain salvation. Unbaptized children have not reached the age of reason and so have committed no actual sins; thus, they avoid the horrors of hell—but without baptism they are deprived of the beatific vision. Within these alternatives of bliss and horror, the *limbo infantium* has developed; this is a concept on which Catholics differ. Since Catholic doctrines are drawn not only from the Scriptures, but also councils, synods, and papal encyclicals, they are tentative and open to revision. (This may be as frustrating to Catholics as it is to others.) As is evident in their confessions, Lutherans present their doctrines with generous references from the early church fathers and councils, but all doctrine must be biblically defensible.

A Reformed Response by Gregg Strawbridge

David Liberto provided a fair and historically insightful overview of the Roman Church's approach to children. He is transparent about his epistemology as a

Roman Christian. To honestly reflect his church's understanding of Scripture as it pertains to children or anything else, he must look to what his church accepts as infallible interpretations of these matters. And as he wrote, Liberto was careful to note the particulars that his church has not yet concluded as dogma. He helpfully points out the possibilities of diversity (within dogmatic boundaries) and traces the historical basis for this. He also freely confesses that certain features of (non-dogmatic) Roman culture have been less than ideal—for instance, that First Communion has too often been postponed until a child reaches age twelve or thirteen. Since I accept paedocommunion, I believe Liberto's preference that First Communion be moved closer to age seven is at least a step in the right direction.

I do, however, have some concerns regarding his presentation. The first two are something of meta-critiques. The latter two are more internal to the system of Roman Catholic theology.

First, at the outset, the primary paradigm problem in the conversation held in this book is that of authority. As a Reformed Protestant, I hold to *sola Scriptura*. Liberto writes, "The Catholic position on any given datum of revelation, therefore, can be found in those magisterial teachings of popes, councils, and synods where the authentic understanding of the Scriptures and the Tradition are expounded for the faithful." But what if these teachings are contradictory in places? Are they still "revelation" from God? Roman Catholicism must maintain a complicated system of justifying such revelatory tensions over the course of church history. One of the most sensible statements on this point is Westminster Confession of Faith 31.4: "All synods or councils, since the apostles' times, whether general or particular, *may err*; and many *have erred*. Therefore they are not to be made the rule of faith, or practice; but to be used as a help in both" (emphasis mine).

Second, the sacramental system of Rome may be richly evidenced in the magisterium; however, in my understanding such views only lightly touch down on the solid ground of the covenants of promise (Eph 2:12). I consider the Roman Catholic substance view of grace through sacraments as an intrusion of Greek philosophical conceptions into the church. Therefore, I cannot accept the view that grace or merit are substances from a depository. Rather, we are clothed with Christ (union with Christ) in baptism (Gal 3:27).[50] A robust covenantal view, therefore, provides both for a model of sacraments as more than mere symbols, as well as the efficacy of the sacraments (in contrast to the Baptist view). It is a reformation of the Catholic view. All of this can be grounded in a fully scriptural theology of the gospel, the sacraments, and familial relations.

Third, Liberto favors the Thomistic view of the destiny of the unbaptized that die in infancy; he believes they experience natural happiness while being ignorant of any supernatural happiness they have lost. However, he does not believe that they are saved, since original sin has not been washed away in baptism. But why are Roman Christians more optimistic about catechumens who die prior to baptism (who receive a "baptism of desire") and even about the unbaptized who are martyred for Christ (who receive a "baptism of blood"), than about their own children who die *en route* to being baptized? God's promise to act in baptism (which I accept) is not God's promise never to act apart from baptism. In Scripture God's posture toward the children of believers is clear.

Finally, it has been most common in the Roman Church for confirmation to precede First Communion. I also understand that the United States Conference of Catholic Bishops disallows confirmation before age seven. But that order is not dogma. On the biblical (and even the Roman) view of baptism, nothing is lacking in the baptized to prevent him from receiving Holy Communion. Eastern Catholics, in full communion with Rome, do confirm infants shortly after their baptisms in order to grant them the "medicine of immortality" within that sacramental order and without delay. If this is possible for some, why not for all?

---

[50] If I have misrepresented Roman Catholicism on this point, I am open to correction.

A Baptist Response by Adam Harwood

David Liberto begins his chapter by explaining the Roman Catholic view of religious authority. His comments reveal why Baptists and Catholics arrive at different conclusions on certain theological matters. Between the Council of Trent and Vatican II, the Roman Catholic Church regarded both Scripture and the church's interpretation to be authoritative. Since Vatican II, they have answered theological questions by discovering the church's official interpretation of Scripture as expressed in councils, synods, and papal documents. Baptists employ a different method for answering theological questions because Baptists affirm a different model of religious authority.

For Baptists, Scripture is the primary authority for Christian faith and practice, overriding all appeals to tradition, reason, and experience. As the Baptist Faith and Message (BFM) declares, Scripture is "the supreme standard by which all human conduct, creeds, and religious opinions should be tried."[51] Building on the cry of the Reformers who affirmed *sola Scriptura* (Scripture alone), Baptists affirm *suprema Scriptura* (Scripture is primary).[52]

---

[51] Baptist Faith and Message (2000), Article 1, available at http://www.sbc.net/bfm2000/bfm2000.asp.

[52] Notice the BFM claims Scripture is "the supreme standard" rather than the sole standard for judging religious opinions. Although Scripture is one of many sources of religious authority, it is the highest and final authority. James Leo Garrett Jr., ST, 2:179–81, argues that the confessions and catechisms of Lutheranism as well as the definitions of *sola Scriptura* by R. C. Sproul and other contemporary Reformed theologians are consistent with *suprema* rather than *sola Scriptura*. Garrett also writes, "The great majority of the Baptist confessions of faith and the great majority of writing Baptist theologians have held to the Bible as the supreme authority for doctrine, conduct, and polity and not to a strictly defined *sola Scriptura*." Quotation from Garrett, 181. For other affirmations of *suprema Scriptura*, see Rhyne R. Putman, *In Defense of Doctrine: Evangelicalism, Theology, and Scripture* (Minneapolis, MN: Fortress, 2015), 214; and Kevin J. Vanhoozer and Daniel J. Treier, *Theology and the Mirror of Scripture: A Mere Evangelical Account* (Downers Grove, IL: IVP Academic, 2015), 81.

Baptists understand that followers of Christ interpreted the Bible for 1,600 years prior to the beginning of the Baptist movement. And we know that core Christian doctrines, such as the Trinity and the union of humanity and divinity in Christ, were articulated centuries after the closing of the New Testament canon.[53] Although Baptists understand that helpful insights can be gleaned from the past, we are not bound to prior theological systems or views—regardless of the originating council, synod, or theologian. Baptists are comfortable rejecting certain theological views, even those affirmed by church councils. Like Calvin, Baptists deny both that councils have *no* authority and that councils have *all* authority. After all, in some cases councils have ruled contrary to one another.[54] We thus examine the judgments of the councils by the standard of Scripture. The Bible is the norming norm. In this way, Baptists are the fullest expression of the Protestant Reformation.[55] As evidence for this claim, consider that neither Luther nor Calvin dispensed with the practice of infant baptism—even when its defense was grounded in tradition and a theological framework rather than explicit commands or examples in Scripture.

Baptists are a maverick group in that we are willing to reject teachings affirmed by other Christians for centuries if we conclude the teachings cannot be established from a plain reading of Scripture alone. Teachings rejected for this reason include baptismal regeneration and the church membership of infants, views which the Roman Catholic Church affirm. This Baptist theological method is influenced by a view that E. Y. Mullins called the competency of the soul in religion, or soul competency.[56] Mullins was *not* affirming

---

[53] For a treatment of the postcanonical development of Christian doctrine by a Southern Baptist scholar, see Putman, *In Defense of Doctrine*.

[54] John Calvin, *Institutes of the Christian Religion*, 4.9.8–9.

[55] E. Y. Mullins, *Axioms of Religion*, ed. C. Douglas Weaver (Macon, GA: Mercer University Press, 2010), 192, went further by stating, "Baptists have been the only adequate interpreters of the Reformation."

[56] For a negative assessment of Mullins's doctrine of soul competency, see R. Albert Mohler Jr., "Baptist Theology at the Crossroads: The Legacy of E. Y.

a humanistic view that people do not need God. Instead, soul competency refers to the competency of the human soul before God in matters of religion. In *Axioms of Religion* Mullins writes, "The idea of the competency of the soul in religion excludes at once all human interference, such as episcopacy and infant baptism, and every form of religion by proxy. Religion is a personal matter between the soul and God."[57] For Mullins, soul competency includes these implications: the right of private interpretation and obedience to the Bible, soul freedom, regenerate church membership, the equality and priesthood of believers, and the separation of church and state. Also, Mullins writes that "the principle of competency assumes that man is made in God's image, and God is a person able to reveal himself to man."[58]

If members of the Roman Catholic Church are considered capable of receiving God's grace and being indwelt by God's Spirit, then why are they not encouraged to read and interpret the Bible? Also, since Jesus is the perfect high priest (Heb 7:25–28) and the only mediator between God and man (1 Tim 2:5), why are members not encouraged to confess their sins to God by the mediation of Jesus Christ alone? Perhaps the answers to these questions reveal the Roman Catholic view of soul competency.

Despite the differences in religious authority and theological method, Baptists and Catholics share many views regarding infants and children in the church. Both traditions trace the problem of sin to Adam's fall in the garden, and both traditions acknowledge that infants share in the devastating

---

Mullins," *Southern Baptist Journal of Theology*, vol. 3, no. 4 (Winter 1999): 19: "The emphasis on soul competency is, as Mullins must have both hoped and expected, the most enduring element of Mullins's legacy. The concept does underscore the necessity of personal religious experience—including repentance and faith—to the Christian life. But soul competency also serves as an acid dissolving religious authority, congregationalism, confessionalism, and mutual theological accountability. This, too, is part of Mullins's legacy." See also Tom Nettles, *The Baptists: Key People Involved in Forming a Baptist Identity*, Vol. One: Beginning in Britain (Ross-shire, Scotland: Mentor, 2005), 12–13.

[57] Mullins, *Axioms of Religion*, 65.
[58] Ibid., 64–67. Quotation on page 67.

effects of the fall although they have not committed personal acts of sin. The Catholic age of reason or discretion appears similar to the Baptist concept of the age of accountability. Although the differences between Baptists and Catholics on infant baptism are obvious, both traditions ground their view of salvation in the work of Christ on the cross. Although Baptists will neither administer the sacraments to infants nor recognize them as members of the church, we share with Catholics a concern for instructing little ones in the Christian faith and nurturing in them a love for and devotion to Jesus.

Infants and Children in the Church:
A Lutheran View

David P. Scaer

Introduction: Baptism—Its Theology, Benefits, and Practice

While the baptism of adults has never been contested, differences over infant baptism have been a cause of division among Protestants since the beginning of the Reformation. Even those who practice infant baptism are not agreed on the sinfulness of children, on their capacity for faith, or even on their need for baptism. Identifying biblical reasons for baptizing infants also presents an issue. Lutherans hold that in one act, baptism destroys sin, arms against Satan, and gives the new life in Christ to the believer. It is the sacrament of rebirth, or regeneration, in which the Holy Spirit is given to create and sustain faith.

Baptism is the foundational sacrament on which the church is built and on which her other rites depend.[1] Its efficacy and benefits last throughout

---

[1] Martin Luther, *Luther's Works: The American Edition*. 55 vols. ed. Jaroslav Pelikan and Helmut T. Lehmann (Saint Louis, MO: Concordia Publishing House; Philadelphia, PA: Fortress, 1955–72), 41:195. "But Baptism is the first and foremost Sacrament, without which all the others are nothing, as they (the papists) must confess." Hereafter cited as *LW*. Contrast this with the Catholic

life.[2] Administered only once, it does not need to be supplemented by other rites. Faith justifies the sinner, but baptism and not faith provides the certainty of salvation. In the midst of his trials and confronted with his personal sin, Martin Luther relied on his baptism by crying out, "I am baptized."[3] Since Christ instituted baptism, it is of divine origin and can no more be disregarded or taken lightly than the Ten Commandments and the Lord's Prayer. Faith receives Christ and his benefits in baptism, but it does not constitute baptism or make its gifts effective. Christ administers baptism, is present in the water, and is to be worshiped there. In confessing the Nicene Creed, "We believe in one baptism for the remission of sins." Believing in baptism is nothing else but believing in Christ.[4] Christ, by whom the world was made, incorporates the baptized into the church, which is his new creation. So as God formed the world by his creating Spirit hovering over the water, so he calls the church into existence out of the water of baptism (Eph 5:26; Titus 3:5); this becomes the boundary between the church and the unbelieving world. God's grace extends to all, so age is not a criterion for who may or may not come to

---

view that holds to the necessity of baptism, but sees the Eucharist as the source of Christian life (*Catechism of the Catholic Church* [Mahwah, NJ: Paulist, 1994], para. 1324).

[2] Lutheran theology allows penance as a third sacrament, but more commonly sees penance as the practice of baptism in the life of the Christian whose sins are daily confessed and forgiven. Baptism is perfect and complete in itself needing no complementary action. Just as baptism is the sacrament of birth, death, and resurrection, so the Lord's Supper is the sacrament in which the believer is nourished with Christ's body and blood.

[3] *LW* 4:165. Some scholars have seen a contradiction between justification by faith as central to Luther's theology and his reliance for salvation on baptism. James Atkinson, *Martin Luther and the Birth of Protestantism* (Baltimore, MD: Penguin Books, 1968), 192. "There is no satisfactory way of reconciling Luther's clear teaching on justification by faith alone with his views on baptismal regeneration. His contemporaries saw this chink in his armor, and so have many radicals who succeeded them."

[4] Heiko Obermann, *Luther: Man Between God and the Devil*, trans. Eileen Walliser-Schwarzbart (New Haven, NJ: Yale University Press, 1989), 225–27.

faith and be baptized. Since baptism is the sacrament of regeneration or the new birth in Christ, it is appropriately administered to infants and young children. In accord with the command of Jesus that to enter the kingdom of God, we must become like children, all candidates for baptism must become like them. In this sense, every baptism is an infant baptism.

Baptism reaches its intended goal in the death of the baptized Christian who remains alive with Christ to await the resurrection of the dead. Baptized believers are relieved of the penalty of sin, but the remnants of sin remain. By their baptism Christians are equipped with the Holy Spirit to confess and overcome their sins and do the good works pleasing to Christ. Since baptism is instituted by God, it remains effective even when the baptized believer falls into sin and unbelief; it calls him back to faith.

Baptizing means using water and can be applied in several ways. In Lutheran theology, the sacramental symbol and its reality constitute one thing. Water in baptism symbolizes creation, birth, death, and resurrection. Large baptismal fonts still in use in the churches built up through the seventeenth century indicate that immersion was the ordinary form of baptizing infants, symbolizing the drowning of the sinful self and the resurrection to a new life in Christ. Pouring water on the head, the more common practice today, signifies a washing in the Holy Spirit and how the believer daily overcomes sin with the Spirit's help. How the water of baptism is applied does not determine its efficacy. A threefold application of the water signifies incorporation into the Father, Son, and Holy Spirit by whose authority the baptism is administered. Luther summarized God's presence in baptism with the Latin phrase *"in baptismo sonat vox Trinitatis"*; it means, "in baptism the voice of the Trinity speaks."[5] Faith finds God in all facets of the baptismal act. Sponsors are customarily used in the baptism of infants to articulate their faith, but

---

[5] *LW* 8:145. "In Baptism the voice of the Trinity is heard, and the words of Baptism must not be understood or received in any other way." For the Latin, see Martin Luther, *D. Martin Luthers Werke: Kritische Gesamtausgabe* (Weimar: H. Böhlau), 44:685. Cited hereafter as WA. This sentence is taken from his Genesis lectures.

they are not absolutely necessary. Remorse over sin and faith in Christ are necessary for the baptism of both adults and little ones.

Lutherans are committed to the Reformation principle of the *sola Scriptura*, that all doctrines are derived from the Bible and show that their teachings and practices are in accord with those of the ancient church with which they identify by use of the Apostles', Nicene, and Athanasian creeds in their liturgies. They distinguish themselves from other Christians by their adherence to the sixteenth-century confessions collected in the 1580 Book of Concord. These confessions are placed alongside the Scriptures not as a separate source of doctrine, but as their correct interpretation. Of these, the chief one is the Augsburg Confession; the best known is Luther's Small Catechism. These confessions present not only biblical expositions of Lutheran doctrine, but in advancing their doctrines generously reference such church fathers as Augustine, Thomas Aquinas, and Peter Lombard.[6]

Question 1: How Are Children Impacted by Sin?

All people—including infants and children—have sinned and have come short of the glory of God but can be redeemed by Christ when called to faith by the Holy Spirit's work in baptism. Thus, the baptism of an infant is fundamentally no different from that of an adult. In accord with their self-understanding of continuing in the Catholic tradition, Article 1 of the Augsburg Confession read before the Emperor Charles V on June 25, 1530, sets forth the Lutheran commitment to the Trinitarian faith of the Nicene Creed. Article 2 on original or hereditary sin is the first article distinguishing Lutherans from Catholics and other Reformation-era Protestants, and it

---

[6] Thus, at the last article of the doctrinal section of the Augsburg Confession (22), they assert that nothing in the confession differs or varies from the Scriptures, the Catholic Church, or the church of Rome—as its writings are known to them.

presents baptism as the remedy for the universality of sin in which children share. Below is the translation of the Latin version.[7]

> Our churches also teach that since the fall of Adam, all human beings who are propagated according to nature are born with sin, that is, without fear of God, without trust in God, and with concupiscence. And they teach that this disease or original fault is truly sin, which even now damns and brings eternal death to those who are not born again through baptism and the Holy Spirit.

The German version of this article of Augsburg Confession paints an even darker picture of the human condition:

> It is also taught among us that since the fall of Adam all who are born according to the course of nature are conceived and born in sin. That is, all men are full of evil lust and inclinations from their mothers' wombs and are unable by nature to have true fear of God and true faith in God. Moreover, this inborn sickness and hereditary sin is truly sin and condemns to the eternal wrath all those who are not born again through Baptism and the Holy Spirit.

From conception all are overcome by sin, are under the power of Satan, and cannot believe in God; thus, they are condemned to God's wrath. The

---

[7] Lutheran pastors and congregations are pledged to the Book of Concord (1580). Included therein are three confessional works written by Philip Melanchthon: the Augsburg Confession, the Apology of the Augsburg Confession, and Treatise on the Primacy and Power of the Pope, as well as three by Luther: the Small and Large Catechisms and the Smalkald Articles. The Formula of Concord (1577) was composed by several theologians, among whom Martin Chemnitz was the most prominent. Citations are taken from *The Book of Concord: The Confessions of the Evangelical Lutheran Church*, trans. and ed. Theodore G. Tappert (Philadelphia, PA: Fortress, 1959). A more recent and critical edition is edited by Robert Kolb and Timothy J. Wengert (Minneapolis, MN: Fortress, 2000). It traces the development of each confession from its composition to its inclusion in the Book of Concord.

only solution is faith in Christ created by the Holy Spirit working in baptism. Sin originates in Adam and by conception it is transmitted from one generation to the next. Just as all believers are incorporated in Christ, so all humanity was incorporated in Adam's transgression of forsaking the divine perfection in which he was created. Since all humanity participated in his perfidy, all now are conceived in sin and have no experience of the state of perfection in which he was created. From conception, children are excluded from God's presence. Adam's sin is theirs and so their thoughts, words, and deeds are innately sinful. No one is born in a state of moral neutrality or only with an inclination to sin that can be rectified with the exercise of a mature will or the use of reason to overcome the evil and do good works.[8] Luther makes this clear in his Small Catechism: no one can by his own reason or strength believe in Jesus Christ and come to him. Faith is worked by the Holy Spirit in the gospel, and humans do nothing to prepare for faith. A middle ground where we can choose between God and Satan,[9] good and evil, belief and unbelief, does not exist in Lutheran theology.[10]

---

[8] Lutherans distinguish between the good works of a Christian and those of which all are capable. The good works of Christians are motivated by Holy Spirit so that they do the works of Christ in loving God and the neighbor. Good works of which all are capable belong to civil righteousness and contribute to the maintenance and improvement of society. These works include honest labor, having friends, building a house, marriage, and establishing a family. See Augsburg Confession 18.

[9] Luther retained the exorcism and the renunciation of the Devil in his revision of the baptismal liturgy. They were removed during the period of eighteenth-century rationalism. With the revival of confessional Lutheranism, the renunciation was restored. The rite of exorcism is less commonly used. These rites signify that without baptism the child is under the reign of Satan.

[10] The Apology to the Augsburg Confession cited Thomas Aquinas, who believed that original sin includes the loss of original righteousness and a disorderly arrangement in all parts of the soul and Bonaventure, who felt that original sin is ignorance in the mind and concupiscence in the flesh (Apology 2:28–29).

Lutherans distinguish between original and actual sins, but actual sin is nothing else than Adam's sin coming to life.[11] From an historical perspective, the Lutheran view of a depraved humanity that envelops children stands in the tradition of St. Augustine, who opposed the Pelagian teaching that a child is born with a morally neutral slate and can choose between good and evil.[12] Lutherans argue that allowing any moral capacity in a person to earn salvation would diminish Christ's works. No work of man is allowed to stand alongside of what Christ has done for salvation. This is an example of how Lutheran Christology penetrates every doctrine. We should be allowed to ask how children are impacted by sin only if we are also prepared to ask about their capacity for faith. This we will do in the following sections.

Question 2: When or How Are Children Considered Members of the Church?

As soon as children are baptized, they are considered members of the church. By incorporating the believer into Christ's death and resurrection, baptism works forgiveness of sins, delivers from death and the Devil, gives eternal salvation, and incorporates the child into the body of Christ—which comes to expression within the church. Since baptism ushers into the covenant and is itself the covenant that God makes in Christ with the believer, it is the entrance rite into Christian community where the infant with other believers receives the benefits earned by Christ's death. Baptized children are no less members of the church than adults.

---

[11] Article 9 of the Augsburg Confession deals with baptism, but it does not specifically address the baptism of infants; however, this is assumed in Article 2, the article on original sin: it condemns all who are not baptized. Since grace is offered through baptism, it is necessary for children who—by being received into God's grace—have their sins forgiven.

[12] This excludes Christ, who was conceived not in an ordinary way but by the Holy Spirit.

In the Old Testament children were included in the covenant God made with Israel and participated in its rites and received their benefits. This anticipated Christ including them in his kingdom. Foundational in understanding the kingdom of God—or as Matthew says, the kingdom of heaven—is what God accomplished by Christ's crucifixion and resurrection. So the church is the manifestation of the kingdom of God on earth and the recipient of its benefits. Inclusion in the kingdom is accomplished by baptism, and baptized children are no less members of the church than other baptized believers.

Jesus and the Children: An Excursus into the Synoptic Gospels

Important for understanding the inclusion of children in the church are the two episodes recorded in the Synoptic Gospels in which Jesus deals directly with children and speaks of their place in his kingdom. Inclusion of these occasions within the Gospel accounts indicates that these episodes were well established in the memories of the apostles who were present, and they continued to hold a prominent place in the church's oral tradition from which the evangelists composed. First in reciting the oral tradition and then in the reading of the Gospels, first-century believers were reminded of what Jesus said of the place of children in his kingdom.

The location of these events in their respective books cannot be overlooked. In all three Gospels, these episodes are placed after the transfiguration of Jesus along with his announcement of death and resurrection. The third and final announcement is placed just before his Palm Sunday entry into Jerusalem. The strategic placement of the children in the Synoptic Gospels reinforces their place in Christ's kingdom.

Each report of the two occasions speaks of the kingdom of God, how it is received by children, and that they serve as examples of faith. In determining when children should be included in the church, it is essential to ask whether the reports of Jesus and the children are only metaphors meant to show how Christians should believe and live. If so, children in the accounts serve as little more than props. The other choice is that these accounts were recorded so the reader would have no doubt of children's inclusion in the church. Providing answers into how these accounts are to be understood is essential for when children can first be considered members.

In the first episode, Jesus resolves a dispute among the disciples about who was the greatest by taking a child to himself and saying the greatest in the kingdom of heaven is the one who humiliates himself like the child (Matt 18:1–5; Mark 9:33–37; Luke 9:46–48). Their entering the kingdom, what we call conversion, requires becoming childlike in faith. But is the only purpose of the pericope didactic, meaning that all believers should become humble like children who depend on their parents and others? Or does it suppose that children, like others in the Christian community, have faith? If children are held up as examples of faith, they can be counted as members of the church at infancy. Disagreements about these passages require additional examination of the episode.

Matthew 18:3 uses the word *paidia* for children, as does Mark 9:37. Mark and Luke 9:48 describe the reception of the child in Trinitarian terms: the one who receives the child receives the Father, who sent Jesus. This parallels the Trinitarian formula of Matt 28:19, that baptism is administered in the name of the Father and the Son and the Holy Spirit. In Matthew 18:5, the writer takes a different tack. Whoever receives the child in Jesus's name receives Jesus himself. Within the context of this Gospel, Jesus reveals the name of the Father, the Son, and the Holy Spirit. What Jesus says about the place of children in the kingdom is reinforced when he actually takes a child in his arms.[13] Since Jesus embraced the child (Gk., *paidion*) in such a manner, the child could have hardly advanced far beyond infancy, if at all (Mark 9:36).

The Greek word for humiliating, *tapeinoō* (Matt 18:4), used to describe the posture of the child over against God, is used to describe the mind of Christ in his facing crucifixion (Phil 2:1–8). Christ was like a child in being

---

[13] The word used for the child by Jesus, *paidion*, is the same word used by Matthew for the child whom the magi worshiped (2:11) as well as for the boys slaughtered by Herod (2:16).

obedient to the death his Father required of him. Elsewhere this word for humiliation is used of submission to the will of God (Jas 4:10; 1 Pet 5:6) that suggests that true Christians are like children listening to the Father's will.

In another account, Jesus does not recruit a child, but children are brought to him; they are as anonymous as those who brought them. Luke speaks of infants (Gk., *brephē*). Some in the crowd were without doubt their parents, but not necessarily so. In the ancient world one household often consisted of several nuclear families. Use of the imperfect in Mark 10:13 and in Luke 18:15 literally means "they were bringing children," suggesting that bringing children to Jesus for a blessing was customary during his ministry. If people ordinarily brought the sick and the demon possessed to Jesus in the hope that he would heal them (Matt 4:24; 8:16), then it can be assumed that those who brought the children wished that the lives of their children would be improved in the kingdom (Matt 19:13). Jesus could give them something they did not already have. His fame rested not only on his miraculous healing powers, but also on what he could do for children by including them in his kingdom that came with baptism (Matt 3:1–2; 4:17). If those who brought the children to Jesus were like the vast majority of others who heard him, some thought of him as little more than an extraordinary prophet. Still others may have known who he really was (Matt 16:13–14). Full comprehension, however, would only follow the resurrection. Faith was a factor in bringing their children to baptism, but the eligibility of children for the kingdom did not depend on the depth or the extent of the faith of those who brought them.

Bringing children to Jesus through baptism now is no different. Children are not entitled to baptism because they are born within a covenant relationship with God, but they are better situated than other children to come into contact with what God promises them. An answer may be found in locating the differences between the two occasions, which though similar are not identical. This would be the case of the first event that all three Synoptic evangelists place in Capernaum, with Mark 9:33 providing the detail that it took place in a house that likely belonged to Peter. So the child may have been his

A Lutheran View 91

or that of another disciple like Andrew, James, or John—all of whom came from the same city; nevertheless, the child remained anonymous.

In contrast to Mark and Luke, Matthew's language used in describing Jesus's blessing the children who are brought to him borders on the sacramental. Matthew 19:13 states, "Then children were brought to him that he might lay his hands on them and pray."[14] This sacramental aspect is enforced at the end of the pericope, "he laid hands on them" (19:15). Throughout the Scriptures, use of the hands has sacramental significance because the gift that one has is shared with another.[15] Mark's description in 9:36 is more earthy in that Jesus gives the child a full arm embrace, "taking him into his arms"; it may reflect the manner in which infants were baptized in the apostolic church. Be that as it may, Jesus literally hugged the child, leaving no doubt that the child has a front row seat in the church. In neither of the two occasions does the child or the children come of their own accord.

When we think of members belonging to a church, we think of believers coming together to worship. But is there any evidence that children are among those who participate in church worship? An episode that took place after Jesus entered Jerusalem on Palm Sunday provides a positive answer to this question:

> But when the chief priests and the scribes saw the wonderful things that he did and the children (*paidas*) crying out in the temple, "Hosanna to the Son of David!" they were indignant, and they said to him, "Do you hear what these are saying?" And Jesus said to them, "Yes; have you never read, 'Out of the mouth of babes and

---

[14] In Greek, *Tote prosēnechthesan auto paidia hina tas cheiras epithē autois kai proseuxētai*. All Scripture references in this chapter are taken from the Revised Standard Version (RSV).

[15] Moses transferred his office as the leader of Israel to Joshua by the laying on of hands (Deut 34:9). Paul gives his authority to Timothy this way (2 Tim 1:6). Aaron transfers the sins of the people to the goat by the laying on of hands (Lev 16:21).

sucklings (*nēpiōn kai thēlazontōn*) thou hast brought perfect praise'?" (Matt 21:15–16)

In the Greek here, one word is used for children and two for infants—all of whom were eyes and ears when Jesus entered Jerusalem on Palm Sunday. They saw Jesus, recognized who he was, and joined in singing what has found its way into the Eucharistic liturgy: "Hosanna to the Son of David. Blessed is he who comes in the name of the Lord."

From the youngest to the oldest, each person, depending on intellect and with emotion and experience, grasps at a level appropriate to his or her development what is happening in a church service. With the crucifix affixed to the processional cross, the candles, and the book of the Gospel, the pastor comes from the back of the church to the chancel at the beginning of the service. Children take it all in and sometimes blurt out an "Amen" at the end of the prayers, especially the Lord's Prayer. Their minds wander, and in this way they are not unlike the rest of us. While some congregations have parallel services for children at the same time as the regular church service, good reason exists that children—as members of the church—should attend the regular services. This is what it means to be members of the church. Children, including infants, have an advantage in believing the gospel.[16]

Question 3: How Does God Treat Those Who Die in Infancy or Childhood?

This question requires an extended answer. Understandably, Christian parents may be concerned that their children receive the blessings of baptism before death, preferably as soon after birth as possible. Non-Christians do not know Christ and his blessings and may be troubled about the fate of their

---

[16] Children praising Christ is reflected in 1 Pet 2:2–3: "Like newborn babes, long for the pure spiritual milk, that by it you may grow up to salvation; for you have tasted the kindness of the Lord." "Newborn babes" might be better translated "just born infants" (*hōs artigennēta brephē*).

deceased children, but not if they share in Christ's blessing. Those living in regions and lands where Christianity is the predominant religion may out of custom have their children baptized, but with the secularization of Europe this custom is falling into disuse. Lutheran concerns about unbaptized children arose in connection to the sixteenth century rise of Anabaptists, who were re-baptizing those who had already been baptized as infants—the custom in Christian lands—and were refusing to baptize their own children. While the Anabaptists held that baptism has no value for salvation, Lutherans held that without baptism children are denied the offer of salvation.[17]

Largely because of the high rate of infant mortality before the advent of modern medicine, infants were taken to the church to be baptized on the same day they were born or the next. With advancements in medical science, infant mortality declined and then often well-meaning parents waited weeks or months before having their children baptized. The secularization of countries with historically Christian cultures has caused a decline in infant baptisms overall.

Ordinarily, the minister of the local congregation administers baptism; when a child is close to death, however, any Christian can administer it and a liturgy for such an emergency baptism is included in the hymnals available to the laity.[18] In situations in which a Christian is unavailable, even a non-Christian may administer a Trinitarian baptism—with the understanding that the administrator is acting not by his own authority, but on the presumed authority of the church to whom the command to baptize has been given. Should the child survive, her baptism is confirmed in the church as soon as possible. At their deaths, baptized children are like other believers; they are received into the presence of Christ to await the resurrection.

---

[17] Augsburg Confession 5:2–3: "They [the Lutheran churches] teach that children are to be baptized. Being offered to God through Baptism, they are received into God's grace. Our churches condemn the Anabaptists who reject the Baptism of children, and say that children are saved without Baptism."

[18] The service for "Holy Baptism in Cases of Emergency" is located at the back of the *Lutheran Service Book* (Saint Louis, MO: Concordia, 2006), 1023.

A matter of real concern to Christian parents is their stillborn children and those who do not survive long enough to be baptized because baptism is not administered after death. Children born within a Christian environment, who through no fault of their own, die before being baptized are also saved. Lutherans hold that while faith can be created in baptism, it can also be created by the spoken gospel before or after birth. An unborn or even a born child can be exposed to the gospel through the mother's participation in the liturgies of the church and on other occasions where the Word of God is spoken.

Evidence that faith can be created before birth in this way is the account of John the Baptist. When he was in the womb of his mother Elizabeth, he heard the greeting of the Virgin Mary and in faith he leapt with joy that he had come into the presence of the unborn Son of God (Luke 1:41–44). Thus, some children may come to faith before they are baptized. Others do so during a church service where the gospel is preached, the creed confessed, and the hymns sung. Other children, especially those not from Christian homes, come to faith during the act of baptism. In situations in which children come to faith before or apart from baptism, baptism confirms this faith.

Lutherans do not pinpoint the moment in which faith is created and in most cases even adult believers become aware of their faith after it is engendered. Funeral and burial liturgies for baptized children and those born within Christian circumstances should not be obsessed with the terrors from which little ones have been saved; instead, they should portray the glories of Jesus those children are enjoying.[19]

---

[19] Consider the following from Theodoret of Cyrus: "If the only meaning of baptism were the remission of sins, why would we baptize newborn children who have not yet tasted of sin? But the mystery of baptism is not limited to this; it is the promise of greater and more perfect gifts. In it are the promises of future delights; it is the type of the future resurrection, a communion with the master's Passion, a participation in His Resurrection, a mantle of salvation, a tunic of gladness, a garment of light, or rather it is light itself." Quoted from John Meyendorff, *Byzantine Theology* (New York, NY: Fordam University Press, 1987), 194.

The Fate of Unbaptized Children: The Crux Theologorum

In working within the boundaries of what God has revealed, we come to questions that in this life escape final resolution. In Lutheran theology such a problem is called a *crux theologorum,* the cross or the burden of theologians, and would most certainly apply to the matter of what happens to those children who because of the circumstances into which they were born had no chance to hear the gospel. Here we are caught between a modified universalism, in which God saves all infants and young children apart from faith, and a modified Manichaeism, in which such children are *ipso facto* sentenced to wrath. Both alternatives are problematic, and only on the last day when the hidden things of God will be revealed will we have an answer to the conundrum. This does not mean that the alternatives cannot be explored—even if we know beforehand that a final answer will escape us.

Universalism, the idea that all are saved, or even a modified form of it that suggests only unbelieving infants and children will be saved in addition to those adults who place faith in Jesus, militates against the Christian belief that salvation is only by faith in Christ. Paul argues that without missionaries receiving financial aid to support their preaching the gospel, those who have not heard it will be lost. In those churches where Universalism has taken hold, enthusiasm for missions has declined. Universalism undercuts not only the church's mission, but its theology.[20] There is no reason to think

---

Theodoret's position is similar to Luther's that a newborn child has committed no actual sin. Also appropriate at the funerals of children would be the following prayer from the Book of Common Prayer: "O Merciful Father, whose face the angels of thy little ones do always behold in heaven; Grant us steadfastly to believe that this thy child hath been taken into the safe keeping of thine eternal love; through Jesus Christ our Lord. *Amen*" (New York, NY: Thomas Nelson & Sons, 1944), 340.

[20] For an analysis of the effect of Universalism on missions, see Arthur Merlin Climenhaga, "Mission and Neo-Universalism," *Evangelical Review of Theology* 28.1 (2004): 4–20; and K. Detlev Schulz, "Universalism: the Urgency of Christian Witness," *Missio Apostolica* 14 (2006): 86–96.

Paul does not include children in the missionary task of the church.[21] If it is countered that God can create faith apart from the preaching of the gospel, this would be another reason to forego missionary endeavors. It would also release Christian parents from the urgency to have their children baptized.

Romans 3:25 may provide a speculative—but not a totally satisfactory—solution in that God passed over what Paul calls "former sins," that is, sins committed by those to whom God's promises to Israel had not reached before the coming of Christ. Such an interpretation would mean that God made an exception to requiring faith for those peoples to whom the prophets were not sent and thus could not hear the gospel and come to faith. If such an interpretation is feasible, it would apply primarily to those who lived before the apostles were commissioned to preach the good news throughout the world. Prior to that time the world population, especially on the American continents, was minuscular in comparison to current figures, so the exceptions would be minimal. This argument can only go so far, however. Such ancient peoples as Egyptians, the Ninevites, the Babylonians, the Assyrians, the Persians, the Canaanites, Greeks, and Romans had come into contact with Israel and had learned of how God was offering salvation to the world through them as his chosen people. Some did believe. By the end of the first Christian century, the gospel was well on its way to being spread throughout the Roman Empire. Still, it is one thing to allow for a modified universalism for those in the ancient world who had not heard the gospel; it is another to say that it applies to all modern children who have not heard and been baptized.

Equally unacceptable is a modified Manichaeism in that to remain faithful to this principle that faith in Christ alone justifies, God excludes from

---

[21] See also Rom 10:12–15: "For there is no distinction between Jew and Greek; the same Lord is Lord of all and bestows his riches upon all who call upon him. For, 'everyone who calls upon the name of the Lord will be saved.' But how are men to call upon him in whom they have not believed? And how are they to believe in him of whom they have never heard? And how are they to hear without a preacher? And how can men preach unless they are sent? As it is written, 'How beautiful are the feet of those who preach good news.'"

salvation all children at least up to the age of reason when faith is first thought possible. Such a proposal is not feasible since it contradicts God's self-revelation as pure love who desires that all should believe and come to the knowledge of the truth. Rather than tackling a question to which only a tentative answer can be given, it would be better to leave it to the inscrutable mind of God. "For God has consigned all men to disobedience, that he may have mercy upon all. Oh the depth of the riches and wisdom and knowledge of God! How unsearchable are his judgments and how inscrutable his ways! 'For who has known the mind of the Lord, or who has been his counselor?'" (Rom 11:32–34)

If we cannot provide a once-and-for-all theological answer to the problem of how God deals with children born into a non-Christian environment, we can explore how the church through its ministers addresses these situations in which a child dies before baptism. Though in the West this is less likely with advancements in medicine, infant mortality rates throughout the world remain high. (Add to the number those infants who are aborted.) The death of an infant is devastating, and parents lacking faith in Christ could hardly ask how their children are included in Christ's salvation. God, Christ, the Holy Spirit, faith and salvation are unknown quantities to them. Unbaptized children of believing parents are another matter. These parents often intended to have their children baptized and did not expect that their little ones would die beforehand.

Luther addresses this issue in his *Lectures on Genesis* in connection with boys who die before circumcision on the eighth day and girls for whom the rite was not intended. Since God is by nature merciful, he will not let their condition become worse because they were unable to obtain circumcision in the Old Testament or baptism in the case of the New Testament.[22]

---

[22] In *LW* 3:103, Luther explains:

But here another question arises. If the uncircumcised males of the Jews are lost, what is one to conclude about infants who died before the eighth day? What about the other sex, the girls? Likewise, what about

Luther understands the benefits of circumcision not in terms of becoming a member of the society of Israel, a chief argument for Ulrich Zwingli, the Enlightenment theologians, and Friedrich Schleiermacher, but in terms of the faith infants have before and apart from circumcision and baptism. Those infants who die without baptism are not condemned, but those who refuse them baptism are held accountable.[23]

> our own infants, either those who are stillborn or those who die shortly after birth, before they are baptized?
>
> Concerning infants who died before the eighth day the answer is easy, just as it easy to give an answer about own infants who die before Baptism. For they do not sin against the covenant of circumcision or of Baptism. Since the Law commands them to be circumcised on the eighth day, could God condemn those who die before the eighth day?
>
> Accordingly, the souls of those infants must be left to the will of the Heavenly Father, whom we know to be merciful. Furthermore, what Paul says in a gentle manner about 'those whose sins were not like the transgression of Adam' (Rom. 5:14) and about Jacob and Esau—'though they were not yet born and had done nothing either good or bad' (Rom. 9:11)—holds true in their case too.
>
> Even though infants bring with them inborn sin, which we call original sin, it is nevertheless important they have committed no sin against the Law. Since God is by nature merciful, He will not let their condition be worse because they were unable to obtain circumcision in the Old Testament or Baptism in the New Testament.
>
> With regard to girls among the Jews the answer is easy. For because this sign was prescribed only for the male sex, it does not pertain to the girls. Nevertheless, since the girls are Abraham's descendants, they are not excluded from Abraham's righteousness; they attain it through faith. But those adults who despised circumcision or who despise Baptism are surely damned.

[23] Luther's discussion is profitable for those concerned with the fate of the unbaptized (*LW* 3:101–7). Jonathan Trigg, commenting on this section, says, "It is those adults who have contempt for circumcision or baptism who are surely damned." *Baptism in the Theology of Martin Luther* (Leiden, Netherlands: Brill, 1994), 41. A question was posed to Thomas Hopko at a Symposium on the Lutheran Confessions at Concordia Theological Seminary, Fort Wayne, about the fate of children baptized with the Modalist-like formula

The Intellectual Life of Infants

Asking about the intellectual life of infants is important as long as some hold that children cannot believe or that they are not held accountable until an age of reason. Some years have passed since an article appeared in *The Boston Globe* entitled "Inside the Baby's Mind."[24] Until then it was assumed that a baby was "missing most of the capacities that define the human mind, such as language and the ability to reason." A baby was thought to be only a lump of need and reflex. Since then science has reversed that understanding and now holds "that the baby brain is abuzz with activity, capable of learning astonishing amounts of information in a relatively short time." While an adult mind "restricts itself to a narrow slice of reality, babies can take in a much wider spectrum of sensation—they are, in any important sense, more aware of the world than we are." The life of an infant is like "being a tourist in a foreign city, where even the most mundane activities are new and exciting." This paragraph from the article might have a familiar ring:

> In fact, in some situations it might actually be better for adults to regress into a newborn state of mind. While maturity has its perks, it can also inhibit creativity and lead people to fixate on the wrong facts. When we need to sort through a lot of irrelevant information or create something completely new, thinking like a baby is our best option.

In light of this, it almost sounds as if Jesus is speaking in secular terms to suggest that to understand anything, we must become like children. In fact,

---

"Creator-Redeemer-Sanctifier." Hopko, perhaps the leading Eastern Orthodox theologian in the United States at the time, responded in virtual Luther-like fashion: "I have no doubt about the salvation of such children, but I do about those who administer that kind of Baptism."

[24] Jonah Lehrer, "Inside the Baby Mind," *The Boston Globe*, April 26, 2009, available at http://www.boston.com/bostonglobe/ideas/articles/2009/04/26/inside_the_baby_mind/. All the quotations in this paragraph were taken from this article.

boundaries between infancy, childhood, adolescence, and adulthood may not be absolute; they may even prove to be artificial and arbitrary. It has been proposed that even the category of childhood has been recently devised.[25] Regardless of the answer to that theory, the matter of how God treats those children who die raises the questions of where the dividing lines between infancy, childhood, and adolescence should be drawn.

Educators, and the Scriptures, know of distinctions based on age differences. In Nineveh, 120,000 persons—assumedly little ones—do not know their left hands from their right (Jonah 4:11). Paul has special instructions for children and parents (2 Cor 12:14; Eph 6:1). John speaks of how fathers and children relate to each other (1 John 2:13–14).[26] Other biblical divisions between old and young, as well as between male and female, married and unmarried, parent and child, pastor and lay person have to do with how Christians relate with one another—not with how they relate to God. So positing an age of accountability when a child is first capable of faith, before which God deals with children apart from their faith, may be little more than a hypothesis. Rather than speak of one kind of sin and faith for children but another for adults, or administering one baptism for infants but another for adults, it might be best to view all people to be under sin—and in need of the one baptism the Lord has made available (Eph 4:5).

The disciplining of children is also a factor in determining when children can be members of the church, since a need for discipline assumes they are morally accountable not just to their parents but to God. Parents can testify

---

[25] James A. Murphy, *Kids and Kingdom: The Precarious Presence of Children in the Synoptic Gospels* (Eugene, OR: Wipf and Stock, 2013).

[26] First John 2:13–14 states, "I am writing to you, little children, because your sins are forgiven for his sake. I am writing to you, fathers, because you know him who is from the beginning. I am writing to you, young men, because you have overcome the evil one. I write to you, children (*paidia*), because you know the Father. I write to you, fathers, because you know him who is from the beginning. I write to you, young men, because you are strong, and the word of God abides in you, and you have overcome the evil one."

that their children have shown themselves to be demanding and self-centered before their first birthdays, and older children are known to do things requiring intervention by the civil authorities. Recognizing that they often misbehave while holding that they are incapable of faith, therefore, attributes more power to Satan than to God. Children brought to a sense of their sin should be allowed to have the faith by which sins are forgiven. By placing baptism in Article 2, the one on original sin, the Augsburg Confession addresses the sinfulness of children by providing a solution in baptism. A counter proposal to the belief that faith requires a certain level of developed intellectual capacity is that reason is more likely an obstacle to faith than an advantage.[27]

Question 4: When or How Are Children Instructed in Christian Doctrine?

As discussed previously, children, as regular participants in the worship within the church, learn their Christian doctrine by hearing the Scripture read and hymns sung. The consistency of the liturgy Sunday after Sunday allows them to commit it to memory. They are often brought to church before they are baptized, but baptism provides a definitive point when their lives within the church begin. Throughout childhood, in Sunday school, in parochial school, and at home, they hear the Bible stories, learn the Ten Commandments, and pray the Creed and the Lord's Prayer.

Traditionally, Lutherans have administered the rite of confirmation around the time of adolescence following one or two years of instruction in

---

[27] Eighteenth-century Rationalist Lutheran theologians raised arguments against infant baptism and allowed it because its cessation would disrupt society since the rite conferred citizenship. The nineteenth-century Reformed theologian Friedrich Schleiermacher, who strongly influenced Lutheran theologians, held to the same view; however, he attributed to baptism a sacramental effect on the child who could later be brought to faith. For a discussion of this, see David P. Scaer, *Infant Baptism in Nineteenth Century Lutheran Theology* (Saint Louis, MO: Concordia, 2011).

Luther's Small Catechism.²⁸ While confirmation is practiced as a reaffirmation of the child's faith confessed at baptism by his sponsors, it also recognizes that the child is prepared to receive the Holy Communion.²⁹ Luther had taken issue with the medieval practice of administering confirmation as a bestowal of grace without prior instruction. He only examined the child to determine fitness for the Lord's Supper. In spite of his concerns, confirmation was so embedded in the lives of the people that other Reformers reinstated it; confirmation was thus again practiced by the end of the Reformation era. As a side benefit, it answered the Anabaptists' objections that Lutherans were baptizing infants who they said were incapable of faith.³⁰

Confirmation, along with instruction, is a nearly universal practice in Lutheran churches. Those baptized as adults are rarely confirmed. More recently, some churches have begun to admit children to the Lord's Supper before confirmation—but this practice is not widespread.

Without biblical command for confirmation, emergency confirmation is unknown. Lacking specific mandate, confirmation incorporates such fundamental elements of the Christian faith as examination in Christian doctrine in front of the congregation or its leading members, a confession of faith based on Luther's Small Catechism, prayer, and a blessing or invocation of the Holy Spirit accompanied by the imposition of the pastor's hands.

---

[28] The Small Catechism has six parts: the Ten Commandments, the Apostles' Creed, the Lord's Prayer, Baptism, "How the Unlearned Should be Taught to Confess," and the Lord's Supper.

[29] For an overview of the several Lutheran understandings of confirmation, see David P. Scaer, "Confirmation as a Sacramental Rite," *Logia* 15.1 (2006): 49–58 and Geoffrey R. Boyle, "Confirmation, Catechesis and Communion: A Historical Survey," *Concordia Theological Quarterly* 79 (2015): 121–42.

[30] For a lively presentation of the presence of faith in infants at the time of their baptism, see Karl Brinkel, *Die Lehre Luthers von der fides infantium bei der Kindertaufe* (Berlin, Germany: Evangelische Verlagsanstalt, 1958). Also see the chapter on infant faith in David P. Scaer, *Baptism*, Confessional Lutheran Dogmatics IX (St. Louis, MO: Luther Academy, 1999), 147–56.

Since the Reformation, the rites of confirmation and their significance have been altered according to the prevalent theology of the times. Pietists, who stressed personal faith, used confirmation to test the sincerity of children's faith. Eighteenth-century Rationalists saw it as a ritual encouraging the confirmands (candidates for religious confirmation) to use their intellects as they assumed the responsibilities of adulthood. Also added at this time was giving each confirmand a Bible passage to be used for lifetime guidance. Beginning with the period of Rationalism, an increasing number of Lutheran theologians no longer held to Luther's doctrine of infant faith, but they were intent in maintaining the practice of baptizing infants. To compensate for this alleged deficiency of faith in a baptized infant, they adopted the view of Friedrich Schleiermacher that confirmation provided the confession of faith that baptism required.[31] With the question in the current rite of confirmation, "Do you this day in the presence of God and of this congregation acknowledge the gifts that God gave you in your Baptism?,"[32] confirmation is presented as a commemoration of infant baptism and not as a supplement to it. The first questions in the rite of confirmation are taken over from the rite of baptism. These are followed by questions requiring promises that confirmands will remain true to the faith.

Conclusion

There is no one moment in life when a person is more human than another, no time when he is less a sinner than another, and no time when he is more capable of faith than another.

That being said, Jesus singled out children as models of faith who are promised a special place in his kingdom. It might have been that their dependence on others made them more vulnerable to others destroying their faith.

---

[31] For a discussion of how Lutherans wrestled with this issue, see Scaer, *Infant Baptism*.

[32] *Lutheran Service Book*, 272–74.

This fits with the warning of Jesus that those who offend the little ones who believe in him face a worse fate than having a millstone tied around their necks before they are dropped into the middle of the sea (Matt 18:6). Clement of Rome (170–220) wrote the hymn "Shepherd of Tender Youth." Its fifth stanza regards infants as members of the church who worship Christ:

> So now, and till we die,
> Sound we your praises high
>   And Joyful sing:
> Infants and all the throng
> Who to the Church belong,
> Unite to swell the song
>   To Christ, our king![33]

Dale Moody, a Baptist theologian, grasped the Lutheran mindset in regard to little ones: "Luther's argument that an infant has faith that is a gift of God leads to the conclusion that infant baptism, not adult baptism, is the norm for all baptism."[34]

Responses to a Lutheran View of Infants and Children in the Church

An Orthodox Response by Jason Foster

David Scaer's chapter on infants and children is well structured and thoughtfully presented. As a Missouri Synod Lutheran scholar, and contrary to many of the

---

[33] *Lutheran Service Book*, 864.

[34] For a fair presentation of baptism by a non-Lutheran author, see Dale Moody, *Baptism: Foundation for Christian Unity* (Philadelphia, PA: Westminster, 1967), 113–61.

contemporary Lutheran jurisdictions that seem to understand their Magisterial Reformer's conclusions and the dogmatic summaries of the Augsburg Confession as merely suggestions, he seeks to uphold the tradition he inherited. In the context of our topic, and dissimilar to the Reformed (Presbyterian) and Baptist positions presented, Scaer's work considers the importance of historical understanding and practice when employing *sola Scriptura*. The Lutheran position on baptism and children offered is theologically derived primarily from biblical references and is influenced by St. Augustine's teachings on original sin or guilt. As mentioned previously, St. Augustine's position on inherited guilt and the Reformation elevation and impregnation of the doctrine of justification is a Latin or Western distinctive not found in the East. Historically, this was evidenced by the nuanced soteriological Lutheran position in the sixteenth century Augustana Graeca that was presented to Patriarch Jeremias II and determined, even with the clarification and moderation of language, not to be within the tradition of the Eastern Church. However, what we do see in Scaer's presentation are certain biblical, theological, and traditional understandings of the sacrament of baptism that the Orthodox Church does confirm as being consistent with the Eastern tradition.

As a matter of practical critique, Scaer's chapter may have been further developed for the reader had he incorporated excerpts of ritual language as well as clerical rubrics describing the performance of the baptismal rite administered for infants. Arguably, the commonalities and divergences of our distinctive views are best realized in what we do in our liturgical praxis. The ancient Latin axiom paraphrased as *"lex orandi, lex credenda"* (the rule of praying is the rule of believing) offers a concise summary of this type of reflection. If we were to juxtapose the Lutheran and Orthodox baptismal service, there are numerous biblical references and ritual similarities that speak to some remnant of a common root system. However, we differ on the mode in which the sacrament is administered and the timing of chrismation (confirmation) and the reception of Holy Communion.

Contrary to the Lutheran act of sprinkling or pouring, in the Orthodox Church, those of all ages are fully immersed in the baptismal waters. This mode seems to be the most consistent with the biblical pattern witnessed throughout the Scriptures and maintains the ancient practice of the church. Furthermore, the ritual act of total immersion arguably communicates the theological significance and sacramental reality of dying and rising with Christ. Scaer's work does not discuss the theological imagery of sprinkling or pouring. The defense of this practice and explanation of it may have served to better develop the Lutheran view of the place and meaning of water in the rite as well as the theological significance of the ritual action according to the Lutheran position—for example, sprinkled with the blood of Christ or pouring forth of the Holy Spirit. When an infant is baptized in the Orthodox Church, again maintaining the ancient practice of the Christian church, he as a new member of the body of Christ, is chrismated (sealed with the gift of the Holy Spirit) and receives Holy Communion. (Notably, the Latin West separated the sacraments of confirmation and Communion over an extended period of time and formally established the practice at the Fourth Lateran Council in 1215; Martin Luther retained it.) Scaer writes, "As soon as children are baptized, they are considered members of the church.... Baptized children are no less members of the church than adults." It seems that to be consistent with this conclusion, infants, who, according to the Lutheran position presented, may have some form of faith and or understanding at a young age and are not withheld from the rite of baptism as infants, should also be confirmed and communed as full members of Christ's church.

Ultimately, the Orthodox and Lutheran Christians desire the same end for their little ones. They want them to grow in the grace and knowledge of our Lord, God, and Savior Jesus Christ and to thus fulfill their baptisms. Sacramentally and theologically, this is comprehended and realized in different ways according to our traditions. However, common to the Orthodox and Lutheran points of view, as noted above by Scaer, is this biblical and theological certainty: "Jesus singled out children as models of faith who are promised a special place in his kingdom."

A Roman Catholic Response by David Liberto

The Lutheran position on the topic of infants and children in the church was presented by David Scaer. My response to it will employ the *modus operandi* of citation and response. I will cite a brief passage from the paper, and then I will respond by way of questions, analysis, and critique. I will cite the various passages in the order in which they are presented in Scaer's essay.

> Citation 1: "Faith justifies the sinner, but baptism and not faith provides the certainty of salvation."

If faith truly justifies the sinner, then isn't this justification certain in and of itself? According to Scaer's explanation, baptism is necessary since it is where faith is received. In the question and answer session of our conference he went on to say that Lutherans hold to baptismal regeneration. If this is the case, although faith is necessary, it proves insufficient since baptism is *also* necessary, as the Augsburg Confession (article ix) states.

> Citation 2: "Remorse over sin and faith in Christ are necessary for the baptism of both adults and little ones."

This statement was puzzling at first, but it is possible that this is the Lutheran understanding that faith is even required of infants who are baptized since the Augsburg Confession states that in "the use of the Sacraments, faith which believes that sins are forgiven, is required" (article xiii). Scaer includes a section on the intellectual life of infants where he quotes a *Boston Globe* article that says that "the baby brain is abuzz with activity, capable of learning astonishing amounts of information in a relatively short time." Scaer, using the support of this article, goes on to conclude that the mind of an infant, as science supports, is capable of much more than we heretofore thought. All of this is brought to bear on the question of whether infants can exercise faith, since, for the Lutheran, faith must be exercised in the recipient of baptism.

A few remarks are in order. First, that the infant brain is abuzz with activity is no clear indication that intellectual activity is taking place. The article itself, in the few quotations cited, is guilty of a gross reductionism whereby the mind/intellect is equated with the brain. Unless we reduce man to a merely physical organism lacking an immaterial intellectual soul, brain activity alone cannot measure intellectual activity. Second, faith is not merely a matter of trust. Faith has content. One must have faith in Christ and in his works on our behalf. Is Scaer saying that infants can have any knowledge of the gospel that is the foundation of faith? Is this required for the Lutheran position on infant baptism?

> Citation 3: "There is no one moment in life when a person is more human than another, no time when he is less a sinner than another, and no time when he is more capable of faith than another."

Although I agree that there is no time when a person is any less a person, still the lack of distinction in the age and ability of the human seems to go against common sense. Why would Lutherans confirm a person during his or her teenage years if there are no difference in the abilities of an infant and a teenager with regard to understanding the faith?

A Reformed Response by Gregg Strawbridge

David Scaer's contribution to this volume is a wonderful exposition. On some of the topics addressed, diversity exists within my own Reformed tradition and his Lutheran one. Some of the elements of this chapter that I appreciate include Scaer's affirmation that baptism does not need to be supplemented by other rites. Although he discusses confirmation, he clarifies that confirmation does not "complete" baptism as though anything were lacking in it. He also states, "Christ . . . incorporates the baptized into the church which is his new creation." I agree that Christ (through the Spirit) is the active agent in baptism and that incorporation into the church is a fundamental accomplishment of baptism. And third, Scaer provides an insightful treatment of children in relationship to Jesus in the Synoptic Gospels. I also like that he gives a helpful discussion of infant faith.

The differences between our views call for delineating a few challenges to the Lutheran position.

First, when addressing Christ's view of children in the Synoptics, Scaer does not ground his view of Jesus on this subject within the Bible that Jesus read. Did Jesus determine that children are heirs to the kingdom? Or does this view arise from the covenant God made with Abraham in Genesis 17? Certainly the Hebrew Scriptures, the Bible Jesus read, did not warrant pagan children to be part of the kingdom. Clearly covenant promises are the foundation for Jesus and for the apostles when they proclaim, "The kingdom of God belongs to such as these" (Luke 18:16) or "The promise is for you and your children" (Acts 2:39, NASB).

Second, Scaer highlights a difference between Lutheranism and the Reformed tradition: "Children are not entitled to baptism because they are born within a covenant relationship with God, but they are better situated than other children to come into contact with what God promises them." Of course, the Christian home provides special contact with the gospel; but, a fully biblical rationale for infant baptism goes far beyond that pragmatic consideration. It also entails the dynamic which Scaer here denies—that the children of believers are born or adopted within a covenant relationship with God (Gen 17:7, Acts 2:39). This in no way detracts from baptism as that which incorporates our children into the church; rather, it establishes the candidacy of our children for baptismal incorporation.

Third, "Lutherans hold that while faith can be created in baptism, it can also be created by the spoken gospel before or after birth." While we agree on the possibility of infant faith, I would trust more in the God of the covenant than in the potential that faith is created "through the mother's participation in the liturgies of the church." In the promises of God, we have explicit biblical statements, as in Gen 17:7, "be God to you and your descendants" (NASB). It seems Scaer unnecessarily goes out of his way to avoid accepting the covenantal truths of the Hebrew Scriptures repeatedly affirmed in the New Testament.

Finally, he notes that in Lutheran practice, "[Confirmation around the time of adolescence] recognizes that the child is prepared to receive the Holy Communion." Although there is disagreement on this within the Reformed community, I have urged that delayed Holy Communion is a significant inconsistency in our theology of children. Scaer argues that in baptism, children are given faith in Christ and are incorporated into him. If this is so, on what basis may they not yet be nourished by Christ at his table? We agree that the sacrament of baptism, to be efficacious, does not require the self-conscious knowledge of the child. But being true in baptism, why is this not true of early participation in Holy Communion as well?

A Baptist Response by Adam Harwood

Baptists share many of the concerns noted in David Scaer's chapter. Both groups affirm child-like faith, depend on God's grace through Christ's work on the cross for salvation, and desire to root their faith and practice in the Scriptures. Baptists affirm the baptism of believers, but they deny that baptism is a sacrament that destroys sin, arms against Satan, and creates or sustains faith. The word *sacrament* (from the Lat. *sacramentum*, which translates the Gk. *mysterion*) refers to the "means by which Christians partake in the 'mystery of Christ.'"[35] Rather than a sacrament, Baptists regard baptism and the Lord's Supper to be *ordinances*, so named because Christ has "ordained" two practices in the church through which one identifies with the death of Christ. As Karl Barth declared, "Baptism is not a sacrament."[36]

---

[35] *The Oxford Dictionary of the Christian Church*, 3rd ed. rev., "Sacrament."

[36] Karl Barth, *The Doctrine of Reconciliation*, in vol. 4, pt. 4 of *Church Dogmatics*, ed. G. W. Bromiley and T. F. Torrance, trans. G. W. Bromiley (Peabody, MA: Hendrickson, 2010), 128.

Like Lutherans, Baptists regard repentance of sin and faith in Christ to be necessary for baptism. The important distinction, however, is that Baptists do not see clear examples in Scripture of proctor faith, also known as sponsor faith. Although our prayers for others can be powerful and effective (Jas 5:16), we do not think a parent or sponsor can repent of sin and believe in Christ for another.

Some Baptists affirm the Lutheran view that infants are condemned by God due to hereditary or original sin. Others reject the view that infants are condemned. But Baptists have affirmed almost universally that all who die in infancy are saved, and they reject the Lutheran solution of baptismal regeneration. Baptists say people are justified by faith, not water. Lutherans stress that infants can have faith. Baptists instead affirm that Jesus pointed to infants and children as examples of how to enter the kingdom of God (Mark 10:13–16). But affirming a child-like faith in a morally capable person should not be confused with affirming the presence of faith in an infant or child who is not yet morally capable. Thus, delaying a child's baptism does not exclude children from God's kingdom. Rather, Baptists will delay a child's baptism until the child seems to understand his own sinful condition and need for Christ, repenting of sin and confessing faith in Jesus. Until such conditions are met, a person is not a proper candidate for baptism—whether her age is one or forty-one.

Despite the theological differences noted, Baptists might benefit from the Lutheran emphasis on catechizing children. Baptist theology is biblically and theologically robust, but it is not always communicated effectively to little ones. Baptist educators would be wise to consider the catechetical tools and methods employed by Lutherans to see if we might glean insights that might strengthen our ministry to infants and children in the church.

Infants and Children in the Church:
A Reformed View

Gregg Strawbridge

A Snapshot of the Reformed View

How might the truth, goodness, and beauty of the Reformed view of children be appraised? The Heidelberg Catechism of 1563 provides a rich summary:

> What is your only comfort in life and death? That I am not my own, but belong with body and soul, both in life and in death, to my faithful Savior Jesus Christ. He has fully paid for all my sins with His precious blood, and has set me free from all the power of the devil. He also preserves me in such a way that without the will of my heavenly Father not a hair can fall from my head; indeed, all things must work together for my salvation. Therefore, by His Holy Spirit He also assures me of eternal life and makes me heartily willing and ready from now on to live for Him.[1]

In this portrait of the Reformed faith, Christians belong to Christ in life and death; he has paid for our sins with his substitutionary atonement; he

---

[1] Heidelberg Catechism (1563), Question 1. This version is approved by the Canadian Reformed Church, available at http://www.heidelberg-catechism.com/en/.

has set us free from the tyranny of the Devil. One of the difficult Reformed doctrines is stated here in terms that surely no Christian can reject. The sovereign care of our heavenly Father protects us in all of life with the purpose of our salvation, a beautiful pastoral truth. As Scripture teaches, all things work together for our salvation (Rom 8:28).

Note therein the immediate nature of assurance in the faith by the Holy Spirit. There is a call to growth, as well. He "makes me heartily willing and ready to live for Him." The personal nature of this teaching has provided clarity, comfort, and strength to many believers. This may be the simplest and perhaps warmest summary of the not so cold orthodoxy of Calvinism. Another way to say it is simply, *God saves sinners*. It is God, not man, who does the saving. We need saving because, as the *New England Primer* said, "In Adam's fall, we sinned all."[2] To paraphrase John Newton, we are all great sinners, but Christ is an even greater Savior. This is the Reformed faith in summary. This is the faith into which believers should earnestly desire to draw their children and the children of their congregations, so that they might know the only true and Triune God, which is life eternal.

Preliminary Qualifications

To orient the reader who may be unfamiliar with the Reformed point of view, here are a few preliminary remarks.

1. *Reformed is an Adjective*. To situate the Reformed church in history is to remember that "reformed" originally described the reforming of the church,

---

[2] This was the first reading primer used in America. It was published around 1687 by Benjamin Harris and constantly revised and republished. For more information on this primer as well as this phrase, see Sämi Ludwig, "'In Adam's Fall / We Sinned All': Puritan Writing and the Making of American Inferiority," In *XVII-XVIII. Revue de la société d'études anglo-américaines des XVIIe et XVIIIe siècles. Diffusion de l'écrit dans le monde anglophone. Spreading the Written Word in the English-Speaking World* (2010): 65–83, available online at http://www.persee.fr/docAsPDF/xvii_0291-3798_2010_hos_2_1_2480.pdf.

the Catholic Church. Of course the Reformation happened in its Western branch. Since the church already existed in the world, it was not the purpose of the sixteenth century Reformers to create a fractured body. Unfortunately, organizational unity was fractured; may the effort of this book bring greater unity and purity to all believers.

2. Creeds and Councils are Useful. The desire for both the peace and purity of the church is captured in such statements as the Belgic Confession of 1561, the Heidelberg Catechism of 1563, the Canons of Dort (1618–19), and the Westminster Confession and Catechisms of 1646.[3] The Reformers had a conciliar view of the authority of the church, which accepted the usefulness of councils and creeds, yet acknowledged their fallibility.[4] Although I will refer to these historic doctrinal statements for clarity and historical accuracy, all of these Reformed statements teach that the Christian's final authority is Scripture. This view is the Protestant principle of *sola Scriptura*.[5] This principle does not exclude the subordinate usefulness of councils and creeds, contrary to some in the Baptist tradition who have said, "No creed

---

[3] There were many more, such as the Confession of Basel, First and Second Helvetic, Genevan Catechism, Gallican Confession, Thirty-nine Articles, and the Scotch Confession. See Philip Schaff, *The Creeds of Christendom*, 3 vols., 6th ed. (Grand Rapids, MI: Baker, 1977). These are the predominant confessions used by Reformed churches today.

[4] The Westminster Confession 31.4 states, "All synods or councils, since the apostles' times, whether general or particular, may err; and many have erred. Therefore they are not to be made the rule of faith, or practice; but to be used as a help in both."

[5] For example, the Westminster Confession 1.6 states, "The whole counsel of God concerning all things necessary for his own glory, man's salvation, faith, and life, is either expressly set down in Scripture, or by good and necessary consequence may be deduced from Scripture." On the matter of authority and history, section 10 says, "The supreme judge by which all controversies of religion are to be determined, and all decrees of councils, opinions of ancient writers, doctrines of men, and private spirits, are to be examined, and in whose sentence we are to rest, can be no other but the Holy Spirit speaking in the Scripture."

but Christ."⁶ My Orthodox and Roman Catholic colleagues may appeal to their additional authoritative traditions, however, to be consistent with the Reformed faith, I must rest the truthfulness of my arguments on Scripture alone.

3. Always Reforming. The view that I will present is Reformed, but it may not sound like American Presbyterianism after the Great Awakening. American Christianity has been affected in a large way by its various revivals. They were not all bad, but they fundamentally altered the Presbyterian view of children. I am appealing much more to the Reformation's historic point of view. Ulrich Zwingli, Heinrich Bullinger, and definitively John Calvin reached deeply into the well of Scripture to defend the inclusion of children in the church, against Anabaptist views.⁷ In doing so, they argued their ecclesiology from the "covenants of *the* promise"⁸ made with Abraham. This provided a strong sense of the right of covenant children to be considered members of the church. However, revivalism's effect caused conversion experience to be virtually the only ground for inclusion. In 1847 Charles Hodge addressed the problem of revivalism:

> It may be highly useful, or even necessary, just as violent remedies are often the only means of saving life. But such remedies are not the ordinary and proper means of sustaining and promoting health. No one can fail to remark that this too exclusive dependence on revivals

---

⁶ This is a self-defeating statement since the statement itself is a simple creed. We cannot avoid creedal activity; we find it in Scripture itself (e.g., 2 Tim 2:11; Phil 2:5–11). What we need are *true* creeds, but by what authority may we know the truth of a creed? The Reformed view says Scripture is that highest authority.

⁷ I address their arguments in "The Polemics of Anabaptism" in *The Case for Covenantal Infant Baptism*, ed. Gregg Strawbridge (Phillipsburg, NJ: P&R, 2003).

⁸ This translation of a phrase from Eph 2:12 reflects the Greek text's definite article on "the promise" (*tēs epangelias*), which is first stated in the protoevangelium (Gen 3:15) and then substantially in the promise to Abraham (Gen 12, 15, 17).

tends to produce a false or unscriptural form of religion. The ordinary means of grace become insipid or distasteful. Perhaps however the most deplorable result of the mistake we are now considering is the neglect which it necessarily induces of the divinely appointed means of careful Christian nurture. Family training of children, and pastoral instruction of the young, are almost entirely lost sight of. We have long felt and often expressed the conviction that this is one of the most serious evils in the present state of our churches.[9]

4. Reformed Tradition. The Reformed faith has a core, but it has always included diversity—sometimes in respect to topics under this book's main heading. The Reformed tradition is like a river with many streams flowing in and out. I am seeking to address the main channel. However, I will try to indicate where my own views may have diverged from its current course.[10]

5. Defining Questions. Our editors have posed several questions about the relation of infants and children to the church. In order to provide a context to answer these questions, I wish to frame this conversation with four foundational topics: biblical covenants, the church defined, the inclusion of children in the sacraments, and spiritual formation by covenant succession.

---

[9] Cited in Robert S. Rayburn's article, "Presbyterian Doctrines of Covenant Children, Covenant Nurture, and Covenant Succession" reprinted in *The Case for Covenant Communion*, ed. Gregg Strawbridge (Monroe, LA: Athanasius, 2006). Hodge's original quotation is found in "Bushnell on Christian Nurture," *Biblical Repertory and Princeton Review* 19 (1847): 520–21.

[10] In terms of a short narrative of this, Zwingli began it; Bullinger and Bucer contributed; Farel saw a vision for it; Calvin nearly perfected it; Ursinus and Oliveanus expressed it; Beza codified it; Turretin explicated it and by the time of the Westminster Assembly, many debates of covenant theology and high Calvinism (surpralapsarianism) had coalesced in a compromise document which sought to retain the organic covenantal insights and the decretal understanding of God's salvation work in history and the church. I think the Westminster standards err on the side of the decretal dimension of theology. Still, these documents carefully and clearly express many Christian dogmas.

Biblical Covenants

As indicated above, it was through excavating the notion of biblical covenants that the Reformers appealing to Scripture alone began to argue for their vision of the inclusion of children in baptism. By thinking through the covenants in the Bible, one can see consistent aspects of covenants: covenantal administrations have signs and the inclusion of descendants. When one goes through the creation covenant,[11] the Noahic covenant, the Abrahamic covenant, the Mosaic covenant, and even the Davidic covenant, there are clear signs associated with these covenants: the tree of life, rainbows, circumcision, a sacrificial system, and Passover, for instance. But other statements indicate that descendants are included: "As in Adam all die" (1 Cor 15:22).[12] So also in the case of Noah, his household was saved. The Abrahamic covenant makes this perfectly explicit: The Lord will be "God to you and your descendants after you" (Gen 17:7).

Covenant (Administration)	Visible Sign	Descendants Included
Creation/Adamic	Tree of Life	yes
Noahic	Rainbow	yes
Abrahamic (Other Patriarchs)	Circumcision Sacrifices/Meals	yes yes
Mosaic	Passover (blood, then meal)	yes
Davidic	Throne	yes
New Covenant	Baptism (entrance) Lord's Supper (continuance)	?

Figure 1: Biblical Covenants[13]

---

[11] Hosea 6:7 states, "But like Adam they have transgressed the covenant."

[12] All scripture references in this chapter are from the New American Standard Bible (NASB).

[13] The chart is taken from my *You and Your Household: The Biblical Case for Infant Baptism* (Brownstown, PA: WordMp3, 2015), available through paedobaptism.com and also on Kindle.

There are discontinuities between the old and new covenants—but not in the way children are to be nurtured or included. There are plain statements throughout Scripture promising the inclusion of children in the new covenant. For example, consider this classic statement of the new covenant:

> "Behold, days are coming," declares the Lord, "when I will make a new covenant with the house of Israel and with the house of Judah...." "I will put My law within them and on their heart I will write it; and I will be their God, and they shall be My people."... Thus says the Lord, Who gives the sun for light by day And the fixed order of the moon and the stars for light by night, Who stirs up the sea so that its waves roar; The Lord of hosts is His name: "If this fixed order departs From before Me," declares the Lord, "Then the offspring of Israel also will cease From being a nation before Me forever." Thus says the Lord, "If the heavens above can be measured And the foundations of the earth searched out below, Then I will also cast off all the offspring of Israel For all that they have done," declares the Lord. (Jer 31:31–37)

The promise to Israel regarding the coming new covenant included their children as indicated in verses 35–37. Implicitly, it is included in "the house of Israel" and "Judah" as well, since this is contextually defined as the "families of Israel" (31:1) with "your children" (31:17). Note above the poetic nature of their inclusion: the fixed order of the universe would have to fail before "the offspring of Israel" are cast off. Certainly this is another way of saying Israel will always be before Yahweh; however, this word includes Israel's children as is indicated in the context. In this case the repeated emphasis is on the offspring. There is no word in this passage that changes the Abrahamic promise's inclusion of children; rather, this inclusion is implicitly and explicitly confirmed. Moreover, there is no word whatsoever that excludes believers' children from inclusion in the New Testament promises.[14]

---

[14] Beyond Jer 31:35–36 there are many more explicit inclusions of children in the new covenant promises: Jer 32:37–40; 33:22–26; Ezek 37:24–26;

The Church Defined

The Westminster Confession says that the church "consists of all those throughout the world that profess the true religion; and of their children: and is the kingdom of the Lord Jesus Christ, the house and family of God, out of which there is no ordinary possibility of salvation" (25.2).[15] Importantly, one must be a member of the church for salvation. But what does this imply for children? If being part of the visible church is normative, then children must be members of the church by default. For Baptists, this leaves little children in "no man's land" in their identity with Christ the only Savior.

So what does the Bible teach about the nature of the church and her children? In the establishment of the covenant with Abraham in Genesis 17, God initiated a covenant with the explicit provision that he would be God to the patriarch and to his descendants after him. This promise to Abraham is recited in Romans, Galatians, and in other passages in the New Testament. A particular passage in Romans clearly states that the inclusion of children is New Testament doctrine:

> For this reason it is by faith, in order that it may be in accordance with grace, so that the promise will be guaranteed to all the descendants, not only to those who are of the Law, but also to those who are of the faith of Abraham, who is the father of us all, (as it is written, "A FATHER OF MANY NATIONS HAVE I MADE YOU") in the presence of Him whom he believed, even God, who gives life to the dead and calls into being that which does not exist. In hope against hope he believed, so that he might become a father of many nations

---

Zech 10:6–9; Joel 2:1–29; Isa 44:3; 54:10–13; 59:20–21; Mal 4:5–6; and New Testament inclusions: Luke 1:17; 2:49–50; Acts 2:39; 3:25; 13:32–33; and Rom 4:13–17, among others.

[15] The Westminster Confession makes a distinction between the visible church and the invisible one. The invisible church is simply all those who will be saved, including elect infants.

according to that which had been spoken, "SO SHALL YOUR DESCENDANTS BE." (Romans 4:16–18)

The promise is guaranteed to all the descendants. This is a reassertion that the Abrahamic covenant is applicable—not only to Jews, but also to believing Gentiles.[16] What, then, were early believing Gentiles to think of their children's identity?

It is difficult to see how Gentiles could have assumed their children excluded from the family of God, especially when believing Jews clearly believed in their inclusion.[17] The New Testament's epistles to churches including those full of Gentiles provides a compelling case for the explicit inclusion of children. For example, in Eph 1:1–2 we read, "To the saints (*hagios*) who are at Ephesus and who are faithful in Christ Jesus: Grace to you and peace from God our Father and the Lord Jesus Christ." And then in chapter six, children are addressed. Saints in Ephesus include husbands, wives, and children. Are children *saints (hagios)*? Yes. Even more, note the greeting: "Grace to you and peace from God." Is this the appropriate greeting for one who is not a member of the church, who is not *in Christ*? No. But is it proper to greet the children of the church in this way? Yes. That's why Paul did so.

An even stronger example of the inclusion of children and their status is found in 1 Cor 7:14. The children of a believing parent are not unclean, "but now they are *holy*" (*hagios*). The same word is translated over fifty times in the New Testament as "saints." They are *hagios*. Children are set

---

[16] Should someone object to this point in terms of the "land promise," Rom 4:13 applies: "For the promise to Abraham or to his descendants that he would be heir of the world (*cosmos*)."

[17] Douglas Wilson argued we find no record of a dispute regarding the apostles excluding the believing Jews' children from the covenant so long established. This is either a remarkable silence or simply not the teaching of the apostles. See *To a Thousand Generations: Infant Baptism—Covenant Mercy to the Children of God* (Moscow, ID: Canon, 1996).

apart as covenantally sanctified.[18] Where did Paul get this notion? From the Abrahamic covenant.

So what is the basis for the church's inclusion of children? The Belgic Confession in 1561 (Article 34) says, "We believe our children ought to be baptized and sealed with the sign of the covenant, as little children were circumcised in Israel on the basis of the same promises made to our children."

This logic is important here: Christ has shed his blood no less for washing the little children of believers than for adults. The idea is that if anyone is going to be saved, it is through what Christ did. And who can assert that no children are saved? The rationale is covenantal and grounded in the promise to Abraham. Similarly, the Heidelberg Catechism (Q. 74) speaks of this in regard to baptism by saying, "Should infants also be baptized? Yes. Infants as well as adults are included in God's covenant and people, and they, no less than adults, are promised deliverance from sin through Christ's blood." John Calvin wrote, "Hence it follows, that the children of believers are not baptised, in order that though formerly aliens from the Church, they may then, for the first time, become children of God, but rather are received into the Church by a formal sign, because, in virtue of the promise, they previously belonged to the body of Christ."[19] In other words, because they are already covenantally included, then baptism is applicable. Baptism does not make a child a member of the covenant; rather, it is a sign and seal of the covenant. This is a rather striking contrast to the views of all of my other colleagues.[20]

---

[18] In perhaps the most persuasive Baptist defense against covenantal paedobaptism, Paul K. Jewett even accepts this sanctification of children (1 Cor 7:14) as due to the "marriage covenant" as in the Jewish/Mishna sources. See his *Infant Baptism and the Covenant of Grace* (Grand Rapids, MI: Eerdmans, 1978), 136.

[19] John Calvin, *Institutes of the Christian Religion*, 4.15.22. This 1845 translation by Henry Beveridge is available from Christian Classics Ethereal Library at http://www.ccel.org/ccel/calvin/institutes.vi.xvi.html.

[20] Orthodox and Roman Catholics differ from Lutherans and from Baptists on how baptism relates to salvation and church membership; but each of these other views misses the relevance and richness of the covenant as the ground of the ecclesiology of children.

There is strong evidence that Martin Luther, Ulrich Zwingli, John Calvin, Zacharias Ursinus (contributor to and writer of the Heidelberg Catechism) accepted that there is a "seed" of regeneration and faith, to use Calvin's term, in infancy.[21] For example, infant regeneration is explicit in the case of John the Baptist (Luke 1:39–44). Infant faith is set forth in Ps 22:9: "Yet You are He who brought me forth from the womb; You made me trust when upon my mother's breasts. Upon You I was cast from birth; You have been my God from my mother's womb." Also, Ps 71:5–6 says, "For You are my hope; O Lord GOD, You are my confidence from my youth. By You I have been sustained from my birth; You are He who took me from my mother's womb; My praise is continually of You."

Speaking of children raised in a faithful home, Bryan Chapell expresses the life-long reality of faith in covenant children: "In this atmosphere, faith naturally germinates and matures so that, *it is possible, even common, for the children of Christian parents never to know a day that they do not believe that Jesus is their Savior and Lord*" (emphasis his).[22]

---

[21] See Rich Lusk, *Paedofaith* (Monroe, LA: Athanasius, 2005); Rayburn's, "The Presbyterian Doctrine of Children"; and Calvin, *Institutes*, 4.16.20. Calvin writes, "In fine, the objection is easily disposed of by the fact, that children are baptised for future repentance and faith. Though these are not yet formed in them, yet the seed of both lies hid in them by the secret operation of the Spirit." Also, "For if fulness of life consists in the perfect knowledge of God, since some of those whom death hurries away in the first moments of infancy pass into life eternal, they are certainly admitted to behold the immediate presence of God. Those, therefore, whom the Lord is to illumine with the full brightness of his light, why may he not, if he so pleases, irradiate at present with some small beam, especially if he does not remove their ignorance, before he delivers them from the prison of the flesh? I would not rashly affirm that they are endued with the same faith that we experience in ourselves, or have any knowledge at all resembling faith (this I would rather leave undecided); but I would somewhat curb the stolid arrogance of those men who, as with inflated cheeks, affirm or deny whatever suits them" (4.16.19).

[22] "A Pastoral View of Infant Baptism" in *The Case for Covenantal Infant Baptism*, 26.

Despite the verses above, many may say, there is no way a little child or infant can have faith. Consider Peter Leithart's argument:

> Is "infant faith" absurd? "Faith" is the human response of trust toward God, a response of allegiance, in a personal relationship, and this has large consequences for our understanding of infant faith. The question of infant faith is not: "Are infants capable of receiving this jolt of divine power?" The question is: "Can infants respond to other persons? Do infants have personal relations? And the answer to this question is obviously yes. Infants quickly (even *in utero*) learn to respond to mother's voice; infants quickly manifest "trust" in their parents; infants quickly distinguish strangers from members of the family.[23]

If one removes all of the scholastic discussions about the nature and content of faith, faith is trust, and trust is a response to a person. The seed of the ability to express allegiance to someone is embedded in us from infancy, as seen in an infant's response to his mother. This is why Calvin used the term "seed faith" to describe the mysterious relationship infants may have to God.

Children Dying in Infancy

But what about the question of a child dying in infancy? The Five Points of Calvinism (total depravity, unconditional election, limited atonement, irresistible grace, and perseverance of the saints) are a rather truncated view of Reformed doctrine, but those five points are originally from the Synod of Dort held in 1618 and 1619. The decisions of this famous Dutch showdown on Calvinism versus Arminianism are contained in the Canons of Dort. Consider Article 17:

---

[23] Peter Leithart, *The Baptized Body* (Moscow, ID: Canon, 2007), 10.

The Salvation of the Infants of Believers

Since we must make judgments about God's will from his Word, which testifies that the children of believers are holy, not by nature but by virtue of the gracious covenant in which they together with their parents are included, godly parents ought not to doubt the election and salvation of their children whom God calls out of this life in infancy.[24]

Calvinists should not doubt the salvation of their children that are lost in early death. I had a poignant opportunity to exercise this doctrine a few years ago. A child was born in our congregation with a severe deformity. It was known that he would not live long, if he lived at all. In consultation with the believing parents, I went to the delivery room prepared to do a baptism. The goal of doing so was not to save the child because the child is in the covenant; rather, I intended to place the sign of the new covenant on that child. In the act of baptizing him, I was declaring with his parents that this was God's baby. Soon thereafter, Hezekiah—only eight days old—died. He is in heaven.

The Reformed tradition strongly affirms the salvation of covenant children, children of at least one believing parent, who die in infancy. Loraine Boettner wrote, "Most Calvinistic theologians have held that those who die in infancy are saved. The Scriptures seem to teach plainly enough that the children of believers are saved; but they are silent or practically so in regard to those of the heathens."[25]

So what about the children of non-Christians? What happens to them should they perish in their first months? The Westminster Confession states, "Elect infants, dying in infancy, are regenerated, and saved by Christ, through the Spirit, who works when, and where, and how He pleases: so also are all

---

[24] This translation is from http://www.crcna.org/welcome/beliefs/confessions/canons-dort.

[25] Loraine Boettner, *The Reformed Doctrine of Predestination* (Phillipsburg, NJ: Presbyterian & Reformed, 1963), 143.

other elect persons who are incapable of being outwardly called by the ministry of the Word" (10.3). At first this may seem only tautological, no more helpful than saying, "Bachelors are unmarried men." However, the context is in the chapter title, "Of Effectual Calling." This is an explanation of *how* God works by his grace, through the Spirit. The Holy Spirit is capable (on a Reformed reading) to regenerate in the womb. Since the Reformed tradition is strong on the salvation of covenant children dying in infancy, another way to read the Confession here is to apply it to all infants, regardless of their covenant inclusion. Assuming the Westminster divines were not apostatizing from previous Reformed views, and read in this way, its meaning would emphasize that there are elect children among unbelievers. The Confession also provides for the mentally handicapped or "other elect persons who are incapable of being outwardly called."

The Confession is careful not to be dogmatic about "all children," yet it leaves the possibility open since all such children *could* be elect. Noted Reformed Theologians such as Charles Hodge, W. G. T. Shedd, and B. B. Warfield held out the hope of salvation for all children dying in infancy.[26] In my own view, I can only say with confidence that *elect* infants who die in infancy will be saved. While I believe in the mercy of God, I cannot cite any text in the Bible to prove a universal hope that all children who die in infancy will be saved. But what I can say is this: believers who lost a child in his or her infancy should claim the promises first made to Abraham and then rest in God's promises for the salvation of their child (Gen 17:7).

In response to the truth that we cannot say with confidence that the infants of unbelievers are admitted into heaven when they die, some may argue that all children are innocent. But the sobering truth is that all have sinned (Rom 3:23). This passage is not speaking of only adults, as every parent knows. Could children sin even in the womb, then? Yes. I believe in the Calvinistic view of the fall and depravity. We are corrupted because of the fall (Romans 3). That means that as soon as we humans are able to sin, we

---

[26] Ibid., 143.

do. Children are "in Adam." And "as in Adam all die" (1 Cor 15:22). Death is an alienation from the Triune God of Scripture. If all in Adam die, then all deserve alienation from God—or else death is an unjust consequence. But nothing God does can be an unjust consequence since he is always righteous and is the standard of justice. This is my most basic argument for the Augustinian conception of original sin.

I would certainly like to think no innocent child goes to hell, just as I would like to think no innocent native goes to hell. But there are no innocent people in Adam. This is because we covenantally participated in Adam's sin, just as we who believe covenantally participated in Christ's redemption. As members of the human family, we have union with Adam; but thanks be to God, we can have union with Christ that unites us as God's family. This covenantal connection to Adam, to Christ, and to the body of Christ is a trinitarian unity.

Despite the devastation of the fall and the severe consequences of sin, the gracious Triune God has determined salvation for every single person in his church. It is my sincere prayer that all the so-called innocent natives, every single child dying in infancy, and every one of the aborted may yet be saved by the mercy of the Lord. Certainly, no more costly sacrifice for them must be made to secure their salvation. No more efficacious Spirit is needed to make them alive in their darkness. God can irresistibly draw them in his grace.

Children and the Sacraments

Another question closely linked with this one is that of children's inclusion in the sacraments of baptism and Communion. First, I must defend the notion of "sacrament." The Shorter Catechism Q. 91 says, "How do the sacraments become effectual means of salvation? A. The sacraments become effectual means of salvation, not from any virtue in them, or in him that doth administer them; but only by the blessing of Christ, and the working of his Spirit in them that by faith receive them." The Westminster Confession 28.6 says, "The efficacy of Baptism is not tied to that moment of time wherein it is administered; yet, notwithstanding, by the right use of this ordinance, the grace promised is not only offered, but really exhibited, and conferred, by the Holy Ghost, to such (whether of age or infants) as that grace belongs unto, according to the counsel of God's own will, in His appointed time."

Both of these Presbyterian and Reformed doctrinal statements clarify that salvation is in some sense *conferred* through baptism (and Communion). Many Presbyterians, influenced by American revivalism, are unaware that this is actually in their catechism or confession. Grace is conferred through baptism, but it is a qualified transmission. In his study of the confession and baptism, David F. Wright stated, "Confession teaches baptismal regeneration." Then he added the various qualifications.[27] The particular qualifications in the above passages are to exclude the notion of any magical property in the water or minister (priest), as well as to protect the Calvinistic view of election—that the blessings of salvation are finally obtained only by the elect, by grace through faith.

Attention should be given to the qualifying phrase, "The efficacy of Baptism is not tied to that moment of time wherein it is administered." This may mean that baptism's efficacy does not necessarily happen at the time of baptism. This is often the way modern Presbyterians take it. However, another way to understand this is more in keeping the historical development of baptism's meaning in Reformation history.

Over against penance (needed to restore one after baptism), the Reformers called the church to a richer view of baptism for life-long grace, duty, comfort, and forgiveness. In other words, believers must "improve" our baptisms throughout all of life.[28] The Belgic Confession (34) says, "Neither does this Baptism only avail us at the time when the water is poured upon us and received by us, but also through *the whole course of our life*" (emphasis mine).

---

[27] "Baptism at the Westminster Assembly," in *Calvin Studies VIII: The Westminster Confession in Current Thought* (Davidson, NC: Davidson College, 1997), 80.

[28] The Larger Catechism of the Westminster Standards (1648), Q. 171.

The Scots Confession (21) also says, "For baptism once received *continues for all of life*, and is a perpetual sealing of our adoption" (emphasis mine). The French Confession (35) concurs: "[Baptism] reaches *over our whole lives and to our death*" (emphasis mine).[29] Most importantly for the Confession's interpretation, the Westminster Directory (for the "Publick Worship of God") gives guidance to ministers teaching on baptism and says, "That inward grace and virtue of baptism is not tied to that moment of time wherein it is administered." At this point one expects to read, "but the Lord in his mysterious sovereignty saves when and where he willith." But what follows instead sounds like the previous Reformed confessions: "That inward grace and virtue of baptism is not tied to that moment of time wherein it is administered; and that the fruit and power thereof reacheth to the whole course of our life." It goes on to teach believers to "look back at their baptism . . . to improve and make right use of their baptism and of the covenant sealed thereby betwixt God and their souls."[30] Baptism is not simply one of the sacraments whose grace may be lost with venial sin; rather, this washing and regeneration extends through all of life—despite our sinfulness—so long as "that grace belongs unto" us.

Baptism in the Bible

As a Baptist I was guilty of thinking baptism started in the New Testament with John the Baptist. This was probably due to the mural of John baptizing in the baptismal of the Southern Baptist church I attended in childhood. Like the stained glass illustrations of medieval cathedrals, the art was intended to

---

[29] This argument is drawn from Rich Lusk, "Baptismal Efficacy and Baptismal Latency: A Sacramental Dialogue," *Presbyterion: Covenant Seminary Review* 32 (Spring 2006): 18–37. In response to a critique, see William B. Evans, "'Really Exhibited and Conferred . . . in His Appointed Time': Baptism and the New Reformed Sacramentalism," *Presbyterion: Covenant Seminary Review* 31 (Fall 2005): 72–88.

[30] Citations are found in *Westminster Confession of Faith* (Glasgow, UK: Free Presbyterian Publications, 1976), 383.

impress upon young minds the teachings of our church. But a deeper look at the Scriptures reveals that the headwaters of the baptismal flood begin in the garden and flow right on through the Old Testament—before the great waterfall of the new covenant era.

In the prototypical garden of Eden are found many of the themes that unfold in Scripture. Gregory K. Beale, in his Revelation commentary, frequently makes use of the garden's prototypical foundation for the meaning of the language in Revelation.[31] Allen P. Ross writes, "It is no surprise that the instructions [for the temple] included many motifs and ideas from creation, notably Paradise. This was true not only of the tabernacle in the wilderness, but also of the Solomonic temple; and it is true also of the prophetic visions of the new creation to come."[32] Gordon J. Wenham, commenting on Gen 2:8–27 notes, "Indeed, there are many other features of the garden that suggest it is seen as an archetypal sanctuary, prefiguring the later tabernacle and temples."[33]

Hence, the tabernacle and the temple are stylized, architectural versions of the garden. Thus, the water God provides for refreshment and cleansing is a theme throughout Scripture. From Eden flowed rivers as boundaries. There are springs in the patriarchal narratives. Israel (including her children) passes through the Red Sea. A laver for priestly cleansing is at the entrance of the tabernacle. Joshua leads Israel across the Jordan into the land. In the temple of Solomon, an ocean and basins of water on chariots create a stylized river flowing out to cleanse the nations. Ezekiel 47 and Zech 14:8 see visions of rivers flowing out in the new covenant. Then in the New Testament, those washings (*baptismos*) in the tabernacle, as well as the crossing of the Red Sea, are explicitly called baptisms (Heb 9:10; 1 Cor 10). Thus, there are many baptisms in the Old Testament. Even more, there are references there to the coming new

---

[31] Gregory K. Beale, *The Book of Revelation* (Grand Rapids, MI: Eerdmans, 1999).

[32] Allen P. Ross, *Recalling the Hope of Glory: Biblical Worship from the Garden to the New Creation* (Grand Rapids, MI: Kregel, 2006), 83.

[33] Gordon J. Wenham, *Genesis 1–15*, Word Biblical Commentary (Waco, TX: Word, 1987).

covenant baptism. The Messiah would come to baptize Israel and the world. Ezekiel 36:24 says, "I will sprinkle clean water on you and you will be clean." Isaiah 52:15 adds, "He will sprinkle many nations." The water flowing out to baptize the nations is promised in the old covenant.

Now enter John the Baptist. He was to go "in the spirit and power of Elijah," who divided the waters of the Jordan (2 Kgs 2:8). John "prepared the way" for Jesus. John was in the wilderness beyond the borders of the land where people "went out to him" (Mark 1:5). To make sense of this, we must call to mind what had happened to Israel in the past.

In the exodus, Israel "passed (Hb. *avar*) through the midst of the sea into the wilderness" (Num 33:8). Paul describes this as a baptism (1 Cor 10:2). Crossing the Red Sea, then, *is* a baptism. Under Joshua, Israel was commanded to "cross (*avar*) this Jordan, to go in to possess the land" (Josh 1:11). Due to Moses's anger, he did not get to cross over (Deut 4:22; 31:2). Crossing language is used again when Elisha is given a double portion of the spirit of Elijah: "Elijah took his mantle and folded it together and struck the waters, and they were divided here and there, so that the two of them crossed over on dry ground" (2 Kgs 2:8). Then in the exile, Judah was expelled out of the land, beyond the borders of the Jordan River (1 Chr 9:1; Joshua 3–4).

In the era just before Jesus arrived, the Jews wanted to know whether the exile was over. On the one hand, they were back "in the land" after a time in Babylon (at least many were). They had walls, a city, and a temple. But on the other hand, they were still oppressed by foreign powers, Herod and Rome. So had God returned to Zion in fulfillment of the prophets (e.g., Isa 40:1–10)? John was "preaching a baptism of repentance" (Mark 1:4). This does not mean John was preaching, "You must be immersed." Rather, given all the history to this point, John was preaching a so-called baptism of the renewal of Israel. The baptism he preached showed this.

Theologian Colin Brown writes, "John was organizing a symbolic exodus from Jerusalem and Judea as a preliminary to recrossing the Jordan as a penitent, consecrated Israel in order to reclaim the land in a quasi-reenactment of the return from the Babylonian exile.... (T)he purity and quantity of the water were of less significance than the historic, symbolic significance of the Jordan itself as the boundary and point of entry."[34] Just as Deuteronomy looked to a time of renewal when they "cross the Jordan" under Joshua's leadership (Deut 4:21), so now—on the verge of the Messiah coming—John was leading them in a symbolic exodus to enter the land in renewal.[35] The rest of the New Testament draws on various threads of this crossing image in baptism. We are baptized into Christ, through death and into resurrection life. We cross into him (Rom 6:3–4; Col 2:11–12).

New Covenant Baptisms

Consider all the biblical examples of Christian baptism, beginning in Acts. A strong argument can be made for the household inclusion into the faith, which would include children. The basic outline of Acts is indicated in the first chapter. The gospel of Christ goes forth: "You shall be My witnesses both in Jerusalem, and in all Judea and Samaria, and even to the remotest part of the earth" (Acts 1:8b). The pattern of baptisms follow this expansion: Jerusalem and Judea, Samaria, and the rest of the world.

Adult Conversion Baptisms	Household Baptisms
3,000 (men) Pentecost (no household present)	Cornelius and household
Samaritans: (both men and women) Simon the Sorcerer	Lydia and household
Ethiopian Eunuch (no household)	Philippian Jailer and household

---

[34] Colin Brown, "What Was John the Baptist Doing?," *Bulletin for Biblical Research* 7 (1997): 37–50. Available here: www.biblicalstudies.org.uk/pdf/bbr/baptist_brown.pdf.

[35] There may be a hint to this crossing when John and his disciples, "looked at Jesus *as He walked*" (John 1:36). This is an odd statement in the context of being a baptism spectator. But, if the baptism setting was a symbolic exodus, then Jesus may have been walking with a crowd of those identifying with this new exodus.

A Reformed View

Adult Conversion Baptisms	Household Baptisms
Paul (no household)	Corinthians: Crispus and household [inferred] Stephanas and household [Gaius below]
Disciples of John (12 men) (no household present)	
Gaius (and household?)	

Figure 2: Adult Conversion and Household Baptisms

In summary of the actual baptisms, we find several interesting points. First, the new covenant promise came "to you and your children" (Acts 2:39) at Pentecost. Only 3,000 men are said to have been baptized in that instance (Acts 2:5, 14, 41). Second, in Samaria "men and women alike" (Acts 8:12) were baptized, including Simon the apostate sorcerer. Third, the Ethiopian eunuch (who had no familial household) was baptized (Acts 8:38). Fourth, Paul—who had no familial household—was baptized (Acts 9:18; cf. 1 Cor 7:7–8). Fifth, Cornelius's household was baptized (Acts 10:48; 11:14). Then, sixth, Lydia's household was baptized (Acts 16:15). Seventh, the Philippian jailer's household was baptized (Acts 16:33). Eighth, many Corinthians were baptized, including Crispus, Stephanas's household, and Gaius (Acts 18:8; 1 Cor 1:14, 16). After that, the adult male disciples of John were baptized (Acts 19:5).

These are the facts about who was baptized. From this we learn of nine people singled-out in the baptism narratives—five clearly had their households baptized, too (Cornelius, the jailer, Lydia, Crispus [inferred], and Stephanas). Two, the eunuch and Paul, had no households. That leaves Simon—who actually turned out to be an unbeliever—and Gaius, who is listed with Crispus, whom Paul baptized (1 Cor 1:14).

As for Gaius, Rom 16:23 says, "Gaius [is] host to me and to the whole church." This implies he was a man of some means (3 John 1 references him as "elder," assuming that Gaius is the same person). As such, he may have had at least household servants, if not his own family, under his roof. Gaius is mentioned with the household head, Crispus the synagogue leader. Crispus "believed in the Lord with all his household" (Acts 18:8). Thus, his household was undoubtedly baptized with him. Yet, Paul said in no uncertain terms, "I baptized *none of you* except Crispus and Gaius" (1 Cor 1:14, emphasis mine). But given that culture, Paul probably spoke of Crispus as representing the household in the administration of baptism.[36] Also, the text goes on to say, "Now I did baptize also the household of Stephanas; beyond that, I do not know whether I baptized any other" (*allos*) (1 Cor 1:16). The referent to the pronoun *allos* is "household" (*oikos*). In other words, Paul did not know whether he "baptized any other [household]." Therefore, if Gaius had a household, it was baptized—just like Crispus's household.

These important biblical points regarding household baptisms are often dismissed. If household inclusion in the new covenant is not the point, did Luke and Paul intentionally include more irregular and anomalous cases of baptism than regular ones? It appears that every baptism beginning with that of Cornelius is a household baptism passage—except where we are told that those present were "twelve men," who were apparently Jews (Acts 19:7).

Gentile Baptisms

A prominent feature of Acts is the inclusion of Gentiles in the Jewish church. When Peter recalls the first case of Gentile conversion (that of Cornelius), it is framed with covenantal words: "And he shall speak words to you by which you will be saved, *you and all your household*" (Acts 11:14, emphasis mine). Then the Gentile households of Cornelius, Lydia, the jailer, Stephanas, and possibly Gaius (see the previous discussion) were all baptized.

---

[36] It is logically possible Paul baptized only Crispus and Gaius, then someone else baptized the households. However, it seems unlikely Paul would baptize Crispus only to turn the proceedings over to someone else.

Outline of Acts The Gospel Goes To ...	Baptisms Follow This Outline
Jerusalem and Judea	3,000 Men at Pentecost
Samaria	Samaritans, Simon, the Eunuch
Ends of the Earth Transition: Apostle Paul (Acts 9) First Gentile: Cornelius (Acts 10) God-fearer: Lydia (Acts 16) New Convert Gentiles: The Jailer (Acts 16) Corinthians (Acts 18) Ephesus (Acts 19)	Saul (apostle to Gentiles) **Cornelius's Household** **Lydia's Household** **Jailer's Household** Corinthians: **Crispus's Household** **Stephanas's Household** Gaius, 12 Men in Ephesus

Figure 3: Baptisms in Acts

Acts is a selective history of thousands of examples of baptisms over the first decades of the church. Surely Luke did not record the only household baptisms of the entire apostolic period. Rather, this was the normative practice of the apostolic church as the gospel went to Gentile families. The gospel and its outward sign went to families because families were to be saved (Acts 16:31b; also 3:25). This is particularly clear in the jailer's case: "Believe in the Lord Jesus, and you shall be saved, *you and your household*" (Acts 16:31, emphasis mine). Again, this is how Luke frames the first case of Gentile conversion: "And he shall speak words to you by which you will be saved, *you and all your household*" (Acts 11:14, emphasis mine).[37]

---

[37] I have addressed the response, "But every member of the household must have believed," more fully elsewhere: see *You and Your Household: The Biblical Case for Infant Baptism* (Brownstown, PA: WordMp3.com, 2015) and on Kindle. In summary, the individuality of faith is not the exegetical point of the two cases, which include statements about the households and faith (the jailer in Acts 16:31–34 and Crispus in 18:8). Consider the nuances of these texts. The Greek texts have singular, not plural verbs, to describe the actions of believing. These texts do not say, the jailer (or Crispus) "and (*kai*)" household members "believed [plural]." Instead, these texts teach what any Old Testament believer might have expected: the jailer, the household head, "rejoiced (singular verb) greatly, with all

In the case of the jailer, the narrative is set up in a covenantal frame: "What must I [individual and singular] do to be saved?" The answer is covenantal: "Believe in the Lord Jesus, and you [individual] shall be saved, *you and your household*" (Acts 16:31). Luke takes some time on this pericope. Why? The jailer's was the first recorded baptism of an outright pagan. Previous Gentiles had been God-fearers, worshiping the true God of Israel before placing faith in Christ. But Philippi was a Roman colony, and many retired soldiers were rewarded with land there. It is likely this jailer was a former Roman soldier; hence, he was about to kill himself. Romans called for the duty of suicide in the face of grave failure, like the loss of one's prisoners. In fear and trembling and after an earthquake, no less, he cried out: "Sirs, what must I do to be saved?" The answer is pregnant with biblical, covenantal concepts.

Further, the exodus images and resonances of this passage should not be missed. This happened at midnight (Acts 16:25). Luke emphasizes the events of washing happened, "the same hour of the night" (16:33). This is an unmistakable Passover allusion (Exod 11:4–5). *Midnight* in Hebrew literally means, "the division of the night," or the point of release between darkness and light. Ironically, with the release of those in bondage (Paul and Silas), the jailer's house would be delivered by the blood of the Lamb to pass through the Red Sea of baptism with rejoicing.[38] By casting the jailer's deliverance (the

---

his house (*panoikei*, an adverb), having believed (*pepisteukos*, participle, singular) in God" (16:34, from the literal rendering of the 1901 American Standard Version). Crispus, the household head, "believed (*episteusen*, verb, singular) in the Lord 'with' (*sun*) all his household" (Acts 18:8). However, observe Luke's careful language in 16:33 indicating baptism is administered to each member of the jailer's household: "He was baptized, he and all his household" (*kai hoi autou pantes*, literally, "those of his all").

[38] The inclusion of Israelite children were essential in the exodus, since this event unfolded the Abrahamic promise (e.g., Gen 18:19). Moses's request to be released was to "go with our young" to "hold a feast to the LORD." Pharaoh was willing to let the men go, but not "your little ones" (Exod 10:7–11). Then came "one more plague," the death of the cherished first-born child "at midnight" (Exod 11:29). "Then [Pharaoh] called for Moses and Aaron by night, and said, 'Rise, go

first converted pagan's baptism) as a Passover/exodus kind of event, Luke strengthens the image of the deliverance of children. It would hardly be a Passover without the salvation of the firstborn. Children were also delivered through the Red Sea of baptism (1 Cor 10:1–4).

Covenant Succession

"Covenant succession" has been used in Reformed circles to indicate the training of Christian children as a chief means of salvation being realized in their lives. It is coordinate with the ecclesiological means of grace, such as the formal ministry of the Word, prayer, and the sacraments. Robert S. Rayburn's article on this topic is helpful.[39] He shows how frequently Scripture shows the nurture of children born to families in the church as a means of bringing about lives of covenant faithfulness in those children. Just as in Abraham's day, the realization of these promises is dependent on covenant nurture. As Gen 18:19 states, "For I have chosen him [Abraham], so that he may command his children and his household after him to keep the way of the LORD by doing righteousness and justice, so that the LORD may bring upon Abraham what He has spoken about him." In Moses's day, the same command was given: "You shall teach them diligently to your sons and shall talk of them when you sit in your house and when you walk by the way and when you lie down and when you rise up" (Deut 6:7). It also appeared in the time of renewal with Joshua's words: "As for me and my house, we will serve the LORD" (Josh 24:15). Many other passages reinforce the idea.

---

out from among my people, both you and the children of Israel'" (Exod 11:30–31). The children were essential then and now.

[39] "Presbyterian Doctrines of Covenant Children, Covenant Nurture, and Covenant Succession" reprinted in *The Case for Covenant Communion*, ed. Gregg Strawbridge (Monroe, LA: Athanasius, 2006). This interesting article draws largely on Lewis Bevens Schenck's 1940 dissertation for Yale University, *The Presbyterian Doctrine of Children in the Covenant: An Historical Study of the Significance of Infant Baptism in the Presbyterian Church in America*.

The Place of Believers' Children: The Same in Both Testaments		
	Old Testament	New Testament
Duties of Parents	"Command...children to keep the way of the Lord." (Gen 18:19)	"Bring them up in the discipline and instruction of the Lord." (Eph 6:4)
Duties of Children	"Honor your father and mother." (Exod 20:12)	"Obey your parents." (Eph 6:2)
Blessings	"Live long in the land." (Exod 20:12)	"Live long on the earth." (Eph 6:3)
Children Must Obey the Word	"Your son and your grandson might fear the Lord your God, to keep all His statutes." (Deut 6:2)	"Continue in the things [Scripture] you have learned from infancy." (2 Tim 3:14–15)
Household Leadership	"As for me and my house, we will serve the Lord." (Josh 24:15)	"Believe in the Lord Jesus, and you will be saved, you and your household." (Acts 16:31)
Promised Reality	"I will pour out My Spirit on your offspring." (Isa 44:3)	"For the promise [of the Spirit] is to you and your children." (Acts 2:39)
Duration of Inclusion	"To a thousandth generation" with those who love Him and keep His commandments." (Deut 7:9)	"His mercy is upon generation after generation toward those who fear Him." (Luke 1:50)
Sign of Inclusion	"All the men of [Abraham's] household...were circumcised." (Gen 17:27)	The jailer "was baptized, he and all his household." (Acts 16:33) (Cornelius's, Lydia's, Crispus's, Stephanas's households were, too.)

Figure 4: The Place of Believer's Children: The Same in Both Testaments

The place of children, then, is not a matter of discontinuity between the old and new covenants—as the chart indicates. So what tools for covenant succession do we see in Scripture? The following tools arise from Christian families ordering their lives to nurture their children in the faith. These are not meant to be in priority order. They are inter-related.

1. Congregational Worship. A formative influence on children is full participation in both Word and sacrament in worship. There is a strong need for the unity of the family in worship. Adult Christians should therefore keep their children alongside them in worship, where they can receive the benefits of all of the liturgy. They too should be singing praise to God and learning to hear God's Word. This takes training. The spiritual formation that takes place in congregational worship significantly shapes children's vision of God, of Christ, and of the faith.

In the congregational gatherings of my faith tradition, a service reflects the historic worship patterns of worship in the church, with a Reformational emphasis in the teaching. In such services there is a continual dialogue between the minister who is leading and the people, including little children. They say after the lectionary readings of Scripture, "The Word of the Lord" and "Thanks be to God." Very early in their lives, children learn the Apostles' and Nicene Creeds. They sing hymns and Psalms and corporately say, "Amen." They learn the *sursam corda:* "Lift up your hearts.... We lift them up unto the Lord." They also sing the Lord's Prayer. These encounters with things of the church are formative.

2. Catechism. Children also learn catechisms of the Reformed faith: this is part of the intentional training of little ones in the faith community. In our congregation, we read through the Heidelberg Catechism and the Westminster Shorter Catechism on a rotating basis to continually encourage families to do the same in their homes. The Shorter Catechism is also in our Christian school curriculum. We have begun utilizing monthly catechism questions and answers for memorization so that the congregation can know central truths by heart. We also have some classes and small groups directed to different ages for study and growth, as do most Reformed congregations.

Most modern Reformed congregations hold communicants classes, but they do not have a rite of confirmation. In so far as Anglicans participate in the Reformed view, most Anglicans continue the tradition of confirmation. This practice is not inconsistent with the Reformed view, so long as the full covenantal membership of the child is not compromised. In this case, confirmation would not be admitting the child into the church, covenant, or kingdom; rather, it is a rite of passage into a deeper discipleship with the Lord.[40] Confirmation may be an unbiblical tradition or a biblical custom that aims to accomplish spiritual formation through another step of maturation. In my church, we have begun conversations about turning our youth discipleship class into this kind of confirmation course. The goal would be to encourage the students to a deeper understanding as they consciously embrace our faith.[41]

3. *Christian Schooling.* Education is worldview-shaping. Therefore, in helping children to form a fully Christian conception of reality, Christian schooling or homeschooling is a key part of the education process—over against an education based solely in a secular government-funded school system. Psalm 127:4–5 holds out the vision: "Children are a gift of the LORD, the fruit of the womb is a reward. Like arrows in the hand of a warrior, so are the children of one's youth. How blessed is the man whose quiver is full of them;

---

[40] Speaking strongly against the confirmation rite, James B. Jordan says, "There is no passage anywhere in the Bible that commands, hints, or shows that children need to go through some ritual before they are included at any religious meal. There is neither 'bar mitzvah' nor 'confirmation' in the Bible." See *The Case for Covenant Communion*, 50. He further argues against the idea that children of the Old Testament era were incorporated into the temple at age twelve, citing Jewish sources to indicate that no such tradition of "bar mitzvah" existed until AD 1400.

[41] I illustrate my view of a "Covenantal Confirmation" with my own college experience. I had studied and played and wrote music from about the age of ten. But in my first semester of music theory, I learned the names for all the sounds that I had experienced. Previously I had understood functional harmony, the sound of the tonic, or the dominant, but then I understood them by the right terms and relations. As we mature in our faith, we may know the music first. But then we learn the lyrics and their full meaning.

they will not be ashamed when they speak with their enemies in the gate." We as believing parents are to raise faithful warriors who by the grace of God use the tools imparted, their talents, and timely opportunities to wage war against evil and to fight the good fight. To overcome their exposure to a secular propaganda machine that spews a false view of reality daily, children will need more than a weekly hour of Sunday school. To truly shape their worldviews, we must engage in grammar and secondary education that imparts the culture (*paedeia*) of Christ (Eph 6:4). That is why I strongly favor the approach to education known as Classical and Christian Education. I believe it combines the best of our civilizational resources with a mature biblical point of view.[42]

Summation

With regard to the matter of how little ones are impacted by sin, the Reformed faith holds that all humankind—including infants and children—are guilty of Adam's sin (Rom 5:14–21). The nature of humans is corrupt because of the fall; sin is universal (Rom 3:23). And this is why all people (regardless of age) need the gracious, salvific work of Jesus.

As discussed within this chapter, the Bible is a covenantal book. Therefore, the two covenant heads are Adam and Christ. People are born in Adam and receive the guilt and penalty (the curse) of Adam's sin. Likewise, those in Christ receive the forgiveness and life of Christ through his obedient life, substitutionary death, and glorious resurrection. If the very young are unable to receive sinfulness through Adam, how then are they able to receive salvation through Christ? Both realities involve covenantal imputation. The case is placed as a parallel in 1 Cor 15:22.

---

[42] See my *Classical and Christian Education*, rev. ed. (Brownstown, PA: WordMp3.com, 2013), which is a booklet that explains this philosophy of education.

As to when and how infants and children are considered members of the church, the Reformed faith holds that because of the covenant, which God promised (Gen 3:15) and established with Abraham, the children of believers are included even in the new covenant. The rites that follow this are baptism and Communion, which are signs and seals of the covenant.[43] Baptism makes a child an official member of the church. Because of covenant inclusion, infants and young children have a right to the rite.

With regard to the question of how God treats those who die in infancy or childhood, the Reformed tradition teaches that Christians who lose a child in infancy should not doubt the salvation of that child. Should such a death take place after baptism, the parents can be even more confident in God's grace in the child's life because the child was signed and sealed in the covenant through that sacrament. In cases involving the premature deaths of the children of unbelievers, we can only say that God is merciful. The judge of all the earth will do right, since he is the standard of righteousness.

And finally, as to the question of when and how little ones are to be instructed in Christian doctrine, the Reformed church holds that God requires parents to be the primary teachers of their sons and daughters (Deuteronomy 6; Eph 6:4). The use of congregational worship, catechetical teaching and classes, as well as family worship, and Christian schooling all play a part in the spiritual formation of young girls and boys.

---

[43] The traditional Reformed pattern is infant baptism, but Communion only on the basis of confession. This generally happens in one's early teen years, though that varies from congregation to congregation. Often, first Communion is given to a baptized child after a communicants' class or in some contexts, a confirmation class. However, a growing number of Reformed churches accept children at the Table earlier, as well as paedocommunion. For example, Tim Gallant, *Feed My Lambs: Why the Lord's Table Should Be Restored to Covenant Children* (Grand Prairie, Canada: Pactum Reformanda Publishing, 2002). See also the book I edited and contributed to, *The Case for Covenant Communion* (currently available at WordMp3.com).

Responses to a Reformed View of Infants and Children in the Church

An Orthodox Response by Jason Foster

Gregg Strawbridge's chapter sets forth a conflation of nuances within the spectrum of Reformed (Presbyterian) theology and its implications for infants and children. His work is based in principle on the Reformation maxim, *sola Scriptura* but, arguably, reflects a modern application of "Scripture alone" that is not found in the Lutheran representative's chapter, that is, one's own interpretation of Scripture does not need to be consistent with the historical conclusions and teachings of Christianity to be valid. Strawbridge's freedom to interpret the biblical texts and alter the ritual practice of his local parish within his current Presbyterian affiliation is demonstrated in his writing. This is contrary to Orthodox ecclesiology in which bishops seek to maintain a common faith, liturgical life, and ritual practice within their respective territories; in that case, the freedom to edit or change what is said and done is not permitted. However, with his freedom, Strawbridge's adherence to a Presbyterian distinctive known as "covenant theology" and how infants and children fit within this schema is well presented and undergirded with numerous biblical citations. He presents a logical argument for the covenantal presupposition and hermeneutic he uses and for the pastoral conclusions he presents regarding little ones in the church.

In the following, I will present certain historical and theological issues pertaining to the Presbyterian view presented in opposition to the Orthodox position and will then conclude with some areas of common practice.

Historical Questions and Assumptions

Strawbridge notes, "The Reformed tradition is like a river with many streams flowing in and out. I am seeking to address the main channel. However, I will try to indicate where my own views may have diverged from its current course." Currently, the Reformed tradition has literally thousands of streams flowing from three very different rivers—the teachings of Luther, Calvin, and Zwingli; each has a distinctive view of the place of infants and children in the church. Therefore, from a pastoral viewpoint, the first question readers may contemplate is how does Strawbridge approach theological issues pertaining to infants and children with a sense of certainty that his current interpretation of the Scriptures and, therefore, current practices are correct? If church councils and creeds are useful but fallible, as acknowledged by Strawbridge and differing from the Orthodox position, how can one build a case for using the Bible as the final authority for matters of faith and practice when the biblical canon was formalized by the Council of Carthage in AD 397? What if that local council erred? If the local council had the authority to canonize the sacred texts, then it seems it may be beneficial to consider their theology of baptism as developed in the various Orthodox baptismal catechisms and liturgical rites of that time.

Theological Considerations

In developing his theological position on baptism, Strawbridge writes this in a footnote: "Orthodox and Roman Catholics differ from Lutherans and from Baptists on how baptism relates to salvation and church membership; but each of these other views misses the relevance and richness of the covenant as the ground of the ecclesiology of children." It should be acknowledged that Strawbridge develops a convincing argument by tracing the covenantal inclusion of children via the faithful family unit from the Old Testament to the New Testament. His conclusion is in agreement with the Orthodox Church. However, where we differ is in how we understand the ecclesiology of children. Strawbridge, in speaking of infants and the covenant, explains, "Baptism does not make a child a member of the covenant; rather, it is a sign and seal of the covenant." In other words, as he clarifies later in his chapter, the sign and seal is empty of any real sacramental meaning. Ultimately, either the child is elect or is not. If he is elect, then he will be received into heaven. If he is not, then he is damned before the moment of his birth. His fate is completely up to the sovereign choice of God. While there is some hope for those born into Christian families, ultimately the infant is guilty before God because of the disobedience of our common patriarch, Adam. This understanding of God's nature, of original sin (guilt), and of salvation is foreign and contrary to the teachings of the Orthodox Church.

In the Eastern Christian tradition, the Holy Trinity pursues all humans out of love, not wrath. The process of salvation begins when an infant, child, or adult truly has his sins washed away in baptism (not for reasons of guilt but of cleansing), and is sacramentally united to Christ in his death and resurrection and is sealed with the gift of the Holy Spirit via chrismation. Baptism, more than a sign and seal of the covenant, is the mystery that establishes the visible church; by it infants and children are full members of the body of Christ and participate in all the sacramental gifts leading unto their salvation through the process of *theosis*. While there are theological differences in our understandings of the sacraments and their efficacy, Strawbridge's view of the need to include children in congregational worship and to catechize them in the faith and to develop classical schools that teach Christian distinctives is in agreement with the Orthodox position in theory. Unfortunately, it is not always realized in Orthodox practice.

A ROMAN CATHOLIC RESPONSE BY DAVID LIBERTO

Gregg Strawbridge presents the Reformed position on the topic of infants and children in the church. My response to his chapter will employ the *modus operandi* of citation and response. I will cite a brief passage from his work, and then I will respond to it by way of questions, analysis, and critique. I will cite the various passages in the order in which they are presented in Strawbridge's essay.

Citation 1: "Infant regeneration is explicit in the case of John the Baptist (Luke 1:39–44). Infant faith is set forth in Ps 22:9: "Yet You are He who brought me forth from the womb; You made me trust when upon my mother's breasts (NASB)."

In the Reformed understanding, the children of believing parents are part of the covenant. Children are baptized as a sign and seal of this. Because of the Reformed faith's understanding that one is saved and made part of the covenanted people by faith alone, Strawbridge goes about trying to demonstrate that infants can exercise faith in some way. The two verses cited above are part of that effort to show that infants—even the unborn as in the case of John the Baptist—can exercise faith in some way. Unfortunately, neither verse states explicitly or otherwise that infants can exercise faith.

In the Lucan passage, although the baby in Elizabeth's womb is stirred, the only person said to be moved by the Spirit in the passage is Elizabeth. Could it be that the baby in her womb is merely reacting to what is primarily the response of the mother? Elizabeth is overwhelmed at what has been revealed to her. Her baby responds to her excitement, which has a biological component. The little one moves about in a way similar to that of other babies who respond to stimuli. This is not to downplay the significance of the mention of the baby stirring. Those stirrings are a precursor to the great work the Baptist will do in preparing for the coming of Christ. Nevertheless, this pericope does not mention the faith of the baby. At best, it is an adumbration of what is to come.

Similarly, the verse from Psalm 22 is not a testimony to infant faith. It is the psalmist's testimony to the providence of God. He is acknowledging as an adult that even when he had no knowledge of God, God was there as his provider and protector. The word "faith" is not used in the Hebrew or Greek text of this passage. One can (and I think should) read this verse as referring to the work of God, not to the exercise of faith in the infant.

> Citation 2: "What does the Bible teach about the nature of the church and her children? In the establishment of the covenant with Abraham in Genesis 17, God initiated a covenant with the explicit provision to be God to the patriarch and to his descendants after

him. This promise to Abraham is recited in Romans, Galatians, and in other passages in the New Testament."

We cannot make a strict correspondence between the Abrahamic covenant and the new covenant. The first was made with a people, an ethnic group. Although a sign was commanded in it, even those who did not have the covenantal sign were still part of the covenant people. Women, for instance, were included in the covenantal people even though they did not receive circumcision. The New Testament covenant is not merely a covenant by propagation in which the exception is someone coming to faith from outside (like a God-fearer who believes in the God of Israel). One is only included in the church, the new Israel, by being born in the Spirit by baptism. Being born into a given family, or a given ethnic group, benefits nothing. The Catholic position reflects this. One is a member of the church not by being born into a Christian home, despite all the benefits that this entails. No, natural birth does not benefit one for eternal life. Only the laver of regeneration, baptism, does that.

> Citation 3: "The sobering truth is that all have sinned (Rom 3:23). This passage is not speaking of only adults, as every parent knows. Could children sin even in the womb, then? Yes. I [Strawbridge] believe in the Calvinistic view of the fall and depravity."

Does the Reformed understanding of total depravity necessarily include that even children in the womb sin? Here the Catholic distinction between original sin and actual sin is helpful. To say that an unborn baby can actively sin seems extreme. For Catholics, concupiscence is a result of original sin: fallen man has his appetites disordered. Catholics would say that infants are in this condition. However, concupiscence is not considered sin in Catholic theology. Actual sin, on the other hand, is a willful disobedience against God and his commands. Infants and children, although they can exhibit signs of their fallen state, do not actively sin until they can recognize the difference between right and wrong.

A Lutheran Response by David P. Scaer

Strawbridge presents his defense of infant baptism in line with Reformed understandings of election and the covenant. Children who were included in the old covenant by virtue of their births are now included in the new covenant for the same reason. Whether the family as family should be equated with the covenant family is open to challenge, but this does not detract from his argument that according to Acts the households to which infants belonged were baptized. Strawbridge is the only one of the five contributors to bring this up for discussion. It might be added that in the ancient world "households" included the head of the household, slaves, and others in the family enterprise—including their children and grandchildren. For this reason, it is highly improbable that any household from the time period was completely without little ones. Since Peter and Paul used households for preaching the gospel, it follows that the other apostles did the same.

Discussion over the propriety of baptizing infants was occasioned by Karl Barth, who argued against it on the grounds that babies are without faith. Barth's concerns were theological, but he opened the way for an historical debate between Joachim Jeremias, who argued for infant baptism as an apostolic practice, and Kurt Aland, who took the opposing position. Had one or the other view prevailed, the propriety of infant baptism would have been closer to resolution, yet no one involved in this debate called for its abolition. Catholic, Reformed, and Lutheran scholars remain on both sides of the historical issue, but the practice or the lack of it is so ingrained in established churches that things will remain the same for the foreseeable future. Due to lower birth rates and the secularization of society, infant baptism has declined in the West, but not because of theological and historical arguments against it. These issues aside, Strawbridge introduced a necessary item into the discussion.

The Reformed, beginning with John Calvin, hold that children born into believing families are by their birth included in the covenant; however, the biblical narratives about the wayward children born to Adam, Noah, Eli, Samuel, and David suggest otherwise. So it was with Jesus's family, who rejected him (Matt 10:36; 13:57). The Reformed concept of the family as a covenant relationship is attractive to a culture that highly prizes family relationships. But the idea that children born within the covenant are excluded from the ravages of original sin is highly problematic. No one can argue that children born and raised in a Christian environment lack an advantage in hearing about Christ and in being brought to baptism early, but birth to Christian parents does not by itself grant inclusion into the household of faith. The Reformed doctrine allows God to elect children born outside the family covenant for salvation through the direct working of the Holy Spirit. In his sovereignty, God is not restricted to working through the Word, but this undermines both biblical and Reformation principles that God creates and confirms faith through Word and sacraments.

Strawbridge holds that infants can have faith, a position he finds in Luther and Calvin; whether these magisterial reformers agreed with each other, however, is another matter. Luther is consistent on infant faith, Calvin less so. In the 1536 edition of the *Institutes*, Calvin spoke of the seed of faith and repentance in infants. But in the 1539 edition he reversed himself in 4.16.19: "I would not rashly affirm that they [children] are endued with the same faith which we experience in ourselves, or have any knowledge at all resembling faith (this I would leave undecided)."

At this point, differences between the Lutheran and Reformed views on faith surface. For Lutherans, faith is trust in Christ and does not necessarily involve self-reflection. For the Reformed, faith is an experience worked directly by the Holy Spirit that provides the assurance of salvation. Calvin's allusion to faith as a seed, a concept that does not appear in later editions of the *Institutes*, seems to be taken from the parable of the Sower in which the seed is the Word of God that creates faith (Luke 8:11), but not faith itself, as Calvin uses the word. Strawbridge falls in line with Reformed doctrine that says that baptism does not give children entrance into the covenant, but only confirms their inclusion in it. Though the Reformed practice infant baptism and the Baptists do not, both agree that faith involves experiencing God's grace and that baptism does not bestow salvation. Ultimately, baptism or its lack is not a factor in the child's salvation.

A Baptist Response by Adam Harwood

Gregg Strawbridge begins his chapter with a section titled, "A Snapshot of the Reformed View." It depicts the Reformed tradition as finding comfort in the life and work of Christ, affirming his substitutionary atonement for sin, declaring that humanity fell in Adam, and proclaiming that God—not man—saves sinners. One wonders, however, whether the section is wrongly titled. Those views are not affirmed exclusively by the Reformed tradition. Rather, the views in that section are affirmed by many Christian groups. Perhaps the section would be better titled, "A Snapshot of the Christian View."

The section titled "Preliminary Qualifications" identifies foundational issues and presuppositions of the Reformed view. Rooted in sixteenth-century reforms that continue today, the Reformed view finds creeds and councils useful, and the Reformed tradition is marked by diversity within its ranks. It might have been helpful for Strawbridge to have limited his work to presenting the Reformed view alone, rather than characterizing the views of other traditions. For example, he notes that the Reformed method "does not exclude the subordinate usefulness of councils and creeds, contrary to some in the Baptist tradition who have said, 'No creed but Christ.'" Although some in the Baptist tradition might have made such a claim, Strawbridge cites no source to support his assertion. Moreover, "No creed but Christ" is not a viewpoint affirmed by the Baptist contributing to this present work. Against the notion that some in the Baptist tradition dispense with creeds, Baptists have drawn up dozens of statements of faith, including several which precede the Westminster Confession and Catechisms (1646) and some that predate even the Canons of Dort (1618–19).[44] It is not the case that Baptists do not incorporate creeds into their theological formulations. Rather, they have repeatedly resisted, even in their Reformed-leaning confessions of faith, the more speculative theological positions such as covenant theology found in documents such as the Westminster Confession.[45]

When defining "the church," Strawbridge appeals to the Westminster Confession's definition of it, which consists of believers "and of their children." Such a position is consistent with the theological framework of covenant theology. However, Baptists root their view of union with Christ and church membership in the weightier and clearer statements of Scripture; these indicate that those who are in Christ, and thus members of his church, have repented of their sin and confessed faith in Jesus. While such a view is disparaged in the chapter as revivalism, Baptists observe in the New Testament a pattern of the conversion of individuals and their subsequent baptism in water. The model following Pentecost is simple: a group of people hear the Word of God; some of those people are converted (they repent and believe in Jesus); then those people identify with the death, burial, and resurrection of Jesus through water baptism by immersion (Acts 2:36–41; 8:4–12; 8:26–38; 10:44–48; 16:13–15; 16:25–34; and other texts).[46] In light of this New Testament pattern, it is not helpful that some in the Reformed tradition

---

[44] See William L. Lumpkin, *Baptist Confessions of Faith*, rev. ed. (Valley Forge, PA: Judson, 1978) for early English Separatist-Baptist confessions such as Smyth's *Short Confession of Faith in XX Articles* (1609) and Helwys's *A Short Confession of Faith* (1610), as well as early English Baptist confessions such as *The London Baptist Confession of Faith* (1644).

[45] For examples of the rejection of certain Reformed views among the Reformed-leaning Baptist confessions, see Steve W. Lemke, "History or Revisionist History? How Calvinistic Were the Overwhelming Majority of Baptists and Their Confessions in the South until the Twentieth Century?" *Southwestern Journal of Theology* 57.2 (Spring 2015): 227–54.

[46] For a classic defense of believer's baptism, see Balthasar Hubmaier, *On the Christian Baptism of Believers in Balthasar Hubmaier: Theologian of Anabaptism,*

would baptize their infants and consider as church members any person who has not repented of sin and confessed Jesus as Lord, regardless of any theological framework or doctrinal statement.[47]

Strawbridge provides a chart and argues that infants were included in the old covenant and its signs and thus should be included in the new covenant and in its respective signs. This argument, however, fails to account for the discontinuity between Israel and the church as well as the proper relationship between covenants and their signs.

Consider a few examples of discontinuity between Israel and the church. The old covenant describes a spiritually mixed community, but the new covenant describes a regenerate one. Under the old covenant, the people of God are distinguished from all other groups by issues such as land and ethnic heritage; under the new covenant, the people of God are distinguished from all other groups by their union with Christ through faith. Consider also that under the old covenant the sign of circumcision does not require the infant's confession of faith, but under the new covenant water baptism serves as the individual's confession of faith. Reasoning by covenantal theologians fails to consider that the meaning of the signs should be derived from one's understanding of the covenants, not the reverse.[48]

Despite the differences noted, the Reformed tradition has always influenced one of the two theological streams that have fed into the Baptist tradition. For this reason, it can be difficult at times to disentangle the Baptist and

---

trans. and ed. H. Wayne Pikpin and John H. Yoder, Classics of the Radical Reformation 5 (Scottsdale, PA: Herald, 1989), 95–149.

[47] For an example of a Baptist who argues for believer's baptism while affirming covenant theology, see Fred Malone, *The Baptism of Disciples Alone: A Covenantal Argument for Credobaptism versus Paedobaptism* (Cape Coral, FL: Founders, 2003).

[48] For a thorough summary and analysis of covenant theology and baptism, see Stephen Wellum, "Baptism and the Relationship Between the Covenants," in *Believer's Baptism: Sign of the New Covenant in Christ*, Thomas R. Schreiner and Shawn D. Wright, NAC Studies in Bible & Theology (Nashville, TN: B&H, 2006), 97–161.

the Reformed views. Some Baptists lean toward Reformed views of soteriology and theology proper, but reject their ecclesiology (especially concerning baptism and church membership). Other Baptists reject all views that are particular to the Reformed perspective. Still others find themselves somewhere between those two theological poles. The Reformed and Baptist views have been partners in theological dialogue for four centuries, and this discussion is likely to continue until the return of our Lord and Savior, Jesus Christ.

Infants and Children in the Church: A Baptist View

Adam Harwood

Introduction

On a Sunday morning I sat on the forest green pew with my six-year old son, Nathan. We were about to witness the baptism of his friend. Knowing this could be a teachable moment for my son, I leaned over and asked, "What do you think about your friend getting baptized?"

He replied, "I want to be baptized."

"Why?" I asked.

"Well, it looks fun," my six-year-old replied. "And I like God!"

I gave him a hug and affirmed that being immersed did indeed look like fun, and I was glad that he liked God. Then I explained that we are not baptized because a friend is baptized or because it looks entertaining, or even because we like God. People are baptized only *after* they place their faith in Jesus to save them from their sins and are publicly committing to follow Jesus for the rest of their lives. We are placed in the water just like Jesus was placed in the grave, and we are raised out of the water just like Jesus was raised from the dead. I whispered, "We'll talk again about baptism." And we did.

The conversation I had with Nathan about baptism is common among Baptists. In this chapter, I will address Baptist ecclesiology, then Baptist views of original sin and infant salvation, and the entrance of infants and children into the church as well as their discipleship within it.

Baptist Ecclesiology

Who are Baptists? What are their distinct theological views? What is their view of the church? The Baptist movement is young. Our historical roots are debated. We began in Europe, either in 1525 or 1609, depending on whether one identifies those roots in European Anabaptists or in English Separatists.[1] In either case, the Baptist tradition is less than five centuries old.

The Baptist view articulated in this chapter includes *baptistic* groups, which are non-Baptist groups like Methodists, Mennonites, those in the Assemblies of God, and those in the Evangelical Free Church, which share a theological affinity with Baptists on certain doctrines. For example, Jack Hayford is a Pentecostal leader, but his views on original sin and infant salvation will be mentioned because his views are *baptistic*.

Distinct Views

Distinctly Baptist doctrines include soul competency,[2] the priesthood of the believer,[3] and religious liberty.[4] The *greatest* distinction between the

---

[1] Although some historians deny any link between Anabaptists and later Baptists, there is widespread agreement that modern Baptists can trace their roots to English Separatists of the early-seventeenth century.

[2] "Soul competency" is the view that because humans are made in God's image, every human soul is competent to receive revelation from God and to deal directly with him. See E. Y. Mullins, *Axioms of Religion*, ed. C. Douglas Weaver (Macon, GA: Mercer University Press, 2010).

[3] "The priesthood of the believer" is the view that the presence of Christ in congregations allows them to mimic the offices of prophet, priest, and king. See Malcolm B. Yarnell III, "The Priesthood of Believers: Rediscovering the Biblical Doctrine of Royal Priesthood," in *Restoring Integrity in Baptist Churches*, ed. Thomas White, Jason G. Duesing, and Malcolm B. Yarnell III (Grand Rapids, MI: Kregel, 2008), 221–44, for five manifestations of the doctrine in church history. Yarnell, 233–39, describes the Catholic sacramental priesthood, Caesarean sacred kingship, Reformation universal priesthood, congregational priesthood, and modern libertarian priesthood. It is the category of congregational priesthood that is particular to Baptists.

[4] Although it could be argued that all Christian views could make such an affirmation today in the United States, it was Baptists who—at the risk of their

perspectives of Baptists and those of the other views in this book is regenerate church membership. This is the view that local church membership should be comprised only of people who are regenerate, or born again. This is regulated by confessor's baptism by immersion.[5] Baptists see in the New Testament a clear pattern for the conversion of individuals and for the formation of local churches. Following Pentecost, the model is simple: people hear the Word of God; some repent and believe in Jesus; *then* those who do so identify with the death, burial, and resurrection of Christ through water baptism by immersion (Acts 2:36–41; 8:4–12; 8:26–38; 10:44–48; 16:13–15, 25–34; and other texts). Those baptized believers meet weekly for prayer, Bible reading, fellowship, and the breaking of bread.

---

lives—argued for this position almost four hundred years ago. In the early sixteenth century, some Anabaptists such as Conrad Grebel (1498–1526), Felix Manz (1498–1527), Michael Sattler (1495–1527), Balthasar Hubmaier (1480–1528), and George Blaurock (1491–1529) suffered persecution because of their arguments with civil authorities against infant baptism and for believer's baptism. Later, Roger Williams (1603–83) established in Providence, Rhode Island, the first Baptist church in the American colonies. His major contribution was in defense of religious conscience against civil government and religious liberty for all people. Baptist pastor John Leland (1754–1841) championed religious liberty during the early days of the United States. Even today, the Baptist ideal for religious liberty is a free church in a free state. The reason this is relevant for considering infants and children in the church is that when the church and state are co-mingled, there is an unhealthy link between civil and ecclesial organizations. For European Christians during the medieval and Reformation periods, infants and children were considered members of the church because they were citizens of the land. That is an alliance that groups such as Anabaptists, Mennonites, and Baptists resisted—even at the threat of their lives. American Christian churches are the beneficiaries of religious liberty largely due to the contributions of Baptists.

[5] The phrase more frequently used for this is believer's baptism, but this alternate term will be used to distinguish it with more precision from all other Christian views of baptism. Nathan A. Finn, "A Historical Analysis of Church Membership," in *Those Who Must Give an Account*, ed. John S. Hammett and Benjamin L. Merkle (Nashville, TN: B&H Academic, 2012), 53–79, uses the phrase "confessor baptism by immersion."

By the medieval period, Augustine's incorrect interpretation of the parable of the Weeds (Matt 13:24–30, 36–43) and equating the church with the kingdom of God resulted in the widely accepted view in the West that the church was a *corpus permixtum*, or a mixed body.[6] Combining this expectation that the church should be a mixture of both believers and non-believers with the practice of baptizing anyone and everyone resulted in the confusion of church membership with national citizenship. Early Baptists (such as Anabaptists and Mennonites) resisted this alliance of church and state by immersing people *after* individuals made a profession of faith in Christ. Thus, they were derided with the label Anabaptist, which means re-baptizer. Their emphasis on the New Testament example of confessor's baptism by immersion put them at odds with both the Roman Catholics and the Magisterial Reformers, who practiced infant baptism for different reasons.[7]

Almost five hundred years ago, Anabaptists noticed that the *only* explicit examples of baptism in the New Testament occurred after people confessed their faith in Christ. Nonetheless, Conrad Grebel, Felix Manz, Michael Sattler, Balthasar Hubmaier, and George Blaurock suffered persecution when they attempted to recover this practice of New Testament baptism. They argued with civil authorities against infant baptism and for confessor's baptism by immersion. The relevance for this discussion is that the differences among Christian views represented today are rooted in long-standing and varied views of the church and its membership.

To develop an understanding of what is meant by "regenerate church membership," it is important to grasp what Baptists believe about the church.

---

[6] Augustine, *City of God* 20.9; and *The Letters of Petilian, the Donatist* 3.4–5. John Calvin, *Institutes of the Christian Religion*, ed. John T. McNeill, trans. Ford Lewis Battles (Philadelphia, PA: Westminster, 1960), 4.1.13, later repeated this mistake. See Gregg R. Allison, *Sojourners & Strangers: The Doctrine of the Church*, Foundations of Evangelical Theology (Wheaton, IL: Crossway, 2012), 89n60.

[7] During the Protestant Reformation, Roman Catholics baptized infants to wash away the guilt of Adam's sin and as a means of God's grace. Magisterial Reformers, however, considered baptism to be the sign of the new covenant.

They believe the church is both universal and local. The universal church is comprised of all who have peace with God through repentance of sin and faith in Jesus. This universal church transcends temporal, cultural, and denominational boundaries. Every person—past, present, and future—who has, is, or will repent of sin and believe in Jesus is (or will be) a member of the invisible, future reality known as the universal church.[8]

However, only a small number of New Testament texts refer to the church in the universal sense; the vast majority of the Bible's references to "church" indicate local churches. In support of this claim, 90 of the 114 occurrences of *ekklēsia* in the New Testament are references to local churches.[9] In other words, the emphasis of the New Testament is on these purposeful assemblies of believers. Local churches manifest the universal church. Baptists define a local church as an autonomous group of believers who unite with one another in confessing personal faith in Christ, in observing confessor's baptism by immersion, and in observing a memorial view of the Lord's Supper.[10]

First, a local church is autonomous (or self-governed) in the sense that no external group directs the local body. Baptist churches answer to no assembly, council, episcopacy, bishopric, or papacy. The Baptist Faith and Message (BFM), the doctrinal statement of the Southern Baptist Convention, states, "Each congregation operates under the Lordship of Christ through

---

[8] The Baptist Faith and Message, Article 6, acknowledges the universal church when it states, "The New Testament speaks also of the church as the Body of Christ which includes all of the redeemed of all the ages, believers from every tribe, and tongue, and people, and nation."

[9] John Hammett, *Biblical Foundations for Baptist Churches: A Contemporary Ecclesiology* (Grand Rapids, MI: Kregel, 2005), 31.

[10] More could be said about offices of the church (pastor and deacon), the gifts of the Spirit manifested in the church, the functions in the church (to worship God, to hear the Word of God, to pray, and to encourage one another), and the mission of the church (the Great Commission, Matt 28:18–20), but these issues do not relate directly to the focus of this study.

democratic processes. In such a congregation each member is responsible and accountable to Christ as Lord" (Article 6).[11]

Second, a local church membership should be comprised of believers only. To review, this is known as regenerate church membership. Non-Christians are welcome in Baptist churches because there they will hear the message of the gospel and meet believers. But non-Christians are not proper candidates for membership in a local church because local churches are manifestations of the universal church. Put another way, non-Christians should not be members of a local church because they are not yet in Christ. Every individual must respond personally to the message and demands of the gospel. Infants and children—even those from Christian homes—who have not yet repented of their sin and confessed personal faith in Jesus through immersion baptism are welcome and included in the Baptist church. They are, however, excluded from its membership.

Baptists emphasize conscious and individual repentance of sin and confession of Jesus as Lord. Grace cannot be received through a sacrament, and faith cannot be passed along through parents or any covenant. Instead, all who desire to identify as Christians must personally repent of their sins and identify with Christ. Whether the moment of salvation is dramatic, like Saul's on the road to Damascus, or subtle, like John Wesley's at Aldersgate, genuine Christians are people who have had their own personal experience in which they hear the message of the gospel, repent, and confess faith in Jesus. A person is not born into Christianity, but must be transferred from the kingdom of Satan into the kingdom of Christ (Col 1:13). A child with Christian parents may benefit from the influence, blessings, and protection of being raised in a Christian home, but it is still necessary for each person to repent of his or her sin and trust Christ in order to be reconciled to God—even if one does so with clear intent in childhood but later is unable to recall all the details surrounding his or her confession.

---

[11] The Baptist Faith and Message is available at http://www.sbc.net/bfm2000/bfm2000.asp

Third, a local church observes confessor's baptism by immersion. Baptists believe the only proper candidate for immersion baptism is someone who has already confessed Jesus as Lord and Savior.[12] Although the biblical example of personal confession *then* baptism has already been stated, it bears repeating because this distinguishes Baptists from all other Christian groups. Acts reveals this paradigm: first, the Word of God is preached; second, some who hear also respond in repentance and faith; third, those who respond are baptized by immersion *after* they confess faith in Jesus.

Immersion is the only valid mode of baptism for several reasons: it is the only mode in the New Testament, observed by John the Baptist, Jesus, and their disciples; the practice best reflects the meaning of the word-group *baptizō*; and it pictures the believer's identification with the death, burial, and resurrection of Christ (Rom 6:3–4). Because an individual confession of faith preceded water baptism in the New Testament, Baptists only baptize people who make their own confession of faith in Jesus—which excludes some individuals, such as infants. Baptists, however, respect other Christian traditions and rejoice in their proclamation of Christ. The subject and mode of baptism is an in-house discussion. Even so, as John Hammett explains, "Since infants cannot place saving faith in Christ, they are not proper candidates for baptism or church membership."[13]

Fourth, a local church observes a memorial view of the Lord's Supper. Article 7 of the Baptist Faith and Message summarizes: "The Lord's Supper is a symbolic act of obedience whereby members of the church, through partaking of the bread and the fruit of the vine, memorialize the death of the Redeemer and anticipate His second coming."

Baptists understand that other Christian traditions hold differing views on many of these matters, but our primary source of authority for faith and

---

[12] Exceptions to confessor's baptism by immersion can be found among a baptistic group such as Methodists, who also practice infant baptism.

[13] John S. Hammett, "Membership, Discipline, and the Nature of the Church," in *Those Who Must Give an Account*, ed. John S. Hammett and Benjamin L. Merkle (Nashville, TN: B&H Academic, 2012), 19.

practice is the Bible. For that reason, although we are aware of the historical and theological arguments for other views, we will not be persuaded by positions that appeal to theological inferences or to historical precedent over arguments primarily derived from Scripture.

Original Sin and Infant Salvation

When a conversation turns to infants and sin, someone inevitably says, "No one has to teach a baby how to sin." The truth of that statement can be found in Scripture (Ps 51:5; Rom 5:12) and can be observed by spending time with young children. Infants often express self-centered behavior. Before little ones can walk, in fact, they sometimes act out in defiant ways. Against those who deny the sinful and fallen nature of humanity, it is important to declare that all people are infected with and impacted by both a sinful nature and a sin-warped environment. Baptists affirm the inevitability and universality of sinfulness in every person except Jesus Christ. They also affirm *two* positions on original sin and *one* position on infant salvation.

Inherited Sinful Nature and Guilt

Some Baptist theologians affirm that all people inherit both a sinful nature and guilt due to Adam's disobedience. Balthasar Hubmaier, for example, traces infant sin and guilt to Adam based on texts such as Ps 51:5; Jer 20:14; and 1 Cor 15:22. Hubmaier declares that "according to the strictness of Scripture" infants are sinful and guilty. Yet although babies are unable to exercise faith since they do not yet know good or evil (Deut 1:39), God can save them by his grace apart from baptism, the faith of their parents, or infant faith.[14]

---

[14] Balthasar Hubmaier, *On the Christian Baptism of Believers* in *Balthasar Hubmaier: Theologian of Anabaptism*, trans. and ed. H. Wayne Pikpin and John H. Yoder, Classics of the Radical Reformation 5 (Scottsdale, PA: Herald, 1989), 140–42.

Also, General Baptist Thomas Grantham (1634–92) affirms the doctrine of inherited guilt. However, Grantham rejects the notion that infants would be judged guilty by God because they have neither "a capacity to believe, nor any liberty to choose."[15]

In his *Abstract of Systematic Theology*, James P. Boyce (1827–88) presupposes a covenant of works (a theological framework handed down to him by Charles Hodge) and describes the federal headship of Adam.[16] God "regards a sinful nature as deserving punishment equally with a sinful act." Also, people "may be punished for the corrupt nature thus inherited, although they may not have been personally guilty of a single transgression."[17] In this way, "Guilt was incurred through Adam."[18] Even so, Boyce affirms that regeneration may exist without faith and conversion, and he specifically mentions infants.[19] Also, through an application of the atonement, "All dying in infancy are redeemed and saved."[20]

Hubmaier, Grantham, and Boyce affirm both that infants inherit the guilt of Adam's sin and that babies who die can (or will) be received by God in heaven.

---

[15] Thomas Grantham in Hugh Wamble, "Historic Practices Regarding Children," in *Children and Conversion*, ed. Clifford Ingle (Nashville, TN: Broadman, 1970), 81.

[16] For the influence of Hodge on Boyce, see Ernest Reisinger and Fred Malone, "Introduction to 1977 edition," in James Boyce, *Abstract of Systematic Theology* (Cape Coral, FL: Founders, 2006), v, who note that Boyce used Hodge's systematic text at The Southern Baptist Theological Seminary for a period of time. Also, see the citation of Hodge's *Outline of Theology* in Boyce, *Abstract*, 235, when explaining the covenant of works. For Boyce on the federal headship of Adam, see *Abstract*, 247–58.

[17] Boyce, *Abstract*, 250.
[18] Ibid., 256.
[19] Ibid., 381.
[20] Ibid., 338.

Inherited Sinful Nature Only

Other Baptists have rejected the doctrine of inherited guilt.[21] Instead, they affirm that people inherit a sinful nature only. Anabaptist Pilgram Marpeck, who died in 1556, explains that until a child matures to a point at which he can distinguish between good and evil, sin has "no damning effect." Also he says, "We excuse young, innocent children from guilt and the remnants of their inheritance through none other than Christ . . . [for] the wrath of God is not upon such children until they reach understanding, that is, the common knowledge of good and evil."[22]

English General Baptist John Smyth (1570–1612) writes, "There is no original sin (lit., no sin of origin or descent), but all sin is actual and voluntary, viz., a word, a deed, or a design against the law of God; and therefore, infants are without sin."[23]

---

[21] An explicit denial of inherited guilt sometimes raises this objection: How can one deny imputed guilt but affirm imputed righteousness? To reply, one must ask what the Bible teaches concerning the conditions required for a person to be counted righteous by God. Romans 3:21–22 states, "But now the righteousness of God has been manifested apart from the law, although the Law and the Prophets bear witness to it—the righteousness of God through faith in Jesus Christ for all who believe." See also Rom 3:28 and 4:5. Consider Rom 4:22–25: "That is why his faith was 'counted to him as righteousness.' But the words 'it was counted to him' were not written for his sake alone, but for ours also. It will be counted to us who believe in him who raised from the dead Jesus our Lord, who was delivered up for our trespasses and raised for our justification." Paul's point in Romans 3–4 is that others are made righteous in the same way as Abraham, by faith. In the Bible, being counted by God as righteous does not require one to affirm the imputation of Adam's guilt; one must only believe in Jesus.

[22] Marpeck, *Response to Caspar Schwenckfeld's Judgment* in *The Writings of Pilgram Marpeck*, ed. Walter Klaassen and William Klaassen, Classics of the Radical Reformation 2 (Scottsdale, PA: Herald, 1978), 89–90.

[23] See "A Short Confession of Faith in Twenty Articles by John Smyth," in William L. Lumpkin, *Baptist Confessions of Faith* (Valley Forge, PA: Judson, 1978), 100–101.

Southern Baptist theologian W. T. Conner (1877–1952) rejects inherited guilt. He reasons that sin implies willful disobedience to God, which requires the knowledge of moral truth. Sin is universal, inevitable, and hereditary due to our relationship to Adam. There are thus "seeds of evil tendency in the child's nature" which will eventually result in the child committing an act of transgression upon reaching an "age of moral responsibility." Prior to that time, though, the child "does not have personal guilt" because he or she has not yet developed personal responsibility, namely "the powers of self-consciousness and self-determination."[24] Conner is clear: "The idea that Adam's sin as an act of sin is charged to his descendants and on that account they are guilty and hence condemned, is an idea too preposterous to be seriously entertained."[25]

The doctrine of inherited guilt is not consistent with the Baptist Faith and Message either. Article 3 explains that Adam's "posterity inherit a nature and an environment inclined toward sin. Therefore, as soon as they are capable of moral action, they become transgressors and are under condemnation." The article affirms an inherited human inclination to commit sinful actions, not inherited guilt. It is reasonable to infer from the BFM that infants and young children have not yet reached an age (or stage) of moral accountability before God. Rather, they will later become capable of moral actions and then will certainly transgress God's laws and fall under just condemnation.[26]

In summary, Baptists affirm two views of original sin, but one view of infant salvation. Regarding original sin, one Baptist tradition affirms that all people inherit both a sinful nature and guilt, but the other tradition affirms that people are born with a sinful nature only. The conclusion among Baptists

---

[24] W. T. Conner, *Christian Doctrine* (Nashville, TN: Broadman, 1937), 131–43. Conner taught theology at Southwestern Baptist Theological Seminary in Ft. Worth, Texas from 1910–49.

[25] Walter T. Conner, *The Gospel of Redemption* (Nashville, TN: Broadman, 1945), 29.

[26] For a treatment of this view, see Adam Harwood, *Born Guilty?: A Southern Baptist View of Original Sin* (Carrollton, GA: Free Church, 2013).

regarding infant salvation is the same: all who die in infancy are safe with God in heaven.[27]

Infant Salvation

God's sin-stained creation awaits its full redemption through the work of Christ on the cross (Rom 8:19–23). Until then, sin, evil, and death are still part of this world, and they afflict the smallest of people. Tragically, some people die in infancy. Prompted by the need to address these awful situations, some pastor-scholars have offered their best accounts for the eternal destiny of those infants or young children. Several suggest, in differing ways, that little ones are not yet guilty of sin.

E. Y. Mullins suggests infants stand uncondemned. To make his case, he distinguishes between an infant's inherited *capacity* for sin and later sinful actions, or *actual* sin.[28] He writes, "Condemnation is not for hereditary sin, but only for actual sin." Mullins then clarifies: "Men are not condemned therefore for hereditary or original sin. They are condemned only for their own sins."[29] He acknowledges that Scripture says little about the salvation of infants, but notes that infants are not "capable of exercising repentance

---

[27] For an example of a Baptist position paper that affirms both inherited guilt and the salvation of all who die as infants, see R. Albert Mohler, Jr. and Daniel Akin, "The Salvation of the 'Little Ones': Do Infants who Die Go to Heaven?" at http://www.albertmohler.com/2009/07/16/the-salvation-of-the-little-ones-do-infants-who-die-go-to-heaven/. For an earlier version of the Mohler-Akin paper, which affirms an inherited sinful nature (without mention of imputed guilt) and the salvation of all who die as infants, see Daniel Akin, "Why I Believe Children Who Die Go to Heaven," at http://www.danielakin.com/wp-content/uploads/2004/08/Why-I-Believe-Children-Who-Die-Go-to-Heaven.pdf.

[28] E. Y. Mullins was a pastor and professor of theology. At various times during the beginning of the previous century, he was president of The Southern Baptist Theological Seminary, the Southern Baptist Convention, and the Baptist World Alliance.

[29] E. Y. Mullins, *The Christian Religion in its Doctrinal Expression* (Valley Forge, PA: Judson, 1917; reprinted 1974), 301–2.

and faith," and they lack "moral discernment." Mullins concludes that people who die as infants will "share in the blessings of Christ's atonement" and thus be saved by God's grace.[30] Mullins believes infants inherit a sinful nature, or capacity to sin; therefore, people who die as infants or young children are free from God's judgment because God judges only *actual* sins.

Jack Hayford says infants are innocent altogether. This Pentecostal pastor articulates a *baptistic* view.[31] First, a fetus in the womb is a real person with an eternal soul (Luke 1:26–56; Jer 1:5; and Ps 139:1). Second, although all infants have "inherent potential for sinning," they are "sinless little ones," who do not enter hell, which is "a self-imposed place of endless abandonment for people who reject [God]." Third, Hayford cites Matt 18:10 ("Their angels always see the face of my Father" NKJV) to explain that "small children, still in their innocence, enjoy an uninterrupted discourse with the heart of God." This union with God will be broken at some point when the person matures and the sin nature leads to sinful actions, but that break has not yet occurred between infants and their Creator.[32]

Alongside the presentation of those points, Hayford cites the examples of David and Abraham. David declared in the Psalms that he would one day be in God's presence; and David declared after the death of his infant that he would one day go to his son (2 Samuel 12). That means David expected to

---

[30] E. Y. Mullins, *Baptist Beliefs* (Louisville, KY: Baptist World Publishing, 1912), 24–25.

[31] Before a reader dismisses Hayford's view as insignificant or unimportant within the Christian community, it should be known that Hayford remains a person of influence in Christianity. His view on this topic has been widely disseminated. He pastored The Church on the Way in Los Angeles for thirty years, founded The King's University, and served from 2004–09 as president of the 8 million member International Church of the Foursquare Gospel. Perhaps most pertinent is that 250,000 copies of his book on this subject are in print. These sales figures are from the cover of a 2007 printing of *I'll Hold You in Heaven: Healing and Hope for the Parent Who Has Lost a Child Through Miscarriage, Stillbirth, Abortion, or Early Infancy Death* (Ventura, CA: Regal, 2003).

[32] Ibid., 20–62.

one day see his son in God's presence. In Genesis, Abraham's appeal for God not to destroy the wicked was based on an appeal to God to be just in his dealings with the righteous. Hayford equates people who die as infants with the righteous. Just as Abraham appealed to God's justice, parents who have lost infants to death can depend on God to be just by allowing them to enter heaven.[33]

For Hayford, the promise of infant salvation extends to the children of non-Christian parents, too. First Corinthians 7:14 teaches that children produced by the union of one believing and one unbelieving parent are "socially and legally acceptable in God's sight." Hayford adds, "The Bible neither declares nor implies that parents determine the eternal destiny of their children. Believing couples do not automatically produce believing children, and conversely, the nonbelief of unbelieving parents does not automatically doom their children to eternal loss." He states, "Salvation is always an individual choice.... Since children have made no moral choices, they have remained innocent."[34]

Some of Hayford's biblical interpretations are questionable. For example, Matt 18:10 refers to angels, but Hayford interprets the verse to mean that infants see the face of God. Also, Hayford states that infants have remained innocent; however, being made righteous by God is different than never having been corrupted by one's sinful choices. Even so, the thrust of Hayford's argument is consistent with a Baptist view: people who die in infancy have not yet committed sinful acts; thus, they are not guilty and are welcomed into God's presence.

Millard Erickson says that infants have not yet reached moral competency; they are incompetent. This Baptist theologian begins his treatment of original sin and infant salvation by affirming a Calvinistic view that all of humanity (excluding Jesus Christ) participated in the sin *and guilt* of Adam

---

[33] Ibid., 62–63.
[34] Ibid., 63–64.

in the garden.³⁵ But, he explains, the Lord excludes from condemnation "infants and those who never reach moral competency." Erickson then points to classic biblical texts for support. First, Jesus held up infants and children as examples of people who would inherit the kingdom (Matt 19:14). Second, David declares that he would one day see his deceased infant (2 Sam 12:23). Erickson writes that people are "not morally responsible before a certain point, which we sometimes call 'the age of accountability.'"³⁶

Some bristle at the idea of an age of moral accountability, asking for biblical support for the concept. Even if 2 Samuel 12 taught that David would be reunited with his son in heaven, they say, that text may support only the view that the children of believers will be there.³⁷ And Matthew 19 may indicate only that Jesus views infants as examples of what it looks like to have child-like faith, not that they are not yet guilty of sin. So is there any stronger biblical support for this idea that an infant is not yet accountable to God but—assuming growth—he or she will later become accountable to God?

Erickson begins his defense of the age of accountability with Deut 1:39, which explains that the Israelite children were not held responsible for the sinful actions of the older generations. Isaiah 7:15–16 and Jonah 4:11 are also references to this period when people do not yet know the difference between good and evil, right and wrong. Erickson then notes the Adam-Christ parallel in Romans 5. Just as one must personally ratify the obedient act of Christ on

---

³⁵ Millard Erickson has been described as "one of the most significant and prolific Baptist and conservative Evangelical theologians" of the last fifty years. Bradley G. Green, "Millard J. Erickson," in *Theologians of the Baptist Tradition*, ed. Timothy George and David S. Dockery (Nashville, TN: B&H, 2001), 317.

³⁶ Millard Erickson, *Christian Theology*, 3rd ed. (Grand Rapids, MI: Baker, 2013), 581.

³⁷ Although David did not have an understanding of heaven informed by New Testament texts that had yet to be inspired, his writings (such as Ps 16:10–11) reflect his hope and expectation that he would be with God after death.

the cross in order to be saved, one must personally ratify the disobedient work of Adam in the garden in order to be condemned.[38]

Erickson affirms a conditional imputation of Adam's guilt with "no condemnation until one reaches the age of moral responsibility." At that point, when we become aware of our "tendency toward sin" and then make a decision to commit a sinful action due to our sinful nature, then our "childish innocence" ends. He explains: "We become responsible and guilty when we accept or approve of our corruption." At that point, we ratify the work of Adam in our own lives and the guilt of Adam is imputed to us.[39] In this way, Erickson affirms that every person who dies before reaching an age of moral responsibility (infants, young children, and mentally impaired individuals) will be with the Lord in heaven.[40]

Mullins, Hayford, and Erickson all argue, in different ways, that infants and young children are not yet guilty of sin. One of the criticisms against this idea is that infants who are not guilty cannot be saved because they are not really in need of saving. In reply, it is only the case that infants and young children who are not yet guilty cannot be saved *in the same way* as older children and adults, who understand the difference between good and evil yet knowingly choose to sin. Those individuals are justly under God's wrath and condemnation, and they need to be saved from God's judgment. Infants and young children, who are not yet guilty of sin, are still in need of the atoning work of Christ to purify them from the stain of an inherited sinful nature.

---

[38] Millard J. Erickson, *How Shall They Be Saved?* (Grand Rapids, MI: Baker, 1996), 250.

[39] Erickson, *Christian Theology*, 582.

[40] In contrast to Erickson and others who affirm that young children are *not* responsible to God for their sin and guilt before an age of moral responsibility, "early conversion" proponents within the Baptist (& baptistic) view argue that young children *are* responsible to God for their sin and guilt. Consider, for example, the teachings of Child Evangelism Fellowship (https://www.cefonline.com/) and see Gideon G. Yoder, *The Nurture and Evangelism of Children* (Scottsdale, PA: Herald, 1959). I am indebted to Kevin Lawson for bringing this view to my attention.

In my view, little ones have committed no sinful actions for which God would condemn them. For that reason, they are not guilty before him. However, their inherited sinful nature, which would later inevitably result in actual sin and condemnation, must be addressed. Perhaps God redeems the sinful nature of infants and young children by including them in his restoration of creation (Rom 8:19–23) and the renewal of all things (Matt 19:28) at the return of Christ. In this way, all who die in infancy will be with God because of his grace and the atoning work of Christ at the cross.[41]

Entrance into the Church

How and at what point do Baptists consider infants and children to be part of the church? In the Old and New Testament, little ones were present and included in the faith communities, but they were not fully accountable for the responsibilities required of the people of God. Important to the upcoming discussion is that Israel is not the church and the church is not Israel, but both are the people of God. Further, the church should be understood as it is defined in the earlier section of this chapter.

God raised up through the seed of Abraham a people who would be his treasured possession and through whom he would bless the nations (Genesis 12; 15). This promise to Abraham (echoes of which were heard by the first couple in the garden in Gen 3:15) was fulfilled in the person and work of Christ (Galatians 2). God did not abandon Israel when he created the church. Instead, he included the Gentiles as his people by grafting them into the tree that he had planted (Romans 9–11). Although the discontinuity is small, there seem to be promises made to Israel that do not apply to the later followers of Christ. Because Israel and the church are both clearly included among the people of God, however, Old and New Testament practices can

---

[41] This is the conclusion presented in Adam Harwood, *The Spiritual Condition of Infants: A Biblical-Historical Survey and Systematic Proposal* (Eugene, OR: Wipf & Stock, 2011).

be examined for indications of how infants and children should be viewed in Christian churches.[42]

Infants and Children Under the Old Covenant

Because of their refusal to e their infants, Baptists have been charged with treating their children as "covenant strangers," creating an "alien mentality," and teaching them "to doubt the promises of God."[43] Against these charges, I will attempt to demonstrate that the Baptists' treatment of children reflects the way little ones are to be treated as described in the Scriptures. At some times during the old covenant, infants and children were present and included—apart from their stated will—among the people of God. At other times, however, they were either absent or unaccountable. Similarly, Baptists usually include infants and children in their faith communities; however, infants are sometimes absent and unaccountable.

First, let us consider the idea of being present and included, apart from the will. During the period of the old covenant, infants and children were

---

[42] For more on the church of the new covenant and various views on the relationship between Israel and the church, see Allison, *Sojourners & Strangers*, 61–89.

[43] For an example of this view, see Douglas Wilson, "Baptism and Children: Their Place in the Old and New Testaments," in *The Case for Covenantal Infant Baptism*, ed. Gregg Strawbridge (Phillipsburg, NJ: P&R, 2003), 286–302. The phrases can be found on pp. 299–301. Wilson, 298–99, writes about a theology of children:

> We are faced with an inescapable reality. God has placed our children in our presence, and we are in covenant with the God who has done so. We will either treat our children as though they are in this covenant together with us, and teach them the terms of it, or we will treat them as strangers to that covenant, as outsiders. If we treat them as strangers to the covenant, if we say it is not possible for us to disciple our children in evangelical faith, bringing them up in it, then we will have to live with the unhappy consequences of covenant members training up covenant strangers.

present and included among the people of God. This can be seen in circumcision, dedication, and festivals. In these instances, little ones were included in the faith community apart from their own decisions, or the use of their wills.

Circumcision was an external physical sign given by God to Abraham for the people of God (Genesis 17). Male children were circumcised during a ceremony on their eighth day of life. Although female children were not included in this ritual, the act permanently marked those young boys as set apart to God. Although Old Testament circumcision should not be equated with New Testament baptism,[44] the Old Testament practice makes it clear that male infants as young as eight days old were present and ceremonially included among the people of God.

Dedication of the first-born male in the Jewish household did not symbolize his entrance into a relationship with God, however. The act was instead the recognition of an already-established covenant between God and that child's family. Consider godly, barren Hannah, who cries out to the Lord and receives a child. She honors her vow to the Lord, delivering young Samuel to the temple and dedicating him. Interestingly, the Scriptures state explicitly that after his dedication the young child "did not yet know the Lord" (1 Sam 3:7). Nevertheless, young Samuel was considered part of the covenant community. He was received by Eli, later he responded to the voice of the Lord, and he grew up to be one of the nation's most distinguished prophets.

Infants and young children in Jewish families participated in religious festivals. These festivals rehearsed the story of God's work among his people in order to teach faith lessons to the younger generations. Two major festivals described in Deuteronomy 16, the Passover and the Festival of Booths, involved the entire family—including young children. The Passover celebrated God delivering his people from Egypt by the sacrifice and meal of an

---

[44] Everett Ferguson, *Baptism in the Early Church: History, Theology, and Liturgy in the First Five Centuries* (Grand Rapids, MI: Eerdmans, 2009), 159n36: "As circumcision was the sign of the covenant for Jews (Rom. 4:11), the Holy Spirit was the sign or seal for Christians (2 Cor. 1:21; Eph. 1:13; 4:30)."

unblemished, year-old lamb and the unleavened bread. The youngest child present at the meal asked questions during it in order to prompt his father to narrate the drama of God delivering his people. The Festival of Booths was another portrayal of God delivering his people from Egypt. In this celebration, families lived in booths for seven days to portray God's provision in the desert. The idea was to let subsequent generations know him as the Lord their God (Lev 23:43).[45]

Next is the idea that children in Scripture sometimes seem absent or unaccountable. Although infants and young children were included among the people of God, there were times in which they were either absent from the group or not held responsible as were the rest of the people of God. Nehemiah describes the group that assembled for religious instruction and commitment:

> All the people gathered as one man into the square before the Water Gate. And they told Ezra the scribe to bring the Book of the Law of Moses that the LORD had commanded Israel. So Ezra the priest brought the Law before the assembly, both men and women and *all who could understand what they heard,* on the first day of the seventh month. And he read from it facing the square before the Water Gate from early morning until midday, in the presence of the men and the women and *those who could understand."* (8:1–3, ESV, emphasis mine)[46]

In chapter 10, only *some* of the Israelites renew their devotion to God. The group is identified as "all who have knowledge and understanding" (Neh

---

[45] Catherine Stonehouse, *Joining Children on the Spiritual Journey: Nurturing a Life of Faith* (Grand Rapids, MI: BridgePoint, 1998), 28–30. For more information on the Jewish festivals and ideas for celebrating them in twenty-first century Christian homes, see Donald and Brenda Ratcliff, *Child Faith: Experiencing God and Spiritual Growth with Your Children* (Eugene, OR: Cascade, 2010), 114–22.

[46] All Scripture references in this chapter are taken from the English Standard Version (ESV).

10:28). Since infants and young children could not understand the Scripture readings and oaths to God, it seems they were not included during those times of corporate worship.

In the story of the twelve spies, the younger generation was present, but unaccountable for the actions of the older generations. Two of the spies urged the people to trust God, who promised to deliver the inhabitants of the land into their hands. But the Israelites failed to trust God. And angered by their actions, God swore that the people in that evil generation would be prohibited from entering the Promised Land. Only Joshua, Caleb and his sons, and the younger generation of Israelites would be allowed to enter. That younger generation is described as having "no knowledge of good or evil" (Deut 1:39b), and they are interestingly identified as those under the age of twenty (Num 14:29). Moshe Weinfeld cites this account, as well as Isa 7:15 and rabbinic tradition, to conclude that these children and youth were not morally accountable for the actions of their parents.[47] John MacArthur agrees: "The Israelite children of sinful parents were allowed to enter fully into the blessing God had for His people. They were in no way held accountable, responsible, or punishable for the sins of their parents. Why? Because they have no knowledge of good and evil, right or wrong."[48]

Although included among the people of God, that younger generation of Israelites was not included in the judgment resulting from the older generation's disobedience. The Scriptures explain precisely why they were excluded from God's judgment: their young age. They had not yet developed the knowledge of good and evil.

---

[47] Moshe Weinfeld, *Deuteronomy 1–11: A New Translation with Introduction and Commentary* in vol. 5 of The Anchor Bible, edited by William Foxwell Albright and David Noel Freedman (New York, NY: Doubleday, 1991), 151.

[48] John MacArthur, *Safe In the Arms of God* (Nashville, TN: Thomas Nelson, 2003), 45.

Infants and Children Under the New Covenant

In the previous section, I attempted to demonstrate that the way Baptists treat infants and children with regard to the church reflects the treatment of infants and children by the Israelite community living under the old covenant. In this section, I will attempt to demonstrate that the way Baptists treat the infants and children in their care reflects the way little ones were treated by Jesus and the early church. Under the new covenant, infants and children were present, but unaccountable.

Infants and children are mentioned throughout the New Testament, but no text clearly indicates how they are to be received into local churches. Jesus welcomes the children (Mark 10:13–16; Matt 19:13–15; Luke 18:15–17) and speaks against anyone hindering them from approaching him. He blesses them and cites them as examples of people to whom the kingdom of heaven belongs. And although these texts are sometimes used to support infant baptism, it is important to note that the Gospels mention Jesus blessing but not baptizing any children. Jesus welcomes little ones, but he does not place on them the same demands he places on adults.

On another occasion, the disciples of Jesus argue among themselves about who is the greatest in the kingdom (Matt 18:1–5; Mark 9:33–37; Luke 9:46–48). Once again, Jesus points to the children to teach the adults.[49] The greatest, Jesus explains, will be the smallest. A person must humble himself like a little child. And to receive children is to receive Jesus. Although the Savior points to children in order to teach the adults, he places no demands on them.

The letter of Ephesians, written to the church in that city, includes instructions for children (6:1–3). But the command for them to obey their parents is God's instruction for them within the home—not a demand regarding church members.

---

[49] William B. Coble, "New Testament Passages about Children," *Children and Conversion*, ed. Clifford Ingle (Nashville, TN: Broadman, 1970), 45.

The New Testament portrays infants and children under the new covenant as present and valued, but unaccountable. They were seen, welcomed, and blessed by Jesus. They would have been present to witness the ordinances of baptism and the Lord's Supper. Even so, no demands were placed on them, and they were unable to fulfill the requirements for participating in the ordinances of self-examination, repentance, and confession.

Summary

The mode and timing of infants and children entering the membership of Baptist churches seems to reflect the practices recorded in the Bible. While infants and children were present and included in the faith communities, they were not fully accountable for the responsibilities required of the people of God.

Discipleship

How and when do Baptists instruct children as disciples of Jesus? The answer is simple: infants and children should be instructed to love and follow Jesus at the earliest possible age. Although little ones are not considered members of a congregation until they confess Christ as Lord and Savior and follow him in confessor's baptism by immersion, Christian instruction should be given to them at the earliest possible time. An example of this practice is found in the life of Timothy. In 2 Tim 3:15 Paul recalls to Timothy "how from childhood (*brephos*) you have been acquainted with the sacred writings, which are able to make you wise for salvation through faith in Christ Jesus."[50] Earlier in the book, Paul names Timothy's grandmother and mother; he then cites the "sincere faith" in Christ that lived in them and now lives in Timothy (1:5).

---

[50] Luke used the word *brephos* to refer to John the Baptist in the womb (Luke 1:41, 44), Jesus in the manger (Luke 2:12, 16), the infants brought to Jesus (Luke 18:15), and the infants killed by the Egyptians (Acts 7:19). Peter used the word as a simile to refer to people as newborn babes, who are eager for spiritual milk (1 Pet 2:2). Second Timothy 3:15 is the only time that Paul used the word.

Whether Paul intended *brephos* to refer to Timothy's infancy (NIV) or childhood (ESV), young Timothy was instructed by his mother and grandmother from an early age.

Scripture at Home

Like Timothy's mother and grandmother, parents today can read the Bible to their children at home. Little ones who hear and are taught the Scriptures at home are provided a solid foundation for their spiritual nurture and growth. Waylan Owens writes of the work of pre-evangelism in a child's life; he says it occurs by the Holy Spirit through the child's hearing of Bible stories. Those Bible stories are taught not merely as moralistic ideals, however (e.g. David was faithful or Jesus obeyed his parents). Rather, they should be presented as arrows pointing to the truths of the gospel message located within each (David was a good king, but Jesus is the perfect king).[51] Parents should present their children with age-appropriate Bibles and read them to their children on a regular basis, emphasizing God's Word as truth rather than allowing it to be confused with fairy tales.

Scripture at Church

Children also should hear and learn about Scripture at church. Although Sunday school for infants and children can include elements of play and crafts, its primary goal should be instructing little ones in age-appropriate biblical truths. In a child's first months, being taught Scripture may involve a nursery worker rocking the infant while she speaks words of truth like "God loves you" to him and sings songs over him that are filled with biblical truths. In his

---

[51] Waylan Owens, "Preparing a child's heart to respond to Christ," 12–17, in a booklet (n.p.: n.p.), "Baptizing Children: When is a Child Old Enough?" originally published in *The Alabama Baptist* (October 2010).

preschool days, a toddler cannot read, but can pray. He should thus be taught by example by that point, listening to and repeating in Sunday school basic truths such as "God made the world" and "God made me." Once he reaches school age, he is prepared to learn that the Bible is God's Word and that Jesus died for him. As he matures, he can understand more complex truths and learn to place the Bible's stories within the larger narrative of Scripture. He can also begin learning how to navigate and study God's Word for himself. Using an integrative approach, Catherine Stonehouse draws on insights from the fields of psychological, cognitive, and moral development to suggest that nuggets of wisdom gleaned from all of these fields can help Christians better nurture a life of faith and engage children with God's Word.[52] Intentionality and consistency are keys.

Whether they attend a corporate worship service with the adults or an age-appropriate children's church meeting, young children should hear God's Word taught in such a way that the content of the message is drawn from the content of the biblical text. Isaiah promised that God's Word would not come back void (Isa 55:11). Paul declared that faith comes by hearing the word of Christ (Rom 10:17). The Bible is the vehicle for spiritual transformation. For that reason, the Bible should be central in teaching and preaching to infants and children, as well as to teenagers and adults. At what age should a child be included in corporate worship? Perhaps an important clue can be found in Ezra's reading the Law to people *who could understand what was read* (Neh 8:2–3).

Witnessing the Ordinances

Children can also learn to be followers of Christ by observing the ordinances of the Lord's Supper and baptism, and they should understand the meaning of baptism *prior* to being baptized. The appropriate time for a young person's

---

[52] See Stonehouse, *Joining Children on the Spiritual Journey*.

baptism is a question that requires attention. Some see a benefit in delaying a child's baptism until after the age of fourteen[53] or even eighteen.[54] Malcolm Yarnell explains why a baptism should be delayed. He writes, "It is all too easy for well-meaning parents to try to rush children into the kingdom of God. If we act hastily, then we may not only contradict the teaching of Scripture that baptism always follows personal conversion but we may also inoculate our children against hearing the gospel in the future." He then notes that rushing children into a baptistery is equally as problematic as infant baptism if God has not already worked repentance and faith in their lives.[55]

Few Baptists ask when children should participate in the Lord's Supper because we consider proper candidates to be those who have personally confessed their faith in Jesus through baptism by immersion. Participants in the Lord's Supper remember the body and blood of Jesus, which was broken and spilled for them (1 Cor 11:24–25). In doing so, they proclaim the Lord's death until his return (v. 26). If we are correct in presuming that such commemoration and proclamation should be made only by genuine believers, and

---

[53] Gordon T. Smith, *Beginning Well: Christian Conversion and Authentic Transformation* (Downers Grove, IL: InterVarsity, 2001), 217. "(W)hen a child under fourteen asks about baptism, we can explain that baptism is for those who are older and that when they are at least fourteen they will be welcome to receive it. Nothing is gained by rushing baptism; and a great deal is gained by waiting until they are at least this age. Many would benefit by waiting even longer. In my judgment, fourteen should be the *minimum* age." Italics his.

[54] This is the published practice of Capitol Hill Baptist Church, in Washington, DC.

[55] Malcolm B. Yarnell III, "Looking at children's baptism through the lens of Christian history," in "Baptizing Children: When is a Child Old Enough?," originally published in *The Alabama Baptist* (October 2010). For other Baptists who encourage delaying the baptism of young children, see John S. Hammett, *40 Questions about Baptism and the Lord's Supper* (Grand Rapids, MI: Kregel, 2016), 165–71, and Mark Dever, "Baptism in the Context of the Local Church," in *Believer's Baptism: Sign of the New Covenant in Christ*, ed. Thomas R. Schreiner and Shawn D. Wright (Nashville, TN: B&H, 2007), 344–50.

that the New Testament assumes that people confess their faith in Christ by baptism, then it follows that the only proper candidates for partaking in the Lord's Supper are confessor's-baptized believers.

Living Examples

Although some aspects of the Christian life need to be taught, much of it is more easily caught through observation. The prophet Micah declared three things that God requires: that people do justly, that they love mercy, and that they walk humbly with God (6:8). Those three things can be observed in action. And children, like adults, can learn to follow Christ by watching other people follow Jesus. They can learn to pray, for instance, by listening to others pray. They can learn how to do justly and love mercy by watching someone lead a godly life in which he or she intentionally chooses to be just and loving.

Although reading books about spiritual disciplines may help older children to solidify their views and to make wise choices, they will learn how to follow Christ best when a person points them first to God's Word and says, "Follow my example, as I follow the example of Christ" (1 Cor 11:1).

Conclusion

The aim of this chapter was to provide a brief account of Baptist ecclesiology, then to present Baptist views of original sin, infant salvation, entrance into and discipleship within the church. I opened with a story about my six-year old at his friend's baptism. When Nathan expressed his desire to be baptized, his mom and I were confronted with a question commonly asked by Baptist parents: When is my child ready to be baptized? The question is significant because Baptists affirm two requirements for membership in a local church: confession of faith in Christ and then baptism by immersion. So, Nathan's question involved not only a request to proclaim faith in Jesus, but also a request to take on the responsibilities of joining our local church.[56]

As explained, all examples of baptism in the New Testament occur only *after* people hear the gospel and respond in repentance and faith in Christ. Infants cannot make that decision. However, if young children seem to understand the essential elements of the gospel and respond in repentance and faith in Christ, why should they be hindered from being baptized?

The Southern Baptist Convention (the SBC) has collected data on the average age of baptismal candidates. The trend is that the lower limit of the age is going down, but the frequency of immersions is going up. Before the 1950s, the SBC did not track baptisms among preschool-age children. But since that time the age of baptismal candidates dropped into the preschool years, so they began to track those younger proclamations of faith. It turned out that many of the people who were baptized at young ages were later re-baptized in their high school or college years, when they gained a better understanding of their commitment.[57]

It would be difficult to establish a standard minimum age for the baptism of children. But parents and church leaders should consider that although the New Testament notes the presence and welcoming of infants and children, it does not appear that those individuals were baptized. In my view, then, the

---

[56] Although one could consider the appropriate conditions for children to partake in the Lord's Supper in a congregation, the focus of the secondary literature is on the other ordinance, baptism. For that reason, this section dealt with that issue.

[57] A 1993 survey of adult baptisms (over age 18) in the SBC found that 36% of those adults had been previously baptized in SBC churches. This high percentage does not count those who had been previously baptized in other denominations or as an infant. Phillip B. Jones, et al., *A Study of Adults Baptized in Southern Baptist Churches, 1993* (Atlanta: Home Mission Board of the Southern Baptist Convention, 1995), 5. For more on baptism trends in the SBC, see Clifford Ingle, "Why the Interest?" *Children and Conversion*, ed. Clifford Ingle (Nashville: Broadman, 1970), 14; and Hammett, *Biblical Foundations for Baptist Churches*, 112, 122–23, 272–73.

professing of faith in Christ by children and the spiritual growth of children should be encouraged—but their baptisms should be delayed until they are mature enough to assume the responsibilities of local church membership. The decision might best be made when they begin making other significant life decisions.[58]

In short, Baptist and baptistic views of original sin lead parents to regard their children as sinners in need of God's grace, because all people inherit either a sinful nature and guilt *or* a sinful nature—which will later lead to their guilt. In either case, all people begin life impacted by sin. By God's grace and Christ's work on the cross, those who die in infancy are safe with God in heaven. Infants and children are always welcome and included in the church, but they are accountable as members only after their own confessions of faith in Jesus through immersion baptism. Little ones should be instructed to love and follow Jesus at the earliest possible age through learning Scripture at home and at church, and by observing the administration of the ordinances and the examples of faithful Christians.

Responses to a Baptist View of Infants and Children in the Church

An Orthodox Response by Jason Foster

Adam Harwood does an excellent job of presenting the history, theology, and place of infants and children in the Baptist and baptistic traditions. Quite often, Southern Baptists in particular are at the forefront of developing quality Sunday school literature, Vacation Bible School curriculum, and other

---

[58] For a constructive and positive view that affirms the spiritual experiences of children but views conversion as an adult experience, see Smith, *Beginning Well*.

educational resources for their young people. There is no doubt there is a genuine concern among Baptists for their children's growth in biblical knowledge and in the things of God. This being said, my critique of Harwood's position on children and the church should not be understood as a dismissal of this Baptist ministry which, in many ways, is challenging and exemplary to Orthodox Christians and others as well.

The Question of Newness, Originality, and Consensus

In his opening chapter on Baptist ecclesiology, Harwood notes that Baptists are "less than five centuries old," thereby acknowledging Baptist faith and practice is based on new understandings of the ancient biblical texts written by the church, for the church, and to the church. Throughout his paper, he acknowledges Scripture and theological ideals flowing from the sixteenth century Radical Reformation, with the exception of a reference to St. Augustine of Hippo whom he believes misinterpreted the parable of the Weeds (Matt 13:24–30, 36–43). From a critical point of view, Harwood's arguments might have been strengthened if he would have attempted, like the early twentieth century Baptist pastor J. M. Carroll did in his work *The Trail of Blood*, to establish a historical and theological continuity within his position on infants and children in the church. To dismiss with silence 1,500 years of church history in which the established and formally unchallenged pattern of infant baptism was practiced and still is among the majority of Christians today is problematic. However, the Baptist understanding of "soul competency" and the "priesthood of all believers" as set forth by Harwood coupled with "solo" as contrasted with *sola Scriptura* and the "autonomous" nature of the local church allows for the self-determination and interpretation of the biblical text. Be that as it may, in the midst of theological strife and division within the sixty or so national Baptist bodies in the United States alone, it seems there is unity on the fundamental understanding of when children should be baptized, as set forth in Harwood's work, but their guilt or innocence before God is disputed. This is a rather significant pastoral issue that he addresses in some detail but, in the end of his discussion, it remains a matter of interpretation among Baptist and baptistic scholars.

Church Membership and Development

The next theological point in Harwood's chapter that needs to be addressed is the issue of "regenerate church membership." According to him, regeneration is the result of placing personal faith in Christ that is followed by and not confused with baptism. However, it can be argued that a quick survey of any Southern Baptist congregation will reveal that many, if not most, of the adults in the gathering have made multiple public professions of faith during their lifetimes and have been baptized, as he notes in his essay, more than once. This begs the question: how, then, can anyone know who is truly regenerate and who is not? This query, in the mind of the Orthodox Christian, is answered in a biblical, historical, and traditional view of the mystery of baptism where there the Spirit of God, as in the beginning, descends on the water of baptism and sanctifies it (John 3:3, 5; Acts 2:38; 1 Cor 6:11; Gal 3:26–27; 4:6–7; Titus 3:5), bringing forth new life in Christ (Romans 6; Colossians 2; 1 Pet 3:21). When the question of where one stands with God arises in a sacramental/liturgical context, the soul is anchored in the God-given rite. But how does a Baptist address the issue of doubt or ongoing sinful habits after a child makes a decision for Christ? Was the decision salvific or not? These are some theological and pastoral questions that arguably need to be explored further. While we disagree on most points regarding infants and children in the church, Orthodox and Baptist do find common ground and agreement on an issue of paramount importance. God entrusts our young ones to us, and they need to grow and mature in their understanding of the Bible and in their faith in Christ.

A Roman Catholic Response by David Liberto

Adam Harwood presents the Baptist position on the topic of how infants and children relate to the church. My response to it will employ the *modus operandi* of citation and response. I will cite a brief passage from the chapter, and then I will respond to it by way of questions, analysis, and critique. I will present the various passages in the order in which they appear in Harwood's work.

> Citation 1: "The *greatest* distinction between the perspectives of Baptists and those of other Christians is ... the view that local church membership should be comprised only of people who are regenerate, or born again."

Since one of the main questions being investigated is whether children are in the church, Harwood begins with outlining a Baptist understanding of the church and its membership. Strictly based on this understanding of the church, then, the children of believers—according to Baptist theology—are not members of the church. This raises the question of the necessity of educating children in the faith. If the children are not understood to be "born again" until they profess Christ at some later age (presumably in their late teens or in early adulthood), how could the gospel message be effective in their hearts before that time? As Harwood explains, a "person is not born into Christianity, but must be transferred from the kingdom of Satan into the kingdom of Christ." Based on this understanding of church membership, it is possible for many children of Baptist parents never to share the convictions of their parents, never to convert to the faith. From a Catholic perspective, this is unthinkable.

> Citation 2: "Although the biblical example of personal confession *then* baptism has already been stated, it bears repeating because this distinguishes Baptists from all other Christian groups."

This statement is not totally accurate. It is common Catholic practice, for instance, to baptize adults who convert to the Catholic faith and who have never been validly baptized previously in some other communion. Of course, such adults must go through Catholic catechesis so they know about the faith they are going to be baptized into during the Easter Vigil. This is what is happening in the New Testament in Acts 2:37. People come to hear the gospel; by God's prevenient grace, they respond to it. Then follows baptism through which the new life in the Holy Spirit is given to them. In Catholic theology, all of this—the calling, the response, and of course, the regeneration in and through the laver of baptism (Titus 3:5)—is the work of God and his saving grace. That the New Testament would only explicitly reference those who profess faith and then are baptized is understandable. The gospel was being preached to adults in the genesis of the church. Adult baptisms in the early church are not unlike adult baptisms now, at least from a Catholic perspective. The adult candidate for baptism is not someone who rejects the faith: infidelity would be an obstacle to God's grace. The evidence that God is preparing the person for baptism is the response of faith seen in the candidate. Note, however, that in Catholic theology, one is not a member of the church merely by assenting to the faith, as a catechumen does. Baptism is the consummation of the divine call to new life in Christ.

> Citation 3: "Regarding original sin, one Baptist tradition affirms that all people inherit both a sinful nature and guilt, but the other tradition affirms that people are born with a sinful nature only."

Harwood cites a plethora of Baptist and baptistic theologians in this section. This raises some questions about what constitutes a Baptist theological methodology. Although he uses the word "tradition" in this context, he surely uses it in a much weaker sense than it is used in Catholic theology. Nevertheless, it is not merely the Bible that informs his position on the question of original sin: a cadre of interpreters are enlisted to fill out the Baptist position being outlined in the chapter on this topic. At one point, he enlists the Baptist Faith and Message as a source that rejects the opinion that original sin also entails inherited guilt. Nonetheless, he ends this section in a summary where both positions on original sin (one including inherited guilt and one excluding the same) are classified as Baptist positions. This is not an unimportant difference since it would seem that one's position on the matter would clearly influence one's position on the question of the fate of children who die without expressing saving faith (and without receiving baptism, since there is no practice of infant baptism in Baptist congregations).

A Lutheran Response by David P. Scaer

Adam Harwood lists three distinctive Baptist beliefs: the preaching of the Word of God, the response of some with repentance and faith, and a confession of faith expressed by baptism by immersion. This paradigm fits the Lutheran rite of baptism for both adults and infants. Before and during the rite, the Word of God is preached, creating repentance and faith in the candidate for baptism. This faith expresses itself in confession, after which water is applied in the name of the Triune God. Immersion is the ancient practice and is still in use in some Lutheran churches, but how the water is applied does not effect what God does in baptism. In spite of these similarities, there are serious differences on how each understands the human condition, faith, baptism, and the church.

Harwood makes the point that arguments offered by Baptists are based primarily on the Bible, a position Lutherans claims for themselves. *Sola Scriptura*, Scripture alone, is the principle that has defined Lutheranism since the Reformation, but claims to biblical fidelity neither guarantee nor make either Lutherans or Baptists immune to critique. Tradition by itself may not be the final arbiter, but doctrines and practices previously unknown in the church are *ipso facto* suspect and in any event the line between Bible and tradition should not be drawn too sharply. Precursors of the Apostles' Creed can be located in the New Testament, indicating that creeds were already in use in apostolic churches—especially in connection with baptism.

Some of Harwood's claims, like "the Gospels mention Jesus blessing but not baptizing any children," need closer attention. Jesus did not baptize anyone—including adults; rather, he left the task to his disciples (John 4:2). Also, nothing is said of Jesus baptizing the Canaanite woman and the Roman centurion, though if anyone was qualified to be baptized, they were qualified. Notably, Jesus held up the children not only as having faith but implied that the faith of adults should be like theirs (Matt 18:6). Matthew's report that Jerusalem and all Judea went out to the Jordan to be baptized raises the haunting probability that the children joined their parents in hearing the message of repentance and being baptized. Households mentioned in Acts as being baptized make no mention of slaves, adolescents, and senior citizens either.

Baptists agree that infants possess a sinful nature, but only when they can distinguish right from wrong are little ones morally accountable and able to decide to believe. Some studies on childhood indicate that children are capable of moral choices much earlier than their teens. The Baptist position that children inherit an inclination to sin without incurring guilt before God is hardly distinguishable from the one proposed by Orthodoxy. For both groups guilt is incurred only when actual sins are committed. This leads Harwood to advocate a modified universalism: "All who die in infancy are safe with God in heaven." In support, he cites the well-respected Millard Erickson, who explains: "The Lord excludes from condemnation infants and those who never reach moral competency." To this we respond that reaching maturity has the disadvantage of possibly rejecting the faith, an option not open to those who have not reached the age of rational discretion. Since, according to the Baptist view, people are accountable for actual but not original sin, it should be noted that this is a distinction without a difference. Actual sins are nothing else than original sin coming to expression. Evil nature is inherent in the human condition from youth, as the Baptists concede (Gen 8:21). Only when individuals decide to commit sin does the innocence of childhood cease, but there is no firm agreement among Baptists of the age when that happens. If the age of moral accountability cannot be definitely determined, it might be that it is nothing else than a philosophical construct. Just as a child is a physical, emotional, and rational creature at the moment of conception, so he is also a spiritual one able to respond to the Word of God.

Part of the Baptist opposition to infant baptism is that only those who have had a personal experience with Christ belong to the local church and so children who are incapable of such are not members. Children blessed by Jesus did not become members of the local church, but it is anachronistic to speak of them and other followers of Jesus joining local churches. They were included in Israel and participated in its rituals and were members of the households that after baptism became the first Christian churches. Basing inclusion in the church on personal experience assumes that the person is qualified to know what the qualifying experience is and that he can believe. Pericopes of Jesus and the children hardly support their exemplary moral character. Read more carefully, they speak of the inclusion of children in the kingdom of God by their faith alone, which is a standard of faith even for the adult disciples. That disagreement about the age of moral competency exists among Baptists is good reason to conclude that it does not exist or at least is so evasive as to serve no useful purpose. Referencing 1 Sam 3:7 that this prophet in waiting "did not yet know the Lord" shows that God had not yet spoken to him, not that he was without faith. As Harwood points out, immersion symbolizes the believer sharing in Christ's death and the resurrection—but Saint Paul says the symbol embraces within itself the reality of these saving events (Rom 6:4). In baptism it is not what we do for God in obeying an ordinance, but what God has done and continues to do in and for the baptized.

A Reformed Response by Gregg Strawbridge

Adam Harwood provides a helpful and lucid summary of the Baptist view. Several commendations are due him for this work. First, I appreciate Harwood's concern that children must own their faith. Second, we agree on *sola Scriptura*, and he seeks to establish his views from the Bible. Third, he is careful in delineating diversity in Baptist views and clearly articulates his own. I do, however, have a few challenges to Dr. Harwood's views.

First, he states that "the *only* explicit examples of baptism in the New Testament occurred after people confessed their faith in Christ" (emphasis his). However, there are no explicit confessions of faith of the household members of Cornelius, Lydia, the jailer, or Stephanus—though they were all baptized. Considering the household baptism cases, the alleged change to an individualistic emphasis is unlikely.

Second, the claim of a "regenerate church membership" is problematic. "Confessor's baptism" does not guarantee a regenerate church membership since confession cannot guarantee regeneration. The assumption lurking here is that infants cannot be regenerate. However, the prime counter example is John the Baptist (Luke 1:15). Would the young, unbaptized, yet *regenerate* John the Baptist be able to be a member of a Baptist church with a regenerate membership policy?[59]

Third, he says, "Immersion is the only valid mode of baptism." A biblical counter-example is Heb 9:10. The term *baptismos* is used of the various washings in the tabernacle; none of these baptisms were immersions. The "pouring out" (*ekkchuno*) of the Holy Spirit is explicitly called baptism (Acts 2:18, 33; 11:16). Baptism "into death" (Rom 6:3) and resurrection is a crossing rite; Christians enter into a different territory, "safely through the water" (1 Cor 10:1–3; 1 Pet 3:18, NASB).[60]

Fourth, Harwood's views of infant salvation are tangled with his denial that we inherit Adam's guilt. If being guilty in Adam is "preposterous" as the cited Walter Connor maintains, then on what basis do Christians have Christ's righteousness applied to them? The principle of covenantal headship

---

[59] My question was answered recently by a Baptist theologian who was discussing "regenerate membership." He said, "No, not if he wasn't baptized by immersion."

[60] The Baptist symbolism in immersion is simply mistaken. Jesus's death was on a cross; he was not plunged into the ground. He was not buried down in a grave (underground); instead, he was laid to rest in the side of a cliff of hewn rock. His resurrection involved simply walking out of that cave (not up from the ground). What actually happened does not conform to the Baptist rite.

functions in both cases: we receive Adam's sin and guilt, and we receive the last Adam's righteousness and forgiveness (Rom 5:16–17; 1 Cor 15:45). "For as in Adam all die, so also in Christ all will be made alive" (1 Cor 15:22, NASB). "People who die as infants or young children are free from God's judgment," Harwood states in his chapter. But is not death itself a judgment? Is God rendering a judgment of death without any judicial basis in the guilt of sin (Rom 3:23)?

Fifth, the argument for universal infant salvation draws upon texts about covenant members' salvation. Would David have taught that Goliath's child was saved? Would Daniel view Belshazzar's child as saved? A number of passages stand in tension with this view: "How blessed will be the one who seizes and dashes your little ones against the rock" (Ps 137:9; also 139:21; 109:12–13).[61] Scripture has not spoken to universal infant salvation, and denying the doctrine of original sin is surely too costly a price for this hope. We should then let God be God in this unknown area.

Finally, on the issue of infants and children in the church, Harwood says, "No text clearly indicates how they are to be received into local churches." We all agree that baptism is the event that provides for officially entering the church. Many households were baptized; children are addressed as congregants (Eph 6:1; Col 3:20; 1 Cor 7:14). Therefore, it seems logically binding to conclude that such children were baptized. They were *accountable* for obedience to parents, yes (Eph 6:1), but also to elders (Heb 13:17). Parents had "of Christ" responsibilities (Eph 6:4). Colossians uses union with Christ language regarding such obedience: "This is well-pleasing in (*en*) the Lord" (Col 3:20, NASB). These children were "in the Lord."

---

[61] These sentiments in the Psalms are difficult, and I am unable to provide a full theodicy of them here. The Bible nowhere promises salvation to all children dying in infancy. In these and like passages there is at least some counter testimony to universal infant salvation.

Welcoming Children

Kevin E. Lawson

> Then children were brought to him that he might lay his hands on them and pray. The disciples rebuked the people, but Jesus said, "Let the little children come to me and do not hinder them, for to such belongs the kingdom of heaven." And he laid his hands on them and went away. (Matt 19:13–15 ESV)[1]

We began this book with a question regarding how Christians are to be faithful stewards of the precious gift of children that God gives to us. How are we to minister to them and encourage their spiritual growth and their own relationships with God, their Creator and Father? Foundational to our response is the way Jesus welcomed children, blessed them, and cautioned his disciples not to hinder them from coming to him (Matt 19:13–15).

As presented through the preceding chapters, views of what it means for Christians to welcome and minister to children are deeply impacted by our perspectives on several key theological issues:

---

[1] All Scripture references in this chapter are taken from the English Standard Version (ESV).

- **Sin:** What is the impact of Adamic sin in the lives of children? How does this affect their ability to be in relationship with God?
- **Child death:** What happens to children who perish in infancy or childhood? Are children held to a different standard than adults in their relationships with God? Is there an age of "accountability" that marks a transition in responsibility for one's sinful actions?
- **Baptism:** What is the meaning of Christian baptism? What is the requirement for baptism? What does it accomplish in the lives of those who are baptized? Are infants fitting candidates? If so, why? If not, why not? How does Christian baptism relate to other baptismal practices and to circumcision?
- **The Church:** What is the church? Who belongs to it? What is required in order for a person to be counted as a part of it? When and how are children to be considered members of the church? How might or should children participate in the life of the church?
- **Instruction:** Who bears the responsibility for instructing children in the Christian faith? When and how should little ones receive this instruction?

The preceding chapters have presented five different theological traditions and their responses to these questions. In addition, their advocates have described the ministry efforts with children that flow from each set of theological convictions. In each case, there is a clear connection and consistency between a tradition's beliefs about children and their ministry efforts to them. This shows how much our theology matters, for theological commitments set Christians' expectations and priorities for life and practice—including the way we interact with the children in our midst.

While there are plenty of areas of difference, both in theological perspective and in our practices with little ones, it is good to see that we are in agreement about so much. In saying that, I do not make light of the differences evident in the preceding chapters of this book; rather, I think it beneficial to consider what we can learn from our areas of agreement.

Areas of Common Ground in Our Understanding

Regardless of differences in particular views on sin, baptism, and the church, there seem to be at least nine areas of agreement among the five traditions represented in this book. I believe they can inform and helpfully guide ministry efforts with children.

1. God loves children and desires for them to know him. In each of the theological perspectives, there is an understanding that God's heart is toward children; he desires that they grow to know him and to live in right relationship with him through placing faith in Christ Jesus. Leaders in the church need to mirror the love that God has for children and do all in our power to help them know the heavenly Father who created and loves them.

2. Infants and children are negatively impacted by sin. Because of the fall, as recorded in Genesis 3, children are negatively impacted because of sin. Some view this truth to mean even infants inherit a bent toward sin and disobedience to God. Others view this as also involving an inherited guilt due to Adam's sin. In either case, all people begin life negatively impacted in some way because of Adam's disobedience. All creation, in fact, groans under the curse of sin (Rom 8:19–22). But that is not the end of the story.

3. God has made provision for the eternal destinies of at least some children. There is agreement among the represented traditions that God has provided a means by which children are able to receive God's saving grace through the sacrificial death and resurrection of Jesus. There is keen disagreement over how this is possible, and to whom it applies, but God's active grace on behalf of little ones is clear. Church leaders, then, should seek to understand how God's grace comes to children and how Christians are to serve little ones by promoting and facilitating their response to the gospel of God's grace.

4. Children are capable of enjoying a genuine spiritual walk with God. While there is recognition that young boys and girls must be instructed in the faith, and learn and grow in their response to the God who has loved them in and through Christ, they are capable of having their own genuine relationships with their heavenly Father. God, through the Holy Spirit, is able to work in the lives of little ones to help them experience his presence for their good. Thus, leaders in the church need to take the spiritual health of children seriously, providing the kind of instruction, spiritual nurture, and encouragement to help them grow and mature in faith and faithfulness. Leaders also need to recognize that they are partnering with God in the process of nurturing his children spiritually and must thus remain attentive to what God may be doing in the lives of those in their care.

5. *In children God sees qualities of faith that should characterize adults who would be part of his kingdom.* In Scripture, children are singled out as having qualities of trust and dependence that should continue to characterize both redeemed humanity's relationship with God and the way in which they live, regardless of age. While little ones need much from the adults in their lives, they also serve as living reminders of the kind of people we are to be if we desire to inherit God's kingdom. Christians' ministry with children, then, should not simply reflect adult efforts on their behalf; adult believers should continually consider children as God's gift that helps those more advanced in age to recognize what type of posture everyone should have before God.

6. *Parents should be equipped and supported in their critical role as children's primary instructors and models of the Christian faith.* All theological traditions are in agreement on this. Although the church has a significant role to play in the lives of children, Christian parents (and those who take on parental roles) are given a primary responsibility for instructing boys and girls in the faith and for encouraging them to respond in faith to the gospel. Church leaders should develop ministries that equip and support parents in this critical role, taking care not to create the impression that the church will do it all.

7. *The church as a whole has a responsibility to help in the spiritual nurture and instruction of children.* Although Christian parents have a primary role in the spiritual upbringing of their offspring, they are also part of the larger body of Christ, which is gifted by God for the spiritual benefit of the entire body (1 Cor 12; Eph 4:11–16). Children, then, can both benefit from the ministry of others in the congregation and can contribute to the spiritual growth of the congregation (more on this below). Ministry leaders need to think carefully about how the church might partner with families in providing not only instruction in the faith, but giving opportunities for them to live it out in the corporate life of the church.

8. *It is important to include children in beneficial ways in the life and practice of the church as they grow.* Each of the traditions described in earlier chapters understands that while young boys and girls may at times benefit from more focused care and instruction designed specifically for their age groups, there is also benefit in having children join with other generations in worship, fellowship, and service. Much can be caught through the modeling and encouragement of adult believers. In addition, a sense of identity as God's child and as a part of the church can develop at a young age, having a deep impact in the years of adolescence and adulthood. Incorporating children into the ministries of the church, therefore, should not be put off until they are considered grown.

9. *It is important for children to grow to own their faith rather than continuing to live it passively as if it were merely some kind of benefit received from their parents.* Regardless of our theological traditions, the writers of this resource share a common goal of raising our children to embrace the Christian faith as their own. We desire that they live their lives as an authentic expression of their personal, faithful responses to God's grace. Because of this, we are all seeking to raise our girls and boys to become adults of faith. We differ greatly in how we think this is best accomplished—especially regarding the role of baptism in the process—but the end goal is one we hold in common.

How to Grow Spiritually with Our Children

In June of 2006, John H. Westerhoff III, presented a plenary session at the Society for Children's Spirituality: Christian Perspectives triennial conference, held at Concordia University. His session was entitled "Growing Spiritually with Our Children." It was a helpful reminder that as Christians, we are all children of God, and *he* asks us to invite little ones to join in the life-long task of growing to know and love him, to respond to and live in light of the gospel of God's grace to us. In Westerhoff's remarks, he framed a three-fold approach to growing spiritually with our children, including ministry "for," "to," and "with" them.[2]

In my reflections since that time, I have added one more aspect of ministry to this model: ministry "by" children. What follows is an explanation of what this kind of four-fold ministry might look like. I think it can fit and work within each of the theological traditions described herein. While our various congregations will have different ways of understanding and carrying out these ministries, remembering our common tasks can help us think more carefully about the full range of what we are to provide the children in our care. I begin by looking at what should characterize ministry "for" children. After that I will move on to address the aspects of ministry "to," "with," and "by" children.[3]

Ministry to Parents/Caregivers FOR Children

If church leaders believe that parents (or other caregivers serving in a parent-like role) have a critical job in the instruction and spiritual nurture of their children, they do well to invest heavily in equipping parents for it. This means that church leaders will strategically design the way they disciple and equip adults.

First, they must pursue strong adult education formation. At a foundational level, churches need to take adult discipleship seriously so that parents

---

[2] John H. Westerhoff III, "The Church's Contemporary Challenge: Assisting Adults to Mature Spiritually *with* Their Children," in *Nurturing Children's Spirituality*, ed. Holly Catterton Allen (Eugene, OR: Cascade Books, 2008), 356–61.

[3] This section of the chapter is adapted from a chapter I contributed to Ronald Habermas's book, *Introduction to Christian Education and Formation: A Lifelong Plan for Christ-Centered Restoration* (Grand Rapids, MI: Zondervan, 2009), 151–60. It is adapted with permission from the publisher.

and other leaders really know the faith, how to live it out, and how to explain it to others—including children. Participation in corporate worship and in Bible study (whether on Sunday morning or during the week) represents one dependable strategy for growing one's adult faith. But actual ministry involvement also shapes adult faith, encouraging greater reflection on Christianity and how it is to be lived out. This leads to more ownership of one's faith in general. Many adults need to be educated on the importance of making such opportunities a priority.

Second, since there are many parents who want to pass their love for their faith on to their children, but some truly do not know how to go about it, churches that value the total needs of children will encourage training opportunities for parents by offering practical classes. They can offer sessions to help parents understand the basic issues of child development, the nature and nurture of faith, and insights for promoting faith at home. As God blesses these church classes, fruitful times of Bible study, prayer, and worship within the family will emerge.

It is difficult for the average parent to keep up with the best available resources for instructing his or her children in the faith. Diversities in subject matter, personal interests, and age range further complicate this challenge. So, third, churches can help parents in this effort by verbally promoting the use of beneficial resources and by offering well-stocked libraries as parenting resource centers. Helpful, biblically sound volumes on everything from how to care for a newborn to how to help one's child navigate puberty are a gift to parents in need of answers. A collection of read-aloud storybooks can encourage parents to spend time with and to talk about God with young children. Books for older children not only help them to address topics like biblical sexuality and life direction in a healthy way but can also encourage their own exploration of God's work in the world. Games, music CDs, DVDs, Christian magazines, other digital media, and various activity books can all help caregivers creatively share the wonderful story of God's love represented in his gift of Jesus Christ.

Fourth, collaboration itself is an effective tool in discipling children, and it is something churches can facilitate strategically. Parents need the encouragement of others as they begin nurturing their children's faith. Church leaders, then, can organize parents' meetings, resource nights, and offer strategies to help parents grow confident in their ability to teach well and rightly.

Advent and Lent are examples of special seasons of the year when churches can provide devotional materials and special activities for use at home, too. These materials help families experience meaningful celebrations during these holy days. For instance, Advent wreaths can be made at church, perhaps even as family projects. The wreaths can then be taken home along with related devotionals that include carols to sing, Scriptures to read, and family activities geared toward putting faith into action. Collaborative efforts like this one promote positive learning experiences between church and home. In fact, these seasonal activities may provide just the opportunity parents need to become more confident and intentional about making their children's year-round instruction in the faith a priority.

Little ones are deeply dependent on the adults in their lives for nourishment and nurture. But while all societies value children in some measure, in too many cases children are neglected or abused. They are some of the first to suffer in times of poverty and times of war.

God makes it clear that he is a defender of the afflicted. In Ps 68:5, the psalmist declares that the "Father of the fatherless and protector of widows is God in his holy habitation." Echoing this, James writes, "Religion that is pure and undefiled before God, the Father, is this: to visit orphans and widows in their affliction, and to keep oneself unstained from the world" (1:27). God's people are to share God's heart and values, acting in ways that mirror his character. The responsibilities of Christians extend beyond seeing to the spiritual nurture and instruction of children to include both advocating and taking action for their physical care and well-being.

Ministry by the Church TO Children

As communities of believers called to share life together, it is appropriate for local church congregations to provide special ministries that nurture the faith of their children. Boys and girls benefit most from attending services that show concern for their particular abilities and needs. Ministries dedicated to intentionally including little ones should supplement what parents provide at home, as well as offering ministry to children in the greater community who lack the benefit of Christian parents.

The biggest investment most churches make is in providing children with diverse and relevant forms of instruction in Scripture and in the basics of the Christian faith. Many of the traditions described herein offer catechetical instruction in the home and through the church. Some Protestant churches have a long and strong history of offering Sunday school classes, vacation Bible schools, and various student club programs during the week. Whatever educational models or designs are utilized within a particular congregation, there needs to be careful, ongoing assessment behind each approach to ensure that the ministry models are genuinely benefiting the children who participate in them and that the efforts are accomplishing their intended goals. Christians must not mistake enjoyment for effectiveness.

Earlier I encouraged churches to include children in their corporate worship, at least up to the point of the sermon. But churches may want to provide specific times and places exclusively for a dedicated children's service, too, allowing boys and girls to more fully praise their Maker according to their abilities. I am not advocating a children's worship that excludes children from corporate church worship. Rather, there is a need for a both/and ministry. One great advantage of creating a distinct worship time for little ones is that many more children can actively participate in such a scenario. More children can join in prayer, learning from Scripture, singing songs of praise, and participating in the sacraments and liturgy. Many publishers of Christian curricula offer resources to aid in the planning of children's worship.

Ministry Together WITH Children

As noted earlier, children want to be part of their church communities so they can experience first-hand the reality of faith at work within the lives of others. That foundation also challenges children to embrace the faith of others as their own. Firsthand experience also enhances children's growing sense of identity, because little ones learn best when they are actively involved in their own instruction. What follows are a couple of suggestions for helping boys and girls grow in meaningful, personal faith as they participate in the activity of the church alongside mature believers.

First, children should be permitted to participate in corporate worship celebrations. It can be a challenge to involve youngsters in corporate worship, but it is worth the effort. Many churches find it beneficial to have young ones present in a common service at least up to the point of the sermon when leaders may then dismiss children for their own worship or Bible study. When children join corporate worship where God is praised, Scripture is read, and prayers are lifted to heaven, they see a total faith community living life together. They begin to understand the nature of worship and are encouraged to participate in it. Because of the numerous variables involved, however, plans for such worship must be formed sensitively. Pastors and worship leaders must consider children's various needs and abilities, along with creating ways to engage them in worship. Providing instructional activity sheets, telling special stories just for little ones, and permitting children to help lead songs are a few methods that help them feel at home among the gathered church.

Second, children should be provided intergenerational learning and fellowship opportunities. When boys and girls are included in intergenerational experiences, they increasingly perceive themselves as part of the church and often grow in admiration of those in elder generations. Helpful experiences may include fellowship dinners, church picnics, family-cluster gatherings, intergenerational Sunday school class sessions, prayer meetings, or group events held at Christmas or Easter. Children who experience opportunities that include people of all ages are prompted to ask more pertinent questions, to see diverse role models outside their families, and to witness multiple sides of church life. When they are given the chance to actively participate in such events, the impact can be great.

My own church organizes community caroling in December. Together young and old share songs, baked goods, and candy with our neighbors before gathering back at the church building for hot chocolate and Christmas cookies. These simple activities bring children together with people of other ages as participants in the body of Christ. Enjoying early experiences within an intergenerational community can positively impact an individual for a lifetime.

Ministry BY Children to Others

One mistake sometimes made is thinking of children only as recipients of the ministry and guidance of their parents and the church rather than realizing that they too can minister to others. Many active adult church members fondly recall that their own involvements in ministry to others began when they were young. And as a result of those early experiences, ministry has been part of their lives ever since.

Even small children can participate in the church's mission projects, like raising funds for World Vision or putting together Samaritan's Purse shoeboxes for needy children. They can join workdays with adults, perhaps doing yard work for those in need within the community. They can also join in visiting homebound church members or in helping to prepare meals for new mothers. Older boys and girls may even help to serve meals to the homeless or might join a parent on a short-term mission trip overseas. Children should be included in the outreach efforts of the church wherever possible in order that they might experience and understand the meaning of compassionate service. They need to see how God has personally gifted them and how he can use them to serve others. Participating in tasks like those mentioned help in addressing children's needs for belonging and identity as they personally contribute within the faith community, too. Such activities help them to see beyond themselves.

Children also can be encouraged to have their own ministries within the church and community. Perhaps the older ones can read stories to smaller children and put on puppet shows for them. They might sing in worship services, pray aloud for church ministries, and visit nursing homes. As important as it is to include children in the general ministry efforts of the church, helping kids take responsibility for planning and carrying out their own ministries encourages the growth of their leadership skills, instills in them a sense of responsibility, and empowers them to take ownership of meeting the needs they will encounter as they grow.

All of this, of course, takes careful planning, coordination, and supervision. It also requires that parents and church leaders avoid the temptation to disregard children's ministries because they seem less effective than what adults may be able to do. The goals and the benefits of allowing boys and girls to serve actively beginning in their early years go way beyond the accomplishment of the ministry task itself. They shape and nurture life-long love and service to God and others.

Recommendations for Further Theological Study, Reflection, and Action

As this book and chapter come to a close, I encourage theologians and church leaders of our various traditions to consider investing time in extended, careful study and consideration of a few important issues that can help the church better understand and respond to the needs of children. The following four areas need our best efforts of research and reflection as we willingly learn from each other's work.

1. The Transition from Infancy to Responsibility: The Age of Accountability, Reason, or Discretion. All of the theological traditions see some kind of difference between young children and adults in their responsibility for sin or for their sin nature. This is shown in attempts to discern whether children are innocent, guilty but not held accountable, guilty but already covered in some way, or guilty but potentially saved through baptism. Scripture notes God's own differential judgment of children compared with adults; for instance, in Deut 1:39 he sends judgment on the older generation of Israel for not entering the Promised Land but allows children to enter.

Jesus welcomes and blesses children, using them as exemplars of those who would receive the kingdom (Mark 10:13–16). We need and would welcome more theological research and writing on these issues to help us understand more clearly both the status of children and how responsibility for one's own nature and life grows. What marks the transition from innocence, or lack of accountability, to accountability? While this is a concept that is frequently discussed, it needs more careful and thorough study. We seem to have been content for some time with a fuzzy understanding, but it limits our careful thinking and discernment in developing ministries with children.

2. The Fate of Children Outside the Community of Faith. Christians wrestle with the implications of our theological positions as we think about those born into this world apart from the Christian community. Some of our traditions focus a lot of attention on the status and fate of those who are born within Christian families, viewing these children as proper candidates for baptism due to the faith of their parents. But our conference interaction in 2015 showed the reluctance of some to discuss the fate of children outside the Christian community who die before both baptism or prior to an opportunity to hear and respond to the gospel message. Those within the church must not, however, be content to simply focus on our own children, content with a tribal approach to the faith. Rather, we must consider carefully the needs of those born outside the church, how they are or are not accepted by God, and what can be done to bring them into right relationship with him (if action is needed). We then need to develop compassionate ministry implications and responses in light of our theological understandings. I'm afraid that our discomfort with thinking in these areas causes us to avoid an area of responsibility for which God will hold us accountable.

3. Fostering an Owned Faith. In each of the represented traditions, we Christians share a desire to raise children who grow into adults who embrace the faith as their own and take responsibility for their walks with God. None of us want to see our children attend worship events as nominal Christians. Rather, we desire them to have a vital and growing faith commitment. We need to continue to study and understand from Scripture, from the history of the church, and even from contemporary social science research what contributes effectively to developing children into adults who fully own their faith.

4. Prioritizing Ministry with Children. This last area is not so much one of new theological research or study, but of living out what we understand from Scripture. If children are loved by God, and are given as a reward to his people, and are to be brought to Jesus, then why are children so often neglected in Christian communities? The church in many parts of the world is focused primarily on adult ministry and worship, with children being seen as some kind of distraction from important ministry efforts. In too many cases church leaders put major financial investments into facilities and programs for adult worship, instruction, outreach, and service but give little thought or attention to the needs of boys and girls. More careful theological study and reflection on the status and needs of children in our congregations and communities should lead us to invest more strategically in ministry for, to, with, and by children. We must sharpen our thinking and understanding so that we might act as more faithful stewards of God's precious gift to us.

May we never be content with a well-defined and defended theological position regarding infants and children. May we instead be moved by God in light of what we believe to a loving ministry designed to benefit those whom Jesus welcomed and blessed.

NAME INDEX

Abbott, Walter M., 48, 69
Akin, Daniel, 166
Albright, William Foxwell, 175
Allen, Holly Catterton, 198
Allison, Gregg R., 158, 172
Amar, Joseph P., 16
Antioch, St. Ignatius of, 28
Aquinas, St. Thomas, 58, 59, 86
Atkinson, James, 82
Augustine, St., 12, 14, 47, 48, 52, 56, 158
Bakke, O. M., 6
Barth, Karl, 110
Battles, Ford Lewis, 158
Beale, Gregory K., 130
Beveridge, Henry, 122
Blaurock, George, 157
Boettner, Loraine, 125
Bonaventure, 86
Bonino, Serge-Thomas, 59
Bouteneff, Peter, 15
Boyce, James, 163
Boylan, Anne M., 7
Boyle, Geoffrey R., 102
Brinkel, Karl, 102
Bromiley, G. W., 110
Brown, Colin, 132
Bunge, Marcia J., 3
Bushnell, Horace, 7, 117
Caesarea, St. Basil of, 18
Calvin, John, 78, 122, 123, 158
Canterbury, Anselm of, 57

Casiday, A. M., 33
Chapell, Bryan, 123
Chemnitz, Martin, 85
Chrysostom, St. John, 17, 18, 26, 35
Climenhaga, Arthur Merlin, 95
Cline, Scott, 41
Coble, William B., 176
Conner, Walter T., 165
Cunningham, Mary B., 15
Cydones, Demetrios, 12
Cyprian, St., 18
Cyrus, Theodoret of, 94, 95
Demacopoulos, George E., 14
Denzinger, Heinrich, 49
Dever, Mark, 180
Dockery, David S., 169
Donaldson, James, 15
Duesing, Jason G., 156
Erickson, Millard J., 169, 170
Estocin, Andrew, 33
Evans, William B., 129
Ferguson, Everett, 17, 173
Fidus, 18
Finn, Nathan A., 157
Fisher, J. D. C., 6
Foley, Michael, 47
Freedman, David Noel, 175
Gallant, Tim, 142
Garrett, James Leo, Jr., 77
George, Timothy, 169
Grantham, Thomas, 163

Grebel, Conrad, 157
Green, Bradley G., 169
Habermas, Ronald, 198
Hammett, John S., 157, 159, 161, 180, 182
Harris, Benjamin, 114
Harrison, Carol, 33
Harwood, Adam, 165, 171
Hayford, Jack, 167
Helwys, Thomas, 151
Herod, 89
Hippolytus, St., 18
Hodge, Charles, 117, 163
Hopko, Thomas, 98, 99
Hubmaier, Balthasar, 151, 157, 162
Hünermann, Peter, 49
Ingle, Clifford, 163, 176, 182
Irenaeus, St., 15, 18, 20
Jewett, Paul K., 122
Johnson, Maxwell, 7
Jones, Phillip B., 182
Jordan, James B., 140
Klaassen, Walter, 164
Klaassen, William, 164
Kolb, Robert, 85
Lawson, Kevin E., 6, 170
Lehmann, Helmut T., 81
Lehrer, Jonah, 99
Leithart, Peter, 124
Leland, John, 157
Lemke, Steve W., 151
Lombard, Peter, 57
Louth, Andrew, 16
Ludwig, Sämi, 114
Lumpkin, William L., 151, 164
Lusk, Rich, 123, 129
Luther, Martin, 81, 82, 83, 95, 97, 98
MacArthur, John, 175
Malone, Fred, 152, 163
Mantzaridis, Georgios I., 16
Manz, Felix, 157
Marpeck, Pilgram, 164
Martyr, Justin, 15, 30
Mastrantonis, George, 31
Mathews, Edward G., Jr., 16
McNeill, John T., 158
McVey, Kathleen, 16
Melanchthon, Philip, 85

Merkle, Benjamin L., 157, 161
Meyendorff, John, 94
Mohler, R. Albert, Jr., 78, 166
Moody, Dale, 104
Moore, William, 29
Mopsuestia, Theodore of, 12, 17
Mullins, E. Y., 78, 79, 156, 166, 167
Murphy, James A., 100
Nazianzus, St. Gregory of, 18
Nellas, Panayiotis, 15
Nettles, Tom, 79
Newman, Henry, 71
Nyssa, Gregory of, 31
Obermann, Heiko, 82
Origen, 6, 19
Owens, Waylan, 178
Papanikolaou, Aristotle, 14
Pelagius, 14
Pelikan, Jaroslav, 81
Pikpin, H. Wayne, 152, 162
Pius, Pope, IX, 53
Ponticus, Evagrius, 33
Pretyman, George, 42
Putman, Rhyne R., 77, 78
Rambut, W. H., 15
Ratcliff, Brenda, 174
Ratcliff, Donald, 174
Rayburn, Robert S., 117, 123
Reisinger, Ernest, 163
Roberts, Alexander, 15
Rome, St. Hippolytus of, 22
Ross, Allen P., 130
Sattler, Michael, 157
Scaer, David P., 101, 102, 103
Schaff, Philip, 29, 115
Schenck, Lewis Bevens, 137
Schleiermacher, Friedrich, 101
Schmemann, Alexander, 23
Schmitt, F. S., 57
Schönmetzer, Adolph, 49
Schreiner, Thomas R., 152, 180
Schulz, K. Detlev, 95
Sheed, F. J., 47
Sherrard, Liadain, 16
Silano, Giulio, 57
Smith, Gordon T., 180, 183
Smyth, John, 164

Name Index

Spinks, Bryan, 17
Sproul, R. C., 77
Stonehouse, Catherine, 174, 179
Strawbridge, Gregg, 116, 117, 137, 172
Sweet, Leonard, 33
Tappert, Theodore G., 85
Tertullian, 6, 17, 18, 25, 30
Theokritoff, Elizabeth, 15
Torrance, T. F., 110
Treier, Daniel J., 77
Trigg, Jonathan, 98
Tugwell, Simon, 33
Turner, Paul, 6
Vanhoozer, Kevin J., 77
Venema, Cornelis P., 41
Wace, Henry, 29

Walliser-Schwarzbart, Eileen, 82
Wamble, Hugh, 163
Weaver, C. Douglas, 78, 156
Weinfeld, Moshe, 175
Wellum, Stephen, 152
Wengert, Timothy J., 85
Wenham, Gordon J., 130
Westerhoff, John H., III, 198
White, Thomas, 156
Williams, Roger, 157
Wilson, Douglas, 121, 172
Wright, David F., 128
Wright, Shawn D., 152, 180
Yarnell, Malcolm B., III, 156, 180
Yoder, Gideon G., 170
Yoder, John H., 152, 162

SUBJECT INDEX

A
ablution, 27
abortion, 8, 97, 127
Abraham, descendants of, 98, 120, 121, 146
accountable (morally), 98, 99, 100, 160, 169, 171, 175, 177, 183, 189, 192, 204, 205
Adam, descendants of, 16, 39, 40, 51, 165
Adam, sin of (or fall of or transgression of or disobedience of), 14, 15, 30, 40, 43, 44, 51, 70, 72, 79, 85, 86, 87, 98, 114, 127, 141, 158, 162, 163, 165, 170, 192, 195
adolescence, 6, 8, 23, 100, 101, 110, 189, 197
adoption, 129
age-appropriate, 65, 67, 178, 179
age of accountability (or age of moral responsibility/competancy), 80, 100, 165, 169, 170, 189, 190, 194, 204
age of reason (or age of rational discretion), 52, 55, 61, 74, 80, 97, 99, 189
altar, 21
Anabaptism, 72, 93, 102, 116, 156, 157, 158, 164
anathema, 51, 53, 54
angel, 40, 47, 57, 95, 167, 168
anoint, 6, 22, 25, 26, 27, 39
Apolysis, 13

apophatic theology, 29
Apostles' Creed, 73, 84, 102, 139, 188
Arminianism, 124
Athanasian Creed, 84
atonement, 12, 113, 124, 150, 163, 167, 170, 171
avar, 131

B
baptism, believer's, 151, 152, 157, 161
baptism, confessor's, 157, 158, 159, 161, 177, 181, 191
baptism, household, 132, 133, 134, 135, 191
baptismos, 130
Baptist Faith and Message, 43, 44, 77, 159, 160, 161, 165, 187
baptizō, 161
beatific vision, 55, 57, 59, 74
birth (physical), 12, 18, 19, 40, 62, 66, 82, 83, 92, 94, 98, 109, 123, 145, 147, 148, 149
blood (of Christ), 6, 20, 34, 42, 76, 82, 106, 113, 122, 136, 180
body (of Christ), 6, 8, 20, 21, 27, 28, 34, 36, 37, 39, 62, 69, 82, 87, 106, 122, 127, 145, 159, 180, 196, 203
born again, 26, 28, 36, 51, 68, 73, 74, 81, 85, 157, 186
brephē, 90, 92

brephos, 177, 178
burial, 25, 27, 28, 54, 94, 151, 157, 161, 191

C

Calvinism, 114, 117, 124, 125, 126, 128, 147, 168
Canons of Dort, 124, 151
catechism, 6, 7, 32, 33, 34, 72, 73, 77, 128, 139, 144, 187
Catechism, Baltimore, 71
Catechism, Heidelberg, 113, 122, 123, 139
Catechism of the Catholic Church (CCC), 50, 51, 52, 53, 54, 55, 60, 63, 64, 71, 82
catechumen, 24, 25, 76, 187
chancel, 92
childlike, 89, 110, 111, 169
children, Israelite, 136, 169, 175, 176
chrismate, 27, 30, 32, 105, 106, 145
churching, 20, 21, 24, 44
church leaders, 5, 6, 182, 195, 196, 197, 198, 199, 200, 202, 204, 206
church membership, 21, 45, 62, 78, 79, 122, 144, 151, 153, 157, 158, 160, 161, 183, 185, 186, 191
circumcision, 18, 19, 42, 97, 98, 122, 138, 147, 152, 173, 194
Concord, Book of, 84, 85
concupiscence, 14, 54, 85, 86, 147
condemnation, 41, 44, 61, 85, 87, 98, 111, 165, 166, 169, 170, 171, 189
confession of faith, 6, 22, 24, 44, 45, 102, 103, 142, 152, 160, 161, 177, 181, 186, 188, 191
confirmation, 6, 7, 32, 62, 63, 70, 71, 72, 76, 101, 102, 103, 105, 106, 108, 110, 139, 140, 142
conversion, 7, 89, 116, 132, 133, 134, 135, 151, 157, 163, 170, 180, 183, 186
corporate worship, 3, 6, 175, 179, 199, 201, 202
corpus permixtum, 158
Council, Fourth Lateran, 6, 72, 106
Council of Carthage (various councils), 42, 51, 52, 144
Council of Constantinople, 12

Council of Orange, Second, 51
Council of Trent, 51, 52, 53, 54, 71, 77
Council, Second Vatican, 49, 62, 68, 77
covenant, Abrahamic (or Abrahamic promise), 120, 121, 122, 136, 147
covenantal headship (or federal headship), 141, 163, 191
covenant children, 42, 116, 123, 125, 126
covenant theology, 117, 143, 151, 152
Creator, 2, 15, 43, 50, 99, 167, 193
crux theologorum, 95
curse (of sin), 37, 141, 195

D

dedication (infant), 44, 173
deification (or *theosis*), 15, 16, 30, 40, 145
demonization (or demon possession; see also exorcism), 45, 90
deposit of faith, 48, 49, 67, 71
depravity, 14, 41, 87, 124, 126, 147
Didache, the, 17
diocese, 63
discipleship, 140, 155, 177, 181, 198

E

ekklēsia, 159
election (the doctrine of), 124, 125, 128, 148
epangelias, 116
eph hō, 56
episcopacy, 79, 159
Eucharist, 2, 6, 62, 63, 64, 82
exodus, the, 131, 136, 137
exorcism (at baptism; see also demonization), 22, 24, 38, 39, 86

G

good and evil, 15, 40, 50, 86, 87, 164, 169, 170, 175
gospel, the, 34, 53, 54, 55, 74, 76, 86, 92, 94, 95, 96, 108, 109, 132, 135, 148, 160, 178, 180, 182, 186, 187, 195, 196, 198, 205

H

heaven, kingdom of (or kingdom of God), 5, 24, 27, 28, 29, 30, 36, 53, 56, 73, 83,

88, 89, 109, 111, 158, 160, 176, 180, 186, 190, 193
hell, 32, 44, 56, 74, 127, 167
Holy Communion, 21, 28, 30, 34, 41, 63, 71, 72, 102, 105, 106, 110
human nature, 5, 13, 39, 51, 52, 72, 74

I

image of God, 15, 16, 25, 50, 79, 156
imputed guilt, 141, 164, 166, 170
inclination to sin, 40, 44, 52, 54, 72, 74, 85, 86, 165, 189
infant baptism (see also paedobaptism), 6, 7, 17, 18, 39, 73, 78, 79, 80, 81, 83, 87, 93, 101, 102, 103, 104, 108, 109, 142, 148, 150, 157, 158, 161, 176, 180, 184, 188, 190
infant damnation, 56, 59, 85, 145, 164
infant faith, 102, 103, 109, 123, 124, 145, 146, 149, 162, 167
infant salvation (or infant regeneration), 44, 45, 123, 125, 126, 127, 145, 155, 156, 162, 163, 165, 166, 168, 181, 191, 192
inherited guilt, 31, 38, 105, 162, 163, 164, 165, 166, 183, 187, 195
inherited sinful nature (or inherited corruption or inherited fallen condition), 8, 17, 30, 44, 162, 163, 164, 165, 166, 170, 171
innocence (of infants and children), 18, 28, 30, 31, 32, 40, 47, 52, 59, 61, 69, 126, 127, 164, 167, 168, 170, 189, 204, 205

J

judgment, God's, 35, 97, 163, 167, 170, 175, 192, 204

L

laver, 54, 56, 130, 147, 187
law, God's, 4, 18, 26, 98, 119, 120, 164, 165, 174, 179
limbo, infant, 56, 57, 58, 59, 60, 72, 74
Lord's Supper, 2, 6, 73, 82, 102, 110, 159, 161, 177, 179, 180, 181, 182

M

magisterium, 48, 49, 62, 71, 75
Manichaeism, 95, 96
massa damnata, 57
mental impairment, 126, 170
Mishna, 122
moral capacity (capable of moral action), 44, 53, 55, 87, 111, 165, 168, 169, 189
mysterion, 110
mystery of baptism, 12, 17, 21, 26, 28, 36, 94, 185

N

new covenant, 19, 119, 125, 130, 132, 133, 134, 142, 147, 148, 152, 158, 172, 176, 177
Nicene Creed, 22, 33, 41, 82, 84, 139

O

oil (anointing), 22, 25, 26, 27, 42
ordinance, 2, 43, 110, 128, 177, 179, 182, 183, 190
original sin, 14, 30, 31, 38, 41, 45, 51, 52, 53, 54, 56, 57, 58, 60, 69, 71, 73, 74, 76, 84, 85, 86, 87, 98, 101, 105, 111, 127, 145, 147, 149, 155, 156, 162, 164, 165, 166, 168, 181, 183, 187, 189, 192

P

paedobaptism (see also infant baptism), 18, 122
paedocommunion, 41, 72, 75, 142
paidia, 89, 91, 100
Passover, the, 136, 137, 173
Pelagianism, 38, 51, 87
penance, 82, 128
Pentecost, 132, 133, 135, 151, 157
Pietism, 7, 103
pouring (of baptism), 54, 83, 105, 106, 128, 191

R

redemption, 20, 25, 30, 69, 84, 127, 159, 163, 166, 171, 196

Reformation, Protestant, 78, 81, 84, 102, 103, 105, 115, 116, 128, 143, 149, 157, 158, 188
regeneration (see also born again), 54, 56, 62, 78, 81, 82, 83, 107, 111, 123, 128, 129, 145, 147, 163, 185, 187, 191
remission of sins, 18, 25, 27, 41, 51, 71, 82, 94
repentance, 44, 45, 79, 111, 123, 131, 149, 151, 152, 157, 159, 160, 161, 166, 177, 180, 182, 188, 189
revivalism, 116, 128, 151
righteousness, 27, 32, 68, 86, 98, 137, 142, 164, 191, 192
rule of faith, 12, 75, 115

S

sacrament, 2, 23, 42, 53, 56, 60, 61, 62, 63, 64, 68, 70, 72, 74, 75, 76, 80, 81, 82, 83, 105, 106, 107, 110, 117, 127, 129, 137, 139, 142, 145, 149, 160, 201
sanctification, 18, 20, 25, 27, 62, 63, 122, 185
Satan (or the Devil), 22, 39, 40, 73, 81, 85, 86, 87, 101, 110, 113, 114, 160, 186
Satan, renouncing, 22, 39, 73, 86
Shema, the, 4
sin, actual, 14, 69, 73, 74, 87, 95, 147, 164, 166, 167, 171, 189
sin, ancestral, 16, 17, 30, 36, 38, 43, 44, 72
sin, venial, 129
sin, voluntary (or voluntary fault), 13, 53, 164
sola Scriptura, 75, 77, 84, 105, 143, 184, 188, 190
soul competency, 78, 79, 156, 184

T

tabernacle, 130, 191
teenager, 108, 142, 179, 186, 189
temple, 13, 14, 19, 20, 21, 42, 44, 91, 130, 131, 140, 173

theodicy, 192
Theotokos, 13
Torah, 42
transformation, 16, 34, 69, 180
transmission (of grace), 128
transmitted (sin), 14, 86
transubstantiation, 6
Trinity, 12, 22, 34, 39, 43, 48, 78, 83, 114, 127, 145, 188
Trisagion, 12

U

unaccountable (people), 172, 174, 175, 176, 177
unbaptized (infants or children), 29, 31, 32, 38, 43, 56, 57, 60, 61, 72, 74, 76, 93, 95, 97, 98, 191
unborn, 4, 94, 146, 147
union with Christ, 12, 17, 21, 22, 24, 27, 36, 41, 44, 45, 62, 71, 76, 127, 145, 151, 152, 192
universalism, modified, 95, 96, 189

V

vespers, 34, 72
vestibule, 20
victims, infants as, 17, 37, 44

W

washing (of baptism), 27, 43, 61, 76, 83, 122, 129, 130, 136, 145, 158, 191
water (of baptism), 24, 25, 26, 27, 28, 36, 39, 42, 44, 45, 53, 54, 61, 68, 69, 82, 83, 105, 106, 111, 128, 130, 131, 132, 151, 152, 155, 157, 161, 185, 188, 191
Weeds, parable of the, 158, 184
Westminster Confession, 43, 75, 120, 125, 127, 150, 151
Wheat, parable of the, 22
womb, 1, 14, 17, 51, 85, 94, 123, 126, 140, 146, 147, 167, 177
wrath (of God), 85, 95, 145, 164, 170

SCRIPTURE INDEX

Genesis
1 *25*
1–3 *15*
2:8–27 *130*
2:16–17 *15*
3 *37, 195*
3:15 *142, 171*
8:11 *26*
8:21 *40, 189*
12 *171*
15 *171*
17 *109, 120, 146, 173*
17:7 *109, 126*
17:27 *138*
18:19 *137, 138*

Exodus
11:4–5 *136*
20:12 *138*

Leviticus
12 *20, 42*
12:3 *42*
23:43 *174*

Numbers
14:29 *175*
33:8 *131*

Deuteronomy
1:39 *162, 169, 204*
1:39b *175*
4:21 *132*
4:22 *131*
6 *142*
6:2 *138*
6:7 *137*
7:9 *138*
16 *173*
31:2 *131*

Joshua
1:11 *131*
3–4 *131*
24:15 *137, 138*

1 Samuel
3:7 *173, 190*

2 Samuel
12 *167, 169*
12:23 *169*

2 Kings
2:8 *131*
2:23–24 *41*

1 Chronicles
9:1 *131*

Nehemiah
8:1–3 *174*
8:2–3 *179*
10:28 *174*

Psalms
5:7 *21*
22 *146*
22:9 *123, 145*
32 *27*
51 *41*
51:5 *14, 40, 43, 162*
68:5 *200*
71:5–6 *123*
104:24 *31*
109:12–13 *192*
127:4–5 *140*
137:9 *192*
139:1 *167*
139:21 *192*

Isaiah
7:15 *175*
7:15–16 *169*
40:1–10 *131*
44:3 *138*
52:15 *131*
55:11 *179*

Jeremiah
1:5 *167*
20:14 *162*
31:1 *119*
31:17 *119*
31:31–37 *119*
31:35–37 *119*

Ezekiel
36:24 *131*
47 *130*

Jonah
4:11 *100, 169*

Micah
6:8 *181*

Zechariah
14:8 *130*

Matthew
3:1–2 *90*
4:17 *90*
4:24 *90*
8:16 *90*
10:36 *149*
13:24–30 *158, 184*
13:30 *22*
13:36–43 *158, 184*
13:57 *149*
15:19–20 *40*
15:28 *45*
16:13–14 *90*
18:1–5 *89, 176*
18:3 *89*
18:4 *89*
18:5 *89*
18:6 *104, 189*
18:10 *167, 168*
19 *169*
19:13 *90, 91*
19:13–15 *176, 193*
19:14 *169*
19:15 *91*
19:28 *171*
21:15–16 *92*
28:19 *26, 89*
28:19–20 *41*

Mark
1:4 *131*
1:5 *131*
2:4–5 *45*
9:33 *90*
9:33–37 *89, 176*
9:36 *89, 91*
9:37 *89*
9:48 *89*
10:13 *90*
10:13–16 *111, 176, 205*

Luke
1:15 *191*
1:26–56 *167*

1:39–44 *123, 145*
1:41–44 *94*
1:50 *138*
2:22–38 *44*
2:22–40 *20*
2:29–32 *21*
8:11 *149*
9:46–48 *89, 176*
9:48 *89*
18:15 *90*
18:15–17 *29, 176*
18:16 *109*
26–27 *29*

John
3:3 *185*
3:5 *26, 27, 53, 185*
3:13–17 *25*
4:2 *189*

Acts
1:8b *132*
2:5 *133*
2:14 *133*
2:18 *191*
2:33 *191*
2:36–41 *151, 157*
2:37 *187*
2:38 *27, 185*
2:39 *109, 133, 138*
2:41 *133*
3:25 *135*
8:4–12 *151, 157*
8:12 *133*
8:26–38 *151, 157*
8:38 *133*
9:18 *133*
10:44–48 *151, 157*
11:14 *134, 135*
11:16 *42, 191*
16:13–15 *151, 157*
16:15 *133*
16:25 *136*
16:25–34 *151, 157*
16:31 *135, 136, 138*
16:31b *135*
16:33 *133, 136, 138*

18:8 *133, 134*
19:5 *133*
19:7 *134*

Romans
3 *41, 126*
3:23 *126, 141, 147, 192*
3:25 *96*
4:16–18 *121*
5 *169*
5:12 *38, 40, 49, 162*
5:14–21 *141*
5:15 *40*
5:16–17 *192*
6 *24, 185*
6:3 *191*
6:3–4 *54, 132, 161*
6:3–11 *27*
6:4 *190*
8:19–22 *195*
8:19–23 *166, 171*
8:28 *114*
9–11 *171*
10:17 *179*
11:32–34 *97*
16:23 *133*

1 Corinthians
1:14 *133, 134*
1:16 *133, 134*
6:11 *185*
7:7–8 *133*
7:14 *24, 121, 168, 192*
10 *130*
10:1–3 *191*
10:1–4 *137*
10:2 *131*
11:1 *181*
11:24–25 *180*
11:26 *180*
12 *196*
15:22 *40, 127, 141, 162, 192*
15:45 *192*

2 Corinthians
5:17 *54*
12:14 *100*

Galatians
2 *171*
3:26–27 *185*
3:27 *76*
4:6–7 *185*

Ephesians
1:1–2 *121*
2:12 *75*
3:17–18 *23*
4:5 *100*
4:11–16 *196*
4:13 *69*
4:22–34 *68*
5:26 *82*
6:1 *100, 192*
6:1–3 *176*
6:2 *138*
6:3 *138*
6:4 *138, 141, 142, 192*

Philippians
2:1–8 *89*

Colossians
1:13 *160*
2 *185*
2:11–12 *132*
3:20 *192*

1 Timothy
2:5 *79*

2 Timothy
1:5 *177*
3:14–15 *138*
3:15 *177*

Titus
3:5 *82, 185, 187*
3:5–6 *26*

Hebrews
7:25–28 *79*
9:10 *130, 191*
13:17 *192*

James
1:27 *200*
4:10 *90*
5:16 *111*

1 Peter
3:15 *32, 69*
3:18 *191*
3:21 *26, 185*
5:6 *90*

2 Peter
1:4 *36, 54*

1 John
2:13–14 *100*

3 John
1 *133*

www.ingramcontent.com/pod-product-compliance
Lightning Source LLC
Chambersburg PA
CBHW021147160426
43194CB00007B/723